POPULAR MAGIC

# Popular Magic

*Cunning folk
in English History*

Owen Davies

hambledon
continuum

Hambledon Continuum
A Continuum imprint

The Tower Building
11 York Road
London, SE1 7NX

80 Maiden Lane
Suite 704
New York, NY 10038

First published as *Cunning-Folk*, 2003 in hardback
This edition published 2007 in paperback

ISBN 1 85285 297 6 (hardback)
ISBN 1 84725 036 X (paperback)

Copyright © Owen Davies 2003

The moral rights of the author have been asserted.

All rights reserved.

Without limiting the rights under copyrights
reserved above, no part of this publication may be
reproduced, stored in or introduced into a retrieval system,
or transmitted, in any form or by any means (electronic, mechanical,
photocopying, recording or otherwise), without the prior
written permission of both the copyright owner and
the above publisher of the book.

A description of this book is available from the
British Library and from the Library of Congress.

Typeset by Carnegie Publishing, Lancaster
and printed in Great Britain by MPG Books, Cornwall.

## *Contents*

| | | |
|---|---|---|
| Introduction | | vii |
| Acknowledgements | | xv |
| 1 | Cunning-Folk and the Law | 1 |
| 2 | For Good or Evil? | 29 |
| 3 | Who and Why | 67 |
| 4 | Services | 93 |
| 5 | Books | 119 |
| 6 | Written Charms | 147 |
| 7 | European Comparisons | 163 |
| 8 | Cunning-Folk in the Twentieth Century | 187 |
| Notes | | 199 |
| Bibliography | | 219 |
| Index | | 239 |

# *Introduction*

The term cunning-folk is little known today. It is recognised by those with an interest in folklore and social history, and is used by some modern practitioners of magic, but for most people it has no meaning. Yet a century ago everyone in rural society would have been familiar with the term, and two hundred years ago the majority of the population, in both town and country, would have known of at least one cunning-man or cunning-woman. Hundreds of thousands of people had personal experience of them over the centuries. The aim of this book is to show the role cunning-folk played in English society over the last five hundred years. Monarchs have condemned them, some swung from the gallows, hundreds were incarcerated, some achieved prosperity, others died in poverty. They were frequently criticised in print, were the subject of plays and novels, and a couple even wrote about themselves, yet they remain elusive characters. Little has been written about them in the last thirty years, and they have never been the subjects of a book. This is therefore the first comprehensive history of English cunning-folk. It seeks to explore both their light and dark sides. While it may disappoint some who have idealised their knowledge, it will enlighten others who believe magic to have been an unmitigated, injurious fallacy. I hope it will entertain, for cunning-folk were consummate performers and no strangers to publicity, and also throw new light on a professional type that for centuries was as integral to English life as the clergyman, constable and doctor.

Cunning-folk was just one of several terms used in England to describe multi-faceted practitioners of magic who healed the sick and the bewitched, who told fortunes, identified thieves, induced love, and much else besides. It is employed in a general sense here not just because it was widely used, but also because it conveniently encompasses both sexes. Wizard and conjuror were also popular terms in some regions, but these were masculine titles, and to refer to wise-women and wise-men all the time becomes unwieldy. White witch, although now a part of common language, was actually little employed in popular speech prior to the twentieth century, except perhaps in Devon.[1] It was frequently used in educated discourse to describe a range of healers, but the indiscriminate way in which it was employed, its restricted popular usage, and the modern context in which it is applied, make it problematic to adopt as a generic term.

The cunning element of cunning-folk comes from the Anglo-Saxon *cunnan*, meaning to know. Wizard similarly derives from the Old English *wis*, meaning wise, so can be seen as a variant of wise-man. Both definitions tell us something fundamental about how these people were perceived. They were individuals who stood out in society for possessing more knowledge than those around them, knowledge that was acquired either from a supernatural source, from an innate, hereditary ability, or from being able to understand writing. Despite their linguistic origins, these terms only appear in documents during the early modern period. In Anglo-Saxon and Viking sources people who would later be described as cunning-folk were usually referred to using the blanket term of *wiccan*, meaning witch, or were described as those involved in *drycræft*, the practice of magic.[2] The ecclesiastical and Christian secular authorities made little distinction between good and bad magic. Both were sinful, and many benign practices were denounced as vestiges of iniquitous pagan worship. There is evidence that the essential services early modern cunning-folk provided were also in demand in the Anglo-Saxon and early medieval period. It can be found in medical manuscripts or leechbooks, some of which demonstrate a potent and indiscriminate blend of religious observance, herbalism and magic.[3] Amongst the many remedies and healing prayers they contain can be found charms to protect one from witches and elves, charms against thieves, and potions to procure love.

The fact that the terms cunning-man and cunning-woman are absent from the Anglo-Saxon sources does not mean they were not in popular usage, only that they were not used in the formal vocabulary of the time. Likewise in the medieval period we hear nothing of them because Latin was the main written language, particularly for official documents. Instead, in the twelfth and thirteenth centuries we find terms such as *incantatrix, incantator, sortilegus,* and *maleficus* being used to refer to a range of magical practitioners including diviners and cunning-folk. There was also *pythonicos*, a Greek word used in the Bible, which was originally applied to the priestess at the oracle of Delphi, but later came to encompass soothsayers, diviners, witches and cunning-folk. During the fourteenth century the vernacular terms enchanter, sorcerer and variations on the word nigromauncer (necromancer) appear more often, but it is only in the second half of the fifteenth century that the terms cunning-man and cunning-woman, as well as wizard, become a part of the written language. It is from this period onwards that this book is concerned.

Considering how central cunning-folk were to the experience of magic for the majority of people in the past it is necessary to say something about what magic means, and how cunning-folk related to various aspects of it. In the historiography of magic a distinction has usually been made between high or learned magic and low or folk magic. Learned magic is generally defined by its sophisticated theoretical, philosophical and ceremonial structure. It can be further broken down into two main categories, demonic and natural. As the name suggests, demonic magic was primarily concerned with the attempt to conjure and command devils and demons, and was thus an explicitly heretical exercise. Its practitioners were usually motivated by a desire for wealth and power, using demons to find treasure, to murder enemies, to prevail over the rich and influential and to have sexual control over women. The practitioners of natural magic, on the other hand, perceived themselves to be acting from purer motives. Natural magic was considered by many intellectuals to be a branch of the sciences, as it dealt with the occult powers within nature. In our period it was primarily influenced by neoplatonism, which held that the universe was suffused and ruled by a hierarchy of spirits. All matter was interconnected by these spiritual influences, and sympathetic relationships governed all matter. Stars and planets possessed evil and good aspects, and radiated their benign or malign influence upon the earth like ripples across water. Natural magicians sought to manipulate the world around them by attracting these benign stellar influences, and adjuring spirits to do their bidding, or beseeching angels to aid them. This could be achieved by means of certain gestures, instruments, words, incantations, and talismans which fused Christian worship with astrological symbolism. In practice, many learned magicians dabbled in both branches of magic, which certainly did not help the defence of natural magic from theological claims that it was equally diabolic.

Low, popular, or folk magic is usually characterised as a rich medley of indigenous beliefs, practices and rituals, some of them dating back to Anglo-Saxon times, perhaps even earlier, perpetuated largely through oral transmission. The use of 'low' does not necessarily indicate that this type of magic was confined to the 'low' elements of society, but those who employed it had no lofty pretensions about what they were doing. The resort to it was purely a means to an end, whether it was employed to negate the effects of witchcraft, to heal ailments, detect thieves or to procure love. Folk magic had no unifying theoretical or philosophical basis, and there were no manuals to instruct the initiate on associated beliefs and practices. Knowledge of it was held in the collective memory of each community, being called upon when necessity required it. Nevertheless, both types of magic shared some of the same principles, most notably the archaic belief in sympathetic associations, and also the incorporation of Christian beliefs and prayers. Furthermore, there were specific individuals who straddled the worlds of both learned and low magic, and who were consequently thought to have more knowledge of the occult than those around them: these people were cunning-folk.

It is axiomatic that wherever there were witches there were cunning-folk. The history of both groups is inextricably bound up with each other. The latter have often been portrayed as the antithesis of the former. From the early modern period onwards this notion led to the convenient but misleading use of colour to distinguish between the two figures – black witches who used magic for malicious, destructive practices, and white witches whose job it was to combat their evil machinations. Such a categorical definition was never, however, a common aspect of the popular perception of cunning-folk. They occupied an ambiguous position both in society and in the realm of magic, which in both moral and practical terms was neither black nor white. The curing of witchcraft was also only one element of the job description of cunning-folk, albeit an integral and crucial one. If we are to appreciate properly the importance of their role in English society, considerable emphasis must also be placed on their other services. The breadth of their activities, both magical and mundane, was well captured in Thomas Heywood's early seventeenth-century play, *The Wise Woman of Hogsdon*, which was possibly based on a real London practitioner. At one point the cunning-woman muses:

> Let mee see how many trades have I to live by: First, I am a wise-woman, and a fortune-teller, and under that I deale in physicke and fore-speaking [bewitchment], in palmistry, and recovering of things lost. Next, I undertake to cure madd folkes; then I keepe gentlewomen lodgers, to furnish such chambers as I let out by the night: Then I am provided for bringing young wenches to bed; and, for a need, you see I can play the match-maker.

She ends with the sly observation, 'Shee that is but one, and professeth so many, may well bee tearmed a Wise-woman, if there bee any'.[4]

All those interested in English cunning-folk owe a great debt to the work of four scholars, George Kittredge, Cecil Ewen, Keith Thomas and Alan Macfarlane. Kittredge was a highly respected American professor of English literature, whose main interests were Shakespeare and Chaucer. He was a prolific writer, and amongst his many academic achievements was an annotated edition of the complete works of Shakespeare. Many people today, though, only know him for his book *Witchcraft in Old and New England*, published in 1929. This was based on an extensive survey of printed records pertaining to a period spanning from Anglo-Saxon times to the nineteenth century. The reference section alone takes up around a third of the book. Despite the title, several chapters are primarily concerned with magic. Although Kittredge never actually discussed cunning-folk as a group, they are the subject of many of the cases he cited involving love magic, thief magic, spirit conjuration, treasure-seeking and divination. Kittredge's research was largely library based, and he did not concern himself with the mass of unpublished archival material relating to the trials for witchcraft and magic. Coincidently, though, around the same time an English contemporary named Cecil Ewen was busy doing just that. Ewen was an eclectic historian who researched and published on a diverse range of topics including lotteries, piracy and Walter Raleigh. During the 1920s he busied himself with an exhaustive search through the assize court records for the home counties, as well as pamphlets, manuscripts and printed records relating to the period of the witch trials between 1542 and 1736. The main result was two books that are still essential research tools for witchcraft historians today, *Witch Hunting and Witch Trials* (1929) and *Witchcraft and Demonianism* (1933). Although Ewen was largely concerned with the trial of witches, his extensive transcriptions also provide a wealth of information concerning the role of cunning-folk.

While recognising the pioneering nature of their work, for the historian of cunning-folk today the witchcraft publications of Kittredge and Ewen are only really useful as source books. Neither scholar attempted detailed analyses of the information they so painstakingly and diligently collated. It was nearly another forty years before a sophisticated examination of English cunning-folk appeared. Keith Thomas's *Religion and the Decline of Magic* (1971) is an immense survey of the role and nature of magic in English society from the medieval period to the eighteenth century. Its author, a now knighted Oxford academic, was the first historian fully to recognise the importance and significance of cunning-folk in early modern English society, and devoted a hundred or so pages to their consideration. Thomas naturally turned to the work of Kittredge and Ewen for information, but also conducted his own equally impressive search through both libraries and archives. He made particularly valuable use of ecclesiastical court records, which, as we shall see later, are one of the most important sources concerning cunning-folk for the sixteenth and early seventeenth centuries. Using this large database of information he painted a revealing picture of who cunning-folk were, what they did, and how they were viewed by various social groups. Thomas's portrait of cunning-folk was not formed in academic isolation, however, as one of his doctoral students, Alan Macfarlane, was also engaged in an innovative regional study of witchcraft and magic in early modern Essex, which refreshingly gave as much emphasis to cunning-folk as to witchcraft accusations and prosecutions. His exhaustive survey of the exceptionally rich court records surviving for the county, both secular and ecclesiastical, enabled him to present, for the first time, some concrete impression of the number of cunning-folk serving the population, their pattern of distribution in the county, and the spatial relationship between them and their clients. As he admitted, the records by no means revealed all of those who practised over the period, but his findings nevertheless served to confirm and highlight the significant role of cunning-folk in early modern society.⁵

In their work on witchcraft and magic, Thomas and Macfarlane did more than anyone before or since to shed light on the world of English cunning-folk, not just in relation to the witch trials but also to the wider context of religion and society at the time. In the last thirty years little more has been written about cunning-folk in early modern England, but much valuable work has been done on society and culture in the period to throw new light on the subject. Hence the appearance of this study and, one hopes, others. Furthermore, Thomas's and Macfarlane's interest in cunning-folk ended prematurely with the termination of the witch trials in the early 1700s. Cunning-folk were as much a part of eighteenth- and nineteenth-century society as they were of the seventeenth, but until recently historians have neglected to investigate their continued social importance.⁶ Considering the popularity of cunning-folk and their centrality to the whole business of witchcraft, their dismissal by British historians is surprising. During the second half of the 1990s there was something of a renaissance in English witchcraft studies, with the publication of some outstanding books and articles, but in all these cunning-folk received only minor consideration.⁷

The main reason for this lack of interest is that historians seem to have difficultly placing cunning-folk. In terms of witchcraft, discussion tends to focus on the trials, the relationship between accuser and accused, and more recently the narrative aspect of accusations, with the role of third party mediators and consultants in these situations often being considered as peripheral. Historians of magic have largely ignored cunning-folk as well. They have been drawn to the world of erudite high magicians, not only because these magicians were intellectual, literate, and left accounts of their experiments, but also because they embraced a coherent and sophisticated philosophy which modern historians can engage with and study within the context of early science. Cunning-folk left little record of their thoughts and experiments, not necessarily because they lacked the intellect to comprehend occult philosophies, but rather because it just did not interest many of them. Cunning-folk applied practical magical solutions to resolve everyday problems. Medical historians, particularly those concerned with the eighteenth and nineteenth centuries, have also shown little interest in cunning-folk. Their debate has concentrated on developments in medical knowledge, the struggle for medical respectability, and the growth of commercialism. On the whole, cunning-folk were rarely engaged in these developments, and so they have largely been sidelined.[8] Consequently, our understanding of the popular experience of illness and cure remains far from complete. Likewise, our knowledge of the popular experience of crime is all the poorer for the historian's reluctance to consider the detective role of cunning-folk.

Cunning-folk, then, have often been air-brushed out of representations of the past. To restore them to our collage of England's cultural history, the reader will be presented with a wide range of sources covering a long period of time. In doing so, I will be looking again at the era of the witch-trials, but this time from the viewpoint of cunning-folk. I will consider their ongoing popularity and social function in an age when the focus on the expansion of orthodox medicine, mass education and industrialisation has often obscured their continued relevance in English society. And I will explore in greater detail than before just who cunning-folk were, how they were perceived and represented over the centuries, and where they stood in relation to their continental counterparts. Finally, to anyone thinking of taking up the 'cunning-profession', this book may serve as a useful historical guide as to the right and wrong ways to go about it.

# Acknowledgements

First and foremost, I would like to thank my family and Céline Chantier for their unceasing support over the years. My brother Angus's pub conversations on matters historical and otherwise require further mention. Next I must thank Ronald Hutton and Willem de Blécourt for providing welcome academic support. Further thanks go to Ronald Hutton for giving me a pre-publication draft of his work on shamanism, and Willem de Blécourt for his valuable comments on a draft of chapter seven, and also for providing synopses of his Dutch publications.

I would also like to express my appreciation to the following who, in conversation or through the provision of source material and publications, have contributed to the writing of this book: Tim Hitchcock, Peter Maxwell-Stuart, Laura Stark-Arola, Steve Mitchell, Linda Oja, Brian Hoggard, Jason Semmens, Darren Oldridge, Jonathan Barry, Jeremy Harte, Robert Lenkiewicz, Tim Tangherlini, Marko Nenonen, Éva Pócs, Sabina Magliocco, Ruth Herman, Soili-Maria Olli, Maureen Perkins, Julie Moore and all the participants in the 'Beyond the Witch Trials' conference. There are others, too, whose help is recognised in the endnotes.

I would like to commend the prompt, professional and friendly service provided by the Rochdale Local Studies Library, Lincolnshire Record Office, Colindale Newspaper Library, Bodleian Library, and British Library. I must also mention the impressive Early English Books Online, which enabled the consultation of several pre-1700 pamphlets that were otherwise difficult to access. Elizabeth Stone, who read the proofs, caught a number of infelicities and suggested many small improvements.

1

## Cunning-Folk and the Law

In the Anglo-Saxon and Viking periods various secular and ecclesiastical legal codes condemned people for using charms to cure the sick, foretelling the future and procuring love. King Alfred decreed that 'women who are wont to practise enchantments, and magicians and witches, do not allow them to live'.[1] His guide was the famous passage in Exodus 22:18, which commanded, 'Thou Shalt not suffer a witch to live'. But there is little evidence indicating the extent to which such edicts were ever invoked. From the twelfth century there were no specific secular laws against magic, but the activities of cunning-folk continued to be seen as a problem by the authorities, and surviving ecclesiastical documents and state papers show that resort to those who practised magic was widespread. There were particular fears in elite circles about its use in aiding political intrigues. Writing in the mid twelfth century, John of Salisbury warned of the dangerous temptations that the promise of magic opened up to courtiers. Over the next three centuries, several accusations of sorcery were made against such high-profile people as Hubert de Burgh, Henry III's justiciar, and Walter Langton, bishop of Lichfield and treasurer to Edward I.[2] The most famous case was that of Eleanor Cobham, duchess of Gloucester, who in 1441 was tried for using magic against Henry VI. To achieve her purposes she was accused of hiring the services of an astronomer and astrologer named Roger Bolingbrooke, Thomas Southwell, a canon of St Stephen's Chapel, Westminster, and a cunning-woman named Margerie Jourdayne. The latter was further accused of supplying the duchess with love potions, and was burned at Smithfield for treason. But such sorcery cases were infrequent in England and rarely involved people, like Jourdayne, who can be confidently identified as cunning-folk.

We really only start getting significant details about cunning-folk, as opposed to learned 'high' magicians, from the second half of the fourteenth century onwards, not necessarily because they were becoming more prevalent or popular, but, rather, because there are more relevant surviving documents from this point onwards, the most important of these being in ecclesiastical records. Unless cunning-folk got mixed up in treasonous plots, poisoning, murder, or were sued for fraud or defamation, their activities were considered to be moral offences, to be dealt with by the church. Until the mid sixteenth century both secular and religious authorities were considerably more concerned with the disruptive, social consequences of magic and deception than with any heretical, satanic complicity cunning-folk might have been involved in. The practice of love magic was one such source of potential social discord, and there are records of several cases heard by the ecclesiastical authorities during the fifteenth and early sixteenth centuries. In October 1446, for example, the 'official' of the priory and convent of Durham heard evidence against Mariot de Belton and Isabella Brome, who were accused of telling women they could magically procure husbands for them.[3] The commissary's court of the London diocese also dealt with several similar cases. In 1492 it heard how Richard Laukiston had offered to find a rich husband for a widow named Margaret Geffrey. Laukiston was going to achieve this by applying to a 'cunning man that by his cunning can cause a woman to have any man that she hath favour to'. In 1526 one Margaret Williamson was examined after it was reported that she possessed certain books from which she concocted love potions.[4]

It was the practice of thief detection, however, which seems to have caused the most concern, as is evident from various surviving court records from London. As early as 1311 the bishop of London, Ralph Baldock, wrote to his archdeacon asking him to investigate the practice of sorcery and theft divination in the city.[5] Later in the century a spate of such cases were brought before the mayor. In 1375, for instance, John Porter of Clerkenwell prosecuted John Chestre for having failed to discover a thief who had stolen some valuables. Chestre admitted that 'he often exercised that art', and claimed to have successfully restored £15 stolen from a man at Garlickhithe. The plaintiff and defendant agreed on a settlement, and the court ruled that, because the defendant's art was held to be a deception of the public, he must swear not to exercise it in future.[6] In 1382 Robert Berewold was accused of defamation and deceit. He had been asked to identify the thief who stole a mazer (drinking bowl) from a house in St Mildred Poultry. Like Chestre he divined by 'turning the loaf'. A wooden peg was sunk into the top of a loaf of bread and four knives were placed in the sides. When a list of names was gone through, either verbally or mentally, the loaf turned at the name of the thief. In this manner Berewold fixed upon a woman named Johanna Wolsy, who subsequently accused him of 'maliciously lying' and of causing a public scandal. For his punishment he was put in the pillory with the incriminating loaf hung round his neck, and was made to go to church on the following Sunday at the hour of mass and confess his crime before Johanna's fellow parishioners and other neighbours. In the same year another practitioner, Henry Pot, was similarly punished for defamation. Nicholas Freman had come to him to find out who had stolen a mazer. Pot made thirty-two balls of white clay and 'over them did sorcery, or his magic art'. From this Pot divined that a married woman named Cristina Freman was the culprit, and it was she who subsequently had him arraigned for falsehood. He confessed before the mayor that 'he had many times before practised divers like sorceries, both within the city and without, through which various persons had undeservedly suffered injury in their character'.[7]

There was particular concern over the detective activities of cunning-folk because their accusations sometimes resulted in embarrassing instances of wrongful imprisonment. This in turn could lead to wider social discord. This fear is apparent from a messy legal situation the mayor and aldermen of London had to sort out in 1390. It involved two men, Robert Mysdene and John Geyte, who had been unfairly arrested and imprisoned for theft upon the word of a cunning-man named John Berkyng. Berkyng was made an example of by the court because 'from such falsehoods ... murders might easily have ensued'. He was placed in the pillory, imprisoned and then banished from the city.[8] Such situations would never have developed if cunning-folk had not been so influential. Officials lower down the legal tier, constables and bailiffs, seem to have considered the word of a cunning-man as sufficient proof of guilt to make arrests. In the fifteenth century John Holond, a husbandmen in the service of the abbey of Woodbridge, Suffolk, was arrested for burglary after having been identified by 'negremaunsers'. While in prison he complained to the court of Chancery that he was being held against 'all lawe, reason and conscience', and that all his neighbours would testify to his 'gode name and fame'. Such arguments cut little ice with his gaolers: his word was deemed inferior to that of a cunning-man.[9]

Despite evidence of the pernicious activities of cunning-folk and diviners, neither church nor state instigated a systematic campaign of suppression, and the victims of theft who felt let down by cunning-folk, and those defamed by them, continued to launch private law suits in various courts throughout the fifteenth and early sixteenth centuries. It was only with the consolidation of monarchical power and centralisation of authority under Henry VIII that a more concerted attempt to suppress cunning-folk and other magical practitioners was possible. In fact, it was the concern over those who practised theft magic, love magic and treasure hunting, rather than witches as they came to be defined later in the century, which led to the first so-called Witchcraft Act of 1542. To be more precise, this statute was directed 'Against Conjuration and Witchcrafts and Sorcery and Enchantments'. Although it made provision for those who used 'witchcrafts, enchantments, and sorceries to the destruction of their neighbour's persons and goods', that is witches, its main target were those who took 'upon them to declare and tell where things lost or stolen should be become', those who practised invocations and conjurations to 'get knowledge for their own lucre in what place treasure of gold and silver should or might be found', and those who 'provoke any person to unlawful love'. The penalty for such activities was death. Although the survival of secular court records for the rest of the decade is very poor, the evidence suggests that the statute was something of a dead letter. There is, at any rate, no record of anyone dying because of it. Prosecutions continued, nevertheless, though not under the conjuration statute. Around 1545, for instance, two practitioners of 'nigramansi', John Lamkyn, master of Holbeach grammar school, and a Cirencester wheelwright named Edmund Nasche, were prosecuted before the Star Chamber – a tribunal consisting of the king's council. The two conjurors had been consulted about the theft of some money and jewels from Holbeach church, and had declared that John Patriche was the guilty party. It was Patriche who subsequently brought a defamation suit against them.[10] Although such cases highlighted the problem posed by cunning-folk, Edward VI repealed the statute of 1542, along with several others, less than six years later. This was a sign that the punishment decreed by the statute was perhaps deemed rather too harsh, and that the problem posed by such people was considered by many to be a moral issue for the church to deal with in its courts rather than a matter for the state.

During the late 1540s and 1550s cunning-folk continued to thrive, and no doubt those aware of the legislation felt relieved that the threat of capital punishment no longer hung over them, although they could still receive lesser punishment in other courts of law. One fascinating piece of evidence for the flourishing state of the trade at this point in time derives from the ecclesiastical examination of a London cunning-man in 1549. William Wycherley, a tailor by trade, of St Sepulchre's, confessed to having conjured up a spirit named Scariot to provide him with knowledge of stolen goods. During his examination he declared that 'there be within England above five hundred conjurers as he thinketh ... and specially in Norfolk, Hertfordshire, and Worcestershire and Gloucestershire'. This was undoubtedly a conservative estimate, but may still have surprised his audience. He also listed numerous practitioners he was personally acquainted with, including 'one Lowth, in Flete-streete, a broderer', Thomas Malfrey, 'of Goldstone besides Yarmouth', a woman 'besides Stoke Clare', a Welshman named John Davye who was 'a prophesier, and a great teller of things lost', and one Durant, a painter in Norwich who did 'use invocation of spirites'. Others he knew in London practising the 'sieve and shears' were a labourer named Thomas Shakilton of Aldersgate Street, Christopher Morgan, a plasterer of Beche Lane beside the Barbican, and a Mrs Croxton of St Giles.[11]

As the prosecution of Wycherley indicates, the absence of statutes against cunning-folk in the years after 1547 was not symptomatic of a lack of concern over the social and moral problem posed by their activities. The 'sooth sayer' that Henry Machyn recorded seeing in a London pillory was certainly not the only practitioner to be punished in this period. The man, a scrivener by trade, had 'a paper sett over ys hed wrytten for sondrys and practyses of grett falsode and muche on-trowthe'.[12] In fact, if anything, the church seemed to increase its vigilance in this legislative void. In 1549 Archbishop Cranmer's Articles of Visitation underlined the responsibility of church officials to report those who practised magic. In 1554, during the brief reign of Mary Tudor, the Catholic bishop of London, Edmund Bonner, reiterated the point. The Royal Articles printed in the first year of Queen Elizabeth's reign, and many times subsequently, demanded that churchwardens and parishioners report anyone 'that do charmes, sorcerye, enchauntmentes, invocations, circles, witchcrafts, southsaying, or any lyke craftes or imaginations invented by the devyll, and speciallye in the tyme of womens travayle'. In the same year Bishop Jewel expressed concern that 'the number of witches and sorcerers had everywhere become enormous'.[13] There were other voices as well, one of the most interesting of which was that of a reformed student of the occult sciences named Francis Coxe. In 1561 he was convicted for his activities, though it is not certain under what law, and did a stint in the pillory. To demonstrate that he was a reformed character he subsequently published a rejection of his former trade in a broadside entitled, *The Unfained Retractation of Frauncis Coxe*. Shortly afterwards he expanded upon the same theme in a *Short Treatise Declaringe the Detestable Wickednesse of Magicall Sciences*. Obviously familiar with the work of the occultist Cornelius Agrippa, 'of whome all the worlde speaketh', he declared all magic to be the work of the devil. According to Coxe, those who practised it became 'infidels, turninge the temple of ye holy Ghoste into a sinagoge of sathan. Therefore deare countryman, flee from these most wicked and damnable sciences of divination'.[14]

In March 1559 there was a failed attempt to restore the laws against conjuration and witchcraft, but it was only in 1563 that a new Bill 'Against Conjurations, Enchantments, and Witchcrafts' was finally passed. The preamble made quite clear that the absence of laws against these 'evils' had been detrimental to the country, and that, since the repeal of the 1542 Act, 'many fantastical and devilish persons have devised and practised invocations and conjurations of evil and wicked spirits, and have used and practised witchcrafts, enchantments, charms and sorceries'. Once again, it was cunning-folk and learned occultists who were the principal targets. The renewed secular action against such people was partly a response to the growing voices of concern, and partly due to suspected magical intrigue in high places. Only the year before, when the countess of Lennox and four others had been prosecuted for treason, it was alleged that they had consulted some 'wizards' to know how long the queen was to live. Again, the law was directed at any person or persons who took:

> upon him or them by witchcraft, enchantment, charm, or sorcery, to tell or declare in what place any treasure of gold or silver should or might be found or had in the earth, or other secret place; or where goods, or things lost or stolen should be found or be come; or shall use or practise any sorcery, enchantment, charm or witchcraft to the intent to provoke any person to unlawful love; or to hurt or destroy any person in his or her body, member, or goods.

The only significant departure from Henry VIII's statute was the absence of the death penalty for a first offence. Those convicted were to face one year's imprisonment and four stints in the pillory. Those convicted of the same offence twice faced life imprisonment. The death penalty was reserved only for those who either committed murder by witchcraft or conjured up evil spirits. If the statute of 1542 proved a damp squib, that of 1563 subsequently sparked a fiery zeal of repression – but not against those who were the original targets of the law. It was witches, those individuals who were thought to use their powers for nothing else than malicious harm against man and beast, who subsequently felt its full force. This is not the place to embark on a consideration of why authoritarian concern over witches now suddenly escalated.[15] Essentially, once the state became determined to suppress all forms of magic, and a statute was put in place and made known, it was left up to the populace to root out all those who came under the law, and the people demonstrated that it was witches who most concerned them.

The attention and focus of the courts shifted away from the activities of cunning-folk and towards the *maleficium* of supposed witches. While for hundreds of innocent women this meant incarceration and death for crimes they had not committed, for cunning-folk this period represented an escape: relatively few were ever prosecuted under the Act. Judicial leniency concerning cunning-folk was, however, in no way representative of much educated opinion at the time. As the campaign against witchcraft took off there were numerous complaints about the profusion of cunning-folk, and many calls for their extermination. The authors of witchcraft pamphlets, who reported trial testimonies and other sensational occurrences for a popular audience, were particularly vocal in their call for the rounding-up of cunning-folk as well as witches. In 1574 a pamphlet recounting a supposed case of diabolic possession began by complaining that the 'Realme is knowen by common experience, and of late, to be troubled with Witches, Sorcerers, and other such wise men and women (as they call them)'. More outspoken was a pamphlet recounting the trial of the Windsor witches in 1579. Referring to cunning-folk, it complained that although 'the Justices bee severe in executyng of the Lawes in that behalfe, yet suche is the foolishe pitie, or slackeness, or both, of the multitude and under-officers that they most commonly are winked at, and so escape unpunished'. Three year later another pamphlet demanded, with sardonic cruelty, that witches and cunning-folk should all be rigorously punished:

> Rygorously, sayd I? Why it is too milde and gentle a tearme for such a mercilesse generation: I should rather have sayd most cruelly executed: for that no punishment can bee thought upon, be it in never so high a degree of torment, which may be deemed sufficient for such a divelish and danable [sic] practise.[16]

Bearing in mind the background to and content of the statutes of 1542 and 1563, historians have been somewhat misleading in referring to them as the Witchcraft Acts. Although that of 1563 came to be invoked predominantly against witches, like its predecessor it by no means placed specific emphasis on maleficent witchcraft. It would, perhaps, be more accurate to describe them as the Conjuration Acts. Even the small but significant changes found in the 1604 Act of James I were as much aimed at cunning-folk and conjurors as witches. Divination for treasure, the detection of lost or stolen property and provoking unlawful love once again became capital offences, though only after a second conviction. Added to the list of magical crimes laid down in the Elizabethan statute was the theft of corpses 'to be employed or used in any manner of witchcraft, sorcery, charm, or enchantment', and the act of entertaining, feeding, consulting or covenanting with any 'evil and wicked spirit'. All were punishable by death in the first instance. The Act basically enshrined in legislation the harsh views on experimental, beneficial and harmful magic that the new king had expressed several years earlier in his *Daemonologie*. Written in the form of a dialogue, King James has a character ask at one point, 'what forme of punishment thinke yee merites these magicians and Witches? For I see that ye account them to be all alike guiltie? ... They ought to be put to death according to the Law of God, the civill and imperiall Law, and municipall law of all Christian nations.'[17] The 1604 Act remained in place for the next 131 years. An attempt was made during the Rump Parliament to bolster the section concerning magical detection by also making it a criminal offence to *consult* cunning-folk in order to find 'goods lost or stolen, or to know who shall be their husbands or wives, or any other such like future contingencies'.[18] The proposal never got beyond the committee stage, but the fact that it was considered at all suggests that there was concern that neither the 1604 Act nor the ecclesiastical courts were making much headway against the popularity of cunning-folk. Around the same time, a pamphlet outlining the *Lawes against Witches and Coniuration* tried to explain to a popular audience why, although wizards and conjurers were different from witches, they were still guilty of the same diabolic crime. Instead of blanketing witches and cunning-folk as 'all alike', a view that the common people could not accept, its author accepted popular discrimination. He acknowledged that the 'Conjurer compacteth for curiosity, to know secrets, or work miracles; And the Witch of mere malice to do mischiefe, and to be revenged', but their 'superstitious, and ceremoniall formes of words (called Charmes)', their 'medicines, herbs, or other things', and their divining of 'things to come' were all still done with the 'Devils help, and covenants made with him'.[19] Such attempts to justify the 1604 Act patently made little impression on those who resorted to magical practitioners.

Although cunning-folk were infrequently prosecuted under the conjuration statutes, the surviving records provide very useful information not only about cunning-folk themselves, but also about the response of the authorities to their activities. It is quite apparent, for instance, that very few cunning-folk were prosecuted at the assizes, which generally dealt with the most serious crimes in England. Only eleven cases out of 503 indictments brought under the conjuration statutes in Essex dealt with cunning-folk or treasure-seekers. A trawl through the published assizes records of other counties does not reveal many more. It is probably safe to say that fewer than a hundred cases of magic, as opposed to malefic witchcraft, were heard in assize courts between 1563 and 1736. It is important to note, however, that the divinatory practices of cunning-folk and fortune-tellers could also be tried under laws against fraud and vagrancy, which entailed a lesser punishment. Thus in 1636 Margaret Snelling was successfully prosecuted at the Devon assizes for 'deceivinge and coseninge of the kinges subjects by fortune telling and deluding them'. She was publicly whipped and pilloried on the next market day, and had to do penance after divine service in three local churches on four consecutive Sundays – not pleasant, but better than a year in prison. In March 1691–92 Elizabeth Powell was brought before a Wiltshire magistrate and charged 'with performing the unlawfull art of Fortune telling and of discovering of hidden treasure'. Although the latter crime was explicitly mentioned in the 1604 Act, Powell was actually prosecuted for the lesser offence of vagrancy, and was sentenced to hard labour in Devizes house of correction.[20]

Only a few of those cunning-folk hauled before the assizes, men such as Nicholas Battersby, of Bowtham, were charged with the crime of detecting stolen goods. In 1663 Battersby was employed by a man languishing in York gaol for the theft of £140 from the study of Lord Fairfax. He professed his innocence and desired the cunning-man to detect the real culprits. Battersby 'tooke instruccions thereof in his booke', and the next day went to the sheriff's gaol to declare formally that the man had been wrongly imprisoned, and that the money had, in fact, been stolen by an old grey-haired man and a young man who were servants in Fairfax's house. Battersby's boldness in appearing before the authorities certainly showed an admirable commitment to both his client and his 'art', but it also led to his own indictment for sorcery.[21] Most assize offences concerned treasure-hunting or the capital offence of conjuring up evil spirits. The two crimes were usually related. One of those unfortunate enough to be charged was Thomas Heather, a yeoman of Hoddesdon in Hertfordshire, who in 1573 was indicted at the assizes for having conjured up spirits in a local wood to help him discover large sums of money. He was found guilty but was later pardoned. Two year later he was further indicted at the Surrey assizes, along with three labourers named William Williamson, Richard Pope and Thomas Twyford, all of Battersea, for invoking evil spirits to assist them in revealing a great treasure. Heather seems to have been the organiser of the escapade, but evaded arrest. His three accomplices were found not guilty, though he was sentenced to hang *in absentia*. Around the same time an Essex tailor, Robert Wallys, was found not guilty of the same crime. In 1591 William Bate was successfully indicted, but was pardoned twenty years later, 'the evidence being found weak'.[22] It needs to be remembered, however, that cunning-folk were certainly not the only ones involved in treasure seeking. The lure of instant wealth attracted people of both high and low birth to explore the avenue of magic. The almost inevitable disappointment involved in treasure conjuration also meant that an itinerant existence was advisable for the professional treasure seeker like Heather, while the cunning-trade generally required a sedentary lifestyle.

Most cunning-folk were prosecuted before the lesser courts of quarter session. Although a few treasure-seeking cases have been found, most quarter sessions cases concerned the detection of thieves and lost property, reflecting the ubiquity of this practice. In 1633, for example, Ann Bellett was brought before the Worcester sessions for 'the evil art that she useth with the juggling trick of the sire and sheves [sieve and shears] to find out goods lost and using the names of Peter and Paule therein in profane manner'. A year later several women of West Ayton appeared before the Yorkshire quarter sessions charged with magically detecting some stolen clothes.[23] In 1669 the Somerset quarter sessions dealt with a cunning-man who helped identify a sheep rustler, and three years later it also heard the case of William Vowles, a cunning-man of Blagdon, who not only identified the man who stole some cloth from a miller named William Allen, but also had the confidence to suggest that a warrant be taken out against the supposed thief.[24] The fact that this crime was rarely deemed worth the attention of the assize judges further indicates that parochial officials considered the 'problem' of cunning-folk as secondary to that of witches. Although theft detection was not a capital crime in the first instance, under the statute of 1604 a second such offence was punishable by death. Yet justices of the peace responded more leniently towards this magical crime than they did towards other aspects of the conjuration laws. Even when the crime of theft detection was brought before the assizes, juries and judges were loath to impose the full weight of the law. Nicholas Battersby was merely bound over to good behaviour.

Not all cunning-folk prosecuted under the Conjuration Acts were tried for what they actually practised; a few found themselves indicted as witches. A lot of nonsense has been written about how many of those persecuted as witches throughout early modern Europe were benign, female folk healers whose skills and influence were resented by misogynistic men in general, and religious and medical interests in particular. Historians have skilfully demolished such claims in recent years.[25] It could be argued, however, that because cunning-folk were well known to possess magical powers, they were more prone to charges of bewitchment than other people. There is, in fact, little evidence to suggest this was particularly so in England. On the other hand, they were certainly no less prone to accusation just because they fulfilled a central role in the popular fight *against* witches. Most accusations of witchcraft arose from neighbourly conflicts, and cunning-folk were as liable as anyone else to be involved in such incidents. If, for instance, they issued threats against someone who failed to pay a debt, and then misfortune subsequently befell those threatened, witchcraft might be suspected. A London cunning-woman, Joan Peterson, one of the few practitioners to be hanged, was convicted in 1652 for bewitching Christopher Wilson under such circumstances. He had been to her for a cure but had failed to pay for services rendered. In retaliation she threatened, 'You had been better you had given me my money for you shall be ten times worse than ever you were'. The implication was quite clear. The worried Wilson subsequently fell into strange fits and became very sick.[26] One of the principal charges against Ursula Kemp, a cunning-woman of St Osyth, hanged in 1582, followed a similar pattern. She had treated a woman named Grace Thurlow, who suffered from 'a lamenesse in her bones', and was promised twelve pence as payment. Five weeks later, Kemp went to see Thurlow, who was now feeling much better, and asked her for the money. Thurlow reneged on her promise, saying 'shee was a poore and needie woman and had no money'. Kemp then asked for some cheese instead, but Thurlow said she had none to give. The frustrated Kemp swore she 'woulde bee even with her', and the next day Thurlow was taken lame. Kemp was subsequently accused of putting a spell on her, even though she had stressed on an earlier occasion that although 'she coulde unwitche' she could 'not witche'.[27]

These two cases demonstrate the classic sequence, from neighbourly dispute to threat – making to accusations of witchcraft, which can be found in many prosecution cases. It is no coincidence, however, that it was usually cunning-women rather than cunning-men who found themselves so indicted. In other words, the relationship between gender and witchcraft was more significant than that between magical ability and bewitchment. Where cunning-folk were more generally vulnerable to accusation was in the field of healing the bewitched. If a cunning-person failed to cure someone of witchcraft, or they got worse after treatment, they might be suspected of doubly bewitching the patient. This seems to have been the case in an accusation levelled at Ann Greene of Gargrave, Yorkshire, in 1653/4. John Tatterson had gone to her to dispel some evil spirits that troubled him at night, and also to cure a related pain in his ear. As part of the cure, she took some hair from his neck without his consent. This made him suspicious, and he asked what she was going to do with it. She replied, 'shee would use it att her pleasure', and that he should go home and forget about it. On his way home, however, his pains increased. No doubt believing she had put a spell on him using the hair, he returned and told her 'to looke to itt or hee would looke to her'.[28] As nineteenth-century sources show, similar cases were not rare. Accusations of witchcraft under such circumstances were certainly one of the hazards of the profession. During the period of the witch trials, however, very few such instances progressed to the level of prosecution. Out of 400 people accused of witchcraft in Essex only four are identifiable as cunning-folk.[29] A figure of one or two per cent can probably be taken as reflecting the situation nationwide.

The question of why there was a witch hunt has often been addressed. As important for our understanding of early modern society is the usually ignored alternative: why there wasn't a cunning-folk hunt. The laws were in place, but ardent critics of beneficial magic waited in vain for the trickle of prosecutions to swell and engulf those who practised it. The simple reason why it never happened is that people did not prosecute cunning-folk in significant numbers. In England the persecution of witches was largely conducted from below, in other words by people who felt threatened by witches in their daily lives: it was they who brought charges. The legal authorities, by and large, did not seek out witches themselves – that was not how English common law worked. Witches were evil but cunning-folk were useful, so there was little cause for people to prosecute them, unless it was felt that they had been cheated or bewitched. As the infamous witch-hunter John Stearne observed, he and Hopkins tackled no cunning-folk, not for want of pursuing them, but because 'men rather uphold them, and say, why should any man be questioned for doing good'.[30] The only way large-scale cunning-folk prosecutions might have happened was if people had swallowed the theological view, pumped out in publications and sermons, that cunning-folk were in league with the devil and therefore a grave menace to Christian civilisation. Those who consulted cunning-folk obviously found this almost impossible to digest, and judging from the leniency meted out to those cunning-folk that were prosecuted, scepticism about their supposed satanic complicity was shared by many in the legal profession as well.

Church court records are one of our most important early modern sources of information. Although relatively few cunning-folk were prosecuted under the secular statutes, many were brought before the church authorities for similar offences: the numbers are difficult to quantify but the figures are smaller than once thought.[31] Amongst those presented were people like Robert Garmann, brought before a Yorkshire court in 1567 because he was 'comonly reputed to be a wiseman or a sorcerer'; Elizabeth Freare of Buttercrambe, in the same county, presented in 1596 for claiming to be a 'wise-woman or a cunning woman'; and John Talbot of Sherifhales, Shropshire, reported in 1623 for being a reputed 'wizard' and finder of lost objects.[32] The reason so many more cunning-folk were brought before church courts is that, while under English common law there was little avenue for the authorities to pursue their own investigations against cunning-folk, ecclesiastical procedure allowed the clergy and their parish officials to be proactive. Whereas the secular courts largely restricted themselves to the crimes of thief detection and treasure seeking, as specifically mentioned in the statutes, the church courts dealt with a wider range of activities, most significantly the detection of witches and the curing of witchcraft.

From a cunning-person's point of view, appearing before the ecclesiastical authorities was far preferable to an encounter with the secular courts, as the punishments that could be meted out by the church courts were far less severe. The worst that the ecclesiastical courts could impose was excommunication. Most transgressors were simply dismissed with an admonishment or ordered to face public penance before the community. This usually involved standing in church, or some other public place, clothed in a white sheet and wearing a paper spelling out the offence committed. It was not just cunning-folk who were targeted. Presentments before the archdeaconry courts were usually gathered by churchwardens in response to articles of visitation that were sent out before the arrival of the courts in each area. These articles frequently referred to all those who used charms, sorcery, soothsaying, witchcraft and 'like craft', so a range of other magical practitioners including charmers, fortune-tellers, astrologers and medical men found themselves called to account before the moral authorities.

Considerable research has been done on ecclesiastical court records in recent decades, much of it concerned with the church's policing of sexual behaviour, though numerous archives still remain untapped.[33] The work that has been done certainly confirms that the Reformation led to little practical change in attitudes towards cunning-folk, in the sense that both Catholic and Anglican clergy considered them pernicious. Generally, however, there was a more overtly Protestant emphasis on the diabolic nature of the popular magical practices dealt with by the church courts. Thus around 1570 Alice Swan was made to confess before a Durham ecclesiastical court that in detecting stolen goods for 'filthie lucre' she followed the 'persuasion of the devell'. What she did could 'not be done without a defection and mistrust to God and some confidence to the devell'. The seven people reported to the visitation of the diocese of Coventry and Lichfield in 1636 for using magic to identify a thief were similarly said to have thereby made an 'implicit compact with the devil'.[34] Indeed, by the late sixteenth century many English theologians held cunning-folk to be no better than the execrable witches they were meant to combat. They were, in fact, often referred to as 'witches' to indicate their diabolic allegiance. The influential Protestant theologian William Perkins (1558–1602) explained that, 'by Witches we understand not those onely which kill and torment: but all Diviners, Charmers, Juglers, all Wizzards, commonly called wise men and wise women'.[35] When the Somerset clergyman Richard Bernard (1568–1641) urged churchwardens to present before 'the Ecclesiaticall Judges, both the Witches themselves, as also all such as resort unto them', he was thinking not of 'hurtful' witches but of cunning-folk.[36]

The aim of the ecclesiastical courts, both before and after the Reformation, was as much to admonish those who resorted to cunning-folk as to punish the cunning-folk themselves. In 1440, for example, William Banastre, a serving-man to William Sadyngstone, abbot of the house of Augustinian canons at Leicester, was accused of taking 'counsel of a wise woman at Harborough for a piece of silver of the house which had been taken elsewhere'. On the eve of the English Reformation, John Welford was sentenced by the Lincoln episcopal court to offer one pound of wax before the image of the Blessed Virgin, for having consulted cunning-men about some stolen money. Jacob Hopkin was presented before the Essex archdeaconry court in 1576 for visiting a 'conninge woman, to knowe by what means his masters cattell was bewytched'. In 1597 Paul Rigden and Alexander Violett were brought before the archdeacon of Canterbury for consulting a female 'sorcerer'. They pleaded that the woman, Mother Chambers, had merely given them some medicine for the 'yelow jandis'. In 1598 one William Taylior was brought before the York Ecclesiastical Commission, for that he sent to 'one widdowe Carre of Darfield reputed wise woman to knowe a remedy for his sicknes and her resolucion was that he was bewitched'. In the following year Thomas Ward of Purleigh, Essex, was presented for 'having lost certain cattell and suspecting that they were bewitched, he went to one Tailer in Thaxted, a wysard'.[37] Such presentments seem to have been numerous. In fact the available evidence suggests that the clients of cunning-folk were actually more prone to ecclesiastical prosecution than cunning-folk. How do we interpret this? Perhaps by considering the personal motivation behind presentments. In many instances, churchwardens acted upon village rumours and tip-offs. One suspects that many of the people who were accused of resorting to magic or magical practitioners were initially reported by neighbours motivated by spite, revenge or maybe even a sense of moral probity. Being brought before the archdecanal courts, which in rural areas were usually held in local churches or inns, may not have been as frightening as being brought before the higher secular courts, but it could still be an uncomfortable experience, and even those found not guilty had to pay court costs. In this sense, such accusations may have had little to do with the consultation of cunning-folk and more to do with neighbourly animosities. This form of mischief-making sometimes backfired on the accuser, for the church court was also the main forum for petty defamation claims. Thomas Veare, of Horndon-on-the-Hill, Essex, was presented in 1602 for slanderously saying that a carpenter named Clarke had been to London to see a cunning-woman about a stolen petticoat.[38] Of course, cunning-folk could also be the victims of malicious reporting, but there were many more people visiting cunning-folk than there were cunning-folk, and unless there was a determined proactive campaign by churchwardens and clergy to suppress them, it would always be the clients who bore the brunt of ecclesiastical censure. There were also practical considerations which militated against large-scale cunning-folk presentments. People did not necessarily consult their nearest practitioner, but often travelled many miles beyond their parishes to visit a preferred cunning-person. Even if a clergyman or churchwarden was concerned by the number of parishioners making such visits, the practical obstacles in dealing with someone ten or even twenty miles outside their ecclesiastical jurisdiction were too great to bother with. Furthermore, the practice of compurgation may also have frustrated clerical attempts to suppress cunning-folk.[39] Cunning-folk could be discharged if they denied the charges made against them and brought before the court a number of parishioners as compurgators to testify to their innocence. Successful compurgation depended on how favourably cunning-folk were considered by their neighbours.

From the early seventeenth century onwards the church courts began to pay less and less interest in cunning-folk and other aspects of popular magic. This pattern of decline was by no means uniform. The ecclesiastical courts in London, a city that abounded with magical practitioners, were apparently the earliest to lose interest in cunning-folk and popular magic, with hardly any relevant cases after 1600. Yet in some counties, including Yorkshire, Durham, Wiltshire and Essex, the courts continued to deal with witchcraft and magic during the first few decades of the seventeenth century. By the outbreak of the Civil War, however, when the courts fell out of use, far fewer cases of popular magic were being heard compared to fifty years before. The available evidence also indicates that following the restoration of the ecclesiastical courts after 1660 the presentment of cunning-folk or their clients became a rare event indeed. The basic reason for this was that the visitation articles issued to vicars and churchwardens, which stated precisely what misdemeanours were to be considered by the courts, largely omitted the practice of sorcery, witchcraft and charming. While a few visitations, such as those of the archdeacon of Shropshire and the bishop of Norwich, continued to call for the presentment of those involved in magic into the early eighteenth century, it seems that most dioceses mirrored the situation in Essex, where popular magic had been dropped from articles by the early 1640s.[40] This was certainly case for the dioceses of Carlisle (1627), Chichester (1634), Rochester (1639) and Lincoln (1641). The articles for the diocese of Gloucester and archdeaconry of Buckingham were still calling for the presentment of magical practitioners during the 1630s, but they too fell silent on the matter when visitations recommenced during the Restoration.

Why was it that at a time when clerical writers like Perkins and Bernard were publicly calling for greater action against cunning-folk, the ecclesiastical authorities began to lose interest in them? Perhaps with the passing of the statute of 1604 the church recognised that witchcraft and magic offences were more properly under the jurisdiction of the secular courts.[41] This makes sense chronologically, and several visitation articles from the 1630s state that only those who had 'used any inchantments, sorceries, witchcrafte, or incantations which are not made felony by the statute of this realme' ought to be dealt with by the church.[42] But the fact that until the 1620s numerous visitation articles continued to call for the reporting of those who practised magic, and that few of these referred to the secular law, counters the notion that the passing of the 1604 Act had a significant impact on presentments for magic. Moreover, there was no secular law punishing those who *consulted* cunning-folk, whereas articles clearly demanded the reporting of 'any that doe goe to seeke helpe at such sorcerers hands'.[43] That the presentment of cunning-folk's clients declined at the same time as those concerning cunning-folk further detracts from an explanation in terms of the 1604 statute. It would seem, rather, that there was a growing gulf between official intent and practice on the ground at this time.

It needs to be realised that, in terms of the number of cases dealt with, popular magic had always been a minor concern for church courts. They were considerably more preoccupied with sexual misconduct, drunkenness, slander, profanation of Sundays and disruption of church services. Furthermore, the weighty theological concerns of learned divines were not necessarily shared by church officials at the parochial level. Add to these two observations the fact that from the late sixteenth century onwards the business of church courts was increasingly taken up with cases of slander litigation, and we get the impression that concern over magic simply became overshadowed by more mundane moral problems. At a time when popular magic was no longer an issue for the London courts, defamation suits – the vast majority sexual in nature – rose from a total of one-third of litigation cases in the 1590s to around three-quarters in the 1630s.[44] It is likely that, with the population expanding significantly over this period, many ecclesiastical courts, particularly those in urban areas, found it increasingly difficult to cope with the volume of cases, and some parish officials simply made a practical decision to reduce the scope of their business. It must have been obvious to churchwardens and many clergymen that prosecuting those who practised magic was neither effective nor popular with the majority of parishioners. The censuring of other moral infringements such as slander, however, had much more popular support, and so made the task of pursuing such cases more practicable. At the local level, action was increasingly only taken against magical practitioners and their clients when they were involved in defamation suits or when their activities were in direct competition with the interests of the church – if, for example, people were resorting to them when they should have been in church. The only case of popular magic to be found in the surviving records of the Buckinghamshire archdeaconry courts for the 1630s concerns a charmer named Edith Clarke who charmed the toothache of Joan Mayes; but the thrust of the presentment was concerned with the point that she did it on the 'Sabbath day' rather than that.[45] The fact is that many early modern clergymen were pragmatically rather than puritanically motivated. Like many of their nineteenth-century counterparts, they recognised that tacit acceptance of popular magic was conducive to a more passive and pliant laity. Besides, not a few clergymen resorted to popular magic themselves.

By the late seventeenth century secular witch-trials had also reduced to a trickle. The last execution for witchcraft took place at Exeter in 1684/5, the last person found guilty was in 1712, and the last indictment for witchcraft occurred five years later. Justices of the peace and assize judges became increasingly cautious about the evidence required to prove guilt, and intellectually the whole basis of witchcraft and magic was being questioned. Unlike those accused of witchcraft, however, cunning-folk actually practised what they were accused of, satanic collusion excepted. Their crimes were, therefore, less problematic both from an intellectual and judicial point of view. There was no reason why prosecutions with regard to them should have diminished. The law did not specify that diabolic collusion in acts of conjuration or thief detection had to be proven. Just carrying out such practices was illegal, so even witchcraft sceptics could have had no qualms about invoking the 1604 Act in this respect. Nevertheless, judicial doubts about witchcraft apparently had an impact on the prosecution of cunning-folk. Just as indictments for *maleficium* under the witchcraft and conjuration statutes declined, so too did those concerning magic. Cunning-folk were presumably conscious of their relative immunity from the law, and the attitude of the eponymous cunning-woman in Edward Ravenscroft's play of 1684, an adaptation of *La devineresse* by Thomas Corneille and Jean Donneau de Vise, well illustrates their pragmatic response to threats of prosecution at this time. 'Nay, let 'em tell all', she remarks, 'if the world upbraid me, it will laugh at them; in this business it is more credit to deceive than be deceived: I can practise yet in remote cities, or live upon what I have already gained'.[46] The surviving records suggest that hardly any cunning-folk were prosecuted at the assizes for conjuration from the 1670s onwards, and there are certainly no extant cases beyond 1700. A trickle of prosecutions under the 1604 Act appeared sporadically before the quarter sessions during the second half of the seventeenth century. One late victim was Anne Kingsbury, who appeared before the Somerset magistrates in 1680 for attempting to speak with a spirit guarding a treasure hidden in a house in Bridgwater. It would seem, however, that the case was dismissed.[47] The suspicion is that the magistracy's growing unease concerning the prosecution of suspected witches made them uncomfortable about invoking any section of the 1604 Act. There was a reluctance to use a law that was increasingly seen as misguided or at least out of date. A new law was needed, one that distinguished between witches and cunning-folk, and between reality and fraud.

Under the Witchcraft Act of 1736 all existing statutes against witchcraft (except that relating to Ireland) were repealed and a new law was introduced for 'punishing such Persons as pretend to exercise or use any kind of witchcraft, sorcery, inchantment, or conjuration'. Those found so guilty faced a maximum sentence of one year's imprisonment without bail, and quarterly appearances in the pillory on market days. Although very few cunning-folk had ever swung from the gallows for their activities, that possibility had now been removed for good. The new Act effectively effaced the witch from the statute books, leaving cunning-folk as the main representatives of illicit magic. The content of the Act, nevertheless, represented a profound official change in attitude towards cunning-folk and their trade. In legal terms, at least, they were no longer considered to be doing the devil's work, and their magical activities were no longer considered as technically feasible but rather explicitly fraudulent pretences designed to fool the credulous. Yet, in practice, exactly the same activities listed in the defunct conjuration statutes remained criminal offences; only the interpretation of those crimes changed. In some respects, the legal position of cunning-folk returned to the way it had been before the early modern statutes against conjuration and the rise of the witch persecution formalised the concept of diabolic inspiration. In other words, cunning-folk were once again tried for what they could not practise rather than for what they could.

With the passing of the 1736 statute one might, perhaps, have expected a partial clamp-down on magical practitioners. There was at least some contemporary confidence in their salutary effect. The author of *Breslaw's Last Legacy*, a book of conjuring tricks, thought that 'witchcraft, witches and wizards, and those tawney sibyls, or gipsey gangs, are less numerous than in former days, and almost totally exploded by a late act of parliament'.[48] Although eighteenth-century assize and quarter session records have not been scrutinised or catalogued as extensively as those of preceding centuries, the evidence still indicates that there was no upsurge in action against magical practitioners. Until the nineteenth-century the rate of prosecution was probably roughly the same as it had been over the previous 200 years. After all, most prosecutions whether before 1736 or after, were the result of complaints brought by dissatisfied clients. So, unless there was an upsurge in popular discontentment with cunning-folk, there was no reason why there should have been a significant rise. This meant, of course, that most were able to carry on their trade with relative impunity. Well-known and prosperous cunning-folk like the Derbyshire-born Richard

Morris (1710–1793) practised for decades, gaining considerable regional notoriety, without ever apparently facing a spell in prison or the pillory. The renowned Yorkshire cunning-man Timothy Crowther (1694–1761) similarly maintained both his magical trade and his post as Skipton parish clerk without any serious legal interference.[49] Yet, as in previous centuries, disgruntled customers periodically sought legal compensation. In 1761, for instance, 'an old sorcerer of thirty years standing' was convicted at the Norwich quarter sessions for pretending to cure a poor woman of witchcraft.[50] Another unsatisfied client was a young man named Hall who, in 1814, summoned the Stroud cunning-man, Benjamin Evans. Hall consulted Evans concerning the theft of some of property, but after several fruitless visits and a few shillings later, all Evans could say was that he was 'getting nearer'. Hall reported him to the local magistrate and Evans was subsequently found guilty under the Witchcraft Act and spent the statutory year in prison, punctuated by four exposures in the pillory at Stroud.[51] A contemporary of Evans, John Jones, who practised his craft across the border in Wales, was induced to make a public recantation in the form of a handbill during his year's imprisonment in Cardiff gaol in 1807:

> This is to acknowledge my total ignorance of, and disbelief in, such matters, and my concern at having so long imposed on weak and credulous individuals, being at the same time thoroughly sensible of the mischievous tendency of such a traffic. I hereby most solemnly promise never to be again guilty of similar offences, and feel myself extremely thankful that I am not to suffer the punishment to its full extent, which the law directs on such occasions; and I most sincerely hope that this my recantation may be a check to the presumption of any person who might hereafter be inclined to exercise such vile arts for the purpose, not only of deceiving, but likewise pocketing the money of the unwary.[52]

It seems as though this published confession was some sort of trade-off with the authorities. Jones's avoidance of punishment 'to its full extent' suggests he escaped the statutory visits to the pillory. Yet, judging from our knowledge of other cunning-folk, it would come as no surprise if he went back on his solemn promise, and took up his trade once again after release from prison. Incarceration was not a particularly effective deterrent to cunning-folk.

Writing a couple of years after the publication of John Jones's prison cell contemplations, the editor of *Cobbett's State Trials*, Thomas Bayly Howell, who was in a good position to know these things, observed that the 1736 Act had resulted in 'very frequent convictions for extorting money, under pretence of telling fortunes, recovering lost or stolen goods etc, by skill in the occult sciences'.[53] This seems to contradict the impression already created that cunning-folk prosecutions were sporadic affairs at this time. But an examination of such prosecutions of the period shows that most of these 'frequent convictions' concerned itinerant or urban fortune-tellers rather than cunning-folk, people like William Turner, of Shaw Cross, near Dewsbury, who was tried at Wakefield quarter sessions in 1801. He was accused of having gone around the town of Halifax and its neighbourhood 'pretending' to be a deaf and dumb fortune-teller. He was found guilty and ordered to be whipped in public. In the same year at least five people were similarly prosecuted in London police courts.[54] Furthermore, such people were usually prosecuted under the laws against vagrancy and not the Witchcraft Act. Even on those occasions when cunning-folk were indicted, and the 1736 Act aptly covered their crimes, the authorities sometimes felt more comfortable invoking other laws. When in 1823 Sarah Roxborough defrauded a tradesman's wife of £25 by pretending to use magic to recover bad debts, she was tried for theft and not for 'pretended' sorcery.[55]

Although Howell's statement seems inaccurate regarding the invoking of the 1736 Act, it is true that during the early nineteenth century there was an increase in the prosecution of urban fortune-tellers and itinerant practitioners, gypsies in particular. This can be seen as symptomatic of wider fears concerning the expansion of the vagrant population at the time, coupled with concerns over vice, popular prophecy, politicisation and unrest during the hardships of the Napoleonic War. The problem became even more acute following the demobilisation of the army and navy after 1815, and the authoritarian response came in 1824 when the vagrancy laws were bolstered. Section four of the new Act reinforced the prosecution of 'every person pretending or professing to tell fortunes, or using any subtle craft, means, or device, by palmistry or otherwise, to deceive and impose on any of His Majesty's subjects'. Those found guilty could be sentenced to imprisonment with hard labour for up to three months. 'Incorrigible' offenders could face up to one year's imprisonment with hard labour, with males also being subjected to a whipping.[56] Although the Witchcraft Act was more explicitly concerned with the activities of cunning-folk, there seems to have been a certain reluctance and embarrassment on the part of magistrates to invoke a law that talked of witchcraft and magic, so the 1824 Vagrancy Act, which makes no mention of magic at all, came to be the main legal weapon against cunning-folk. It was under this law rather than the Witchcraft Act that the majority of cunning-folk were prosecuted over the ensuing decades. The implementation of the statute led, on occasion, to the absurd situation where prosperous, home-owning cunning-folk were ostensibly being prosecuted for vagrancy. It was only from the mid nineteenth century onwards, that there was a discernible increase in such cunning-folk prosecutions, the consequence not of further laws or even a concerted campaign against the agents of 'superstition' but of more effective policing. The majority of cunning-folk were based in rural areas and provincial towns where, unlike the cities, professional policing was only introduced following the County and Borough Police Act of 1856. The inception of organised, uniformed and full-time police forces, and the setting up of police stations, gave people more incentive and opportunity to resort to the law, and complaints about cunning-folk were more likely to be acted upon and investigated. Yet there was certainly no deluge of indictments after 1856: the drips merely became a trickle.

We should not always think of cunning-folk as the 'victims' of the legal system. Many were obviously familiar with the workings of the courts and, despite the illegality of their trade, felt quite comfortable with using the same formal instruments of justice to pursue their own grievances. Some, in fact, had a remarkably litigious streak. This might take the form of appeals against conviction. Take, for example, the Cheltenham cunning-woman Mrs Niblett. In 1830 she was brought before the petty sessions for using pretended sorcery, and was sentenced to six weeks' confinement in the Northleach house of correction. She hired a lawyer and appealed against the conviction at the following quarter sessions. The ensuing tribunal at Gloucester, chaired by a local clergyman, the Rev. Cooke, heard 'many ancient cases and convictions for sorcery produced pro and con', but unsurprisingly upheld the conviction.[57] Of more significance were those instances where cunning-folk resorted to the law against their clients. This sometimes occurred after assaults committed upon them by unhappy customers. In 1881 William Henry Hillman, a cunning-man of Ottery, Devon, prosecuted a farmer's son for scratching him with a wooden dart. The young man had originally consulted Hillman concerning the bewitchment of his family, but subsequently conceived the idea that Hillman had also put a spell upon them. Two years later the Somerset wizard James Stacey indicted nine villagers of West Mudford for beating him up after receiving unsatisfactory services.[58] Cunning-folk also resorted to the law to retrieve unpaid debts or damages. In 1846 the Exeter cunning-man James Tuckett unsuccessfully sued a client for repossessing a horse that had been given to him in lieu of payment. In the same year the Bideford 'white witch', William Salter, tried to sue a Barnstaple policeman for unlawful arrest after being apprehended for causing a disturbance, and two years later he lodged a complaint against a coal merchant whose cart had damaged his wagon.[59] One wonders whether such lawsuits were counter-productive, having negative repercussions in terms of the cunning-folks' reputations: some clients may have pondered why such powerful magicians had not used their magical powers rather than the law courts to achieve their aims.

Few cunning-folk had as many brushes with the law as Maria Giles, the 'Newbury Cunning Woman'. Between 1853 and 1871 she appeared in court no less than eleven times, though not always as a defendant. She was surely the most convicted cunning-person in history. As a result, she, and her residence in Bartholomew Street, were not only well known to the town's magistrates but also to the local press and the wider populace. The *Berkshire Chronicle* wearily reported each new court appearance with the preface 'Maria Giles Again.' In 1853 alone she was prosecuted on three separate occasions for assault, wilful damage to property and detecting stolen goods. In the same year, she, in turn, prosecuted a female neighbour for assaulting her daughter, and in a separate and far more serious incident charged her next-door neighbour with sexually assaulting the same daughter. In 1856 she was found guilty under the Vagrancy Act for deceiving a man whom she said she could cure of witchcraft. In May 1858 she was convicted at the assizes for perjury. In May 1864 she was brought before the Newbury petty sessions and charged under the Vagrancy Act for pretending to recover magically the property of a client's deceased mother. In 1865 she appealed against another conviction, this time under the statute against false pretences, but the court of Queen's Bench upheld the conviction. In 1868 she was tried at the Berkshire assizes for having received money to recover a stolen watch and identify the thief. In 1871 she received possibly her last sentence, once again for detecting stolen property. The case was initially heard by the borough police court. On being committed to trial at the next quarter sessions, she requested bail, which was a matter for the magistrates' discretion. Although they were well aware of her string of convictions, they recognised that she had always respected bail conditions, so they granted it her on condition of £20 personal surety and two lots of £10 from second parties. The fact that she managed to post it suggests that she had been doing rather well in her trade. Up until this point, Giles had spent nearly five out of the last eighteen years in prison, but she had taken up her profession again after each spell of incarceration. As the recorder at the quarter sessions remarked, 'Reform in her case seemed perfectly hopeless'. He felt that the only thing to do was to 'make an example of her by passing such a sentence as would effectually prevent her returning to her old course of life, at least for a long period, if she survived the punishment'. She was sentenced to five years penal servitude.[60]

One of several issues arising from the criminal history of Maria Giles concerns her vulnerability to prosecution. No other contemporary cunning-folk, either urban or rural, appeared before magistrate or judge. It has to be remembered, of course, that cunning-folk were only prosecuted when clients made official complaints. Maria Giles was not persecuted by the local police, even though they were well aware of her activities. Perhaps it was her individual personality that got her into so much trouble. She certainly had a provocative streak and took things too far. We can see this from her relations with a neighbour named Ann Wherrall. In 1853 she had been convicted at the local police court for assaulting Ann and her husband, and was fined £1 and twelve shillings. Maria would not let the matter lie, however, and straight after returning home from court sent her daughter, Clara, to the Wherralls' house to ask them for two shillings to help her pay the fine. This audacious request went down badly with the Wherralls, and a physical altercation ensued. Maria consequently launched her own prosecution for assault against Ann Wherrall. A couple of weeks later she was back in the same court for maliciously damaging the rented tenement she had just been asked to leave. One gets the impression that her landlady, Mrs Griffin, had ordered her out in response to her neighbourly disputes. If Giles also carried on in a similarly belligerent manner with her clients, no wonder they resorted to the law. It may also be that successive, effective convictions gave confidence to other dissatisfied clients to take legal action.

Another question arising from the story of Maria Giles is how, despite spending a year or more in prison on three separate occasions, she managed to maintain her client base. Such long spells in prison usually had a detrimental impact in trade terms, particularly as a removal was often a practical necessity after release. What Giles did, however, was to go back to the same street each time. That is where her rural clients knew they could find her. When Emma Gregory of Tadley lost some goods, a Mrs Swain of Aldermaston recommended a cunning-woman in Newbury: 'She didn't mention her name, but said if I inquired a little way down Bartholomew-street I should find her out.'[61] The notoriety she gained from the reporting of her trials further advertised both her business and where she could be found. Giles undoubtedly knew this: despite having a poor reputation in the street she refused to set up elsewhere. For cunning-folk bad press was, evidently, not always bad news. Even before the days of newspapers, word of mouth concerning the trial of a cunning-person could help boost his or her clientele. It was said of the infamous Stuart wizard John Lambe that 'his fame was never truly great, till he came to bee questioned by the lawes of the kingdome at assises and sessions', his presence at which 'did raise an opinion of his abilitie among the people'.[62] He was, however, beaten to death by a London mob some years later.

Giles's criminal history is exceptional. Even with a fully functioning police force from the mid nineteenth century onwards, only a fraction of what must have been hundreds if not thousands of unhappy customers ever resorted to the law. This fact was not lost on those who continued to see cunning-folk as social pests. Sabine Baring-Gould, for example, recognised what he saw as their 'immunity' from prosecution, but hoped that 'some day certain of these gentry will be tripped up, and then, though magistrates can no more send them to the stake, they will send them to cool their heels in gaol, and richly they will deserve the punishment'.[63] This call for action was belated. By the time it was made the role of cunning-folk in society was weakening. Writing in 1922 the folklorist John Udal believed this was due to the 'salutary effect' of the 'firmer application of the wholesome laws relating to "rogues and vagabonds"'.[64] But this was not the case. Few cunning-folk were convicted after 1900 because the basis of their trade was being undermined by broader social and economic changes. When the Fraudulent Mediums Act of 1951 consigned the Witchcraft Act to the dustbin of history, and expunged the crime of pretended sorcery and conjuration, there were no cunning-folk left anyway.

2

## *For Good or Evil?*

The previous chapter will have given the reader a good idea of the range of forces lined up against cunning-folk, but now we need to explore in greater detail the reasons why cunning-folk were considered in such a bad light over the centuries. It is easy to understand why there was so much fear and concern regarding witches, but the hostility towards to those who practised beneficial magic is less easy to comprehend. What was so bad about doing good? To answer this question the debate over cunning-folk needs to be traced not only through trial documents and clerical diatribes, but also through a wide variety of other literary forms. They were the subject of plays in the seventeenth century, biographical accounts in the eighteenth century and novels in the nineteenth century. As the educated fear of the devil subsided, they also became objects of antiquarian curiosity and figures of rustic romance, though they remained bogey figures to those preoccupied with the religious and moral well-being of the poor.

It has already been mentioned that cunning-folk were often described as 'white' witches in opposition to harmful 'black' witches. The identification of cunning-folk with such a benign colour may have been acceptable to their satisfied clients, even if it was not a term widely used in popular discourse, but the distinction was one that sorely exercised sixteenth- and seventeenth-century clergymen. For them no such distinction could be made. Cunning-folk were as black as the blackest witches. In fact, Protestant anti-witchcraft literature, both in England and elsewhere in Europe, was as much concerned with the diabolic threat posed by cunning-folk as with witches.[1] For some clergymen, including William Perkins and Richard Bernard, cunning-folk were actually *more* pernicious than those they referred to as 'hurting' or 'cursing' witches. One relevant section in Perkins's *A Discourse of the Damned Art of Witchcraft* is headed, 'The good witch, the worser of the two'. He went on to explain how the 'more horrible and detestable monster is the good witch, for look in what place soever there be any bad Witches that hurt onely, there also the devil hath his good ones, who are better knowne than the bad, beeing commonly called wisemen, or wise-women'.[2] In Perkins's view these people did 'a thousand fold more harme', and represented a grave threat to Christendom.[3] For Bernard the 'curing witch' or 'good witch' was likewise 'in many respects worse than the other'.[4] Another clergyman, Thomas Cooper, believed 'good witches' were 'verie dangerous instruments for the restoring and encrease of the kingdome of Antichrist'.[5] Writing several decades later the Huntingdonshire vicar, John Gaule, asserted, 'the accounted Good witch, is indeed the worse and more wicked of the two'.[6] The witch-hunter John Stearne recognised the popular distinction between 'those called bad witches, and those called white or good witches', but personally considered 'all witches be bad, and ought to suffer alike, being both in league with the Devill'.[7] Shortly after the Restoration the physician Thomas Ady, a man sceptical of much that was said about witchcraft, still believed that those 'commonly called cunning men, or good witches' were 'themselves right witches, that cause men to seek to the Devil for help'.[8] Even later in the century, the Somerset gentleman Richard Bovet felt it necessary to assert that, 'Tho these wretched artists are commonly distinguished into those of the Black, and White orders; they are certainly the same, and cannot be said to differ in deeds of darkness, which admit of no difference of colour. They are certainly both alike guilty in compounding with the Devil.'[9] Why did cunning-folk generate such vehement dislike during the late sixteenth and seventeenth centuries? The answer obviously lies in the perceived relationship between cunning-folk and the devil.

According to the clergyman Henry Holland, there were three types of satanic covenant: 'some have an open, expresse, and evident league and confederacie with Sathan: some a more hid and secret: some a mixt and meane betweene both'. Under the first belonged all 'manifest conjurations', under the second 'divining, astrologie, palmestrie, and such like', and under the third 'all practises of superstitious magicke in all sorceries whatsoever'.[10] Cunning-folk were, therefore, guilty of entering into all three diabolic alliances, whereas the witch was usually only involved in either the first or third. In this sense cunning-folk were thought to have sunk even deeper into hellish sin than harmful witches. But what was most iniquitous about cunning-folk was the insidious way that the devil used them to ensnare not only the bodies but also the very souls of unwitting Christians. As William Perkins explained, the bad witch 'did onely hurt the bodie, but the devil by meanes of the other, though he have left the bodie in good plight, yet he hath laid fast hold on the soule, and by curing the body, hath killed that'.[11] Herein lay the threat they posed to Christendom. The bad witches may have harmed or killed their victims, but at least their souls remained otherwise uncorrupted. Cunning-folk, however, enticed people into an implicit bargain with the devil by encouraging them to seek magical aid instead of putting their faith in God's will. To seek their aid was to sup at the devil's table. As one pamphleteer wrote concerning a cunning-man named Marsh, of Dunstable, 'the Divel is never blacker, and more to be abhorr'd than when hee transforms himself into an Angel of Light'.[12] Cunning-folk, and those who consulted them, basically broke the First Commandment concerning the worshiping of false gods, and so, according to Henry Holland, they committed 'a most horrible and dreadful sinne ... for the contempt of God and his Word'. Moreover, those bewitched who sought a cure from cunning-folk were doubly cursed as 'they seeke helpe of the same serpent that stung them ... they would have Sathan to drive out Sathan'.[13]

It is important to establish that 'demonologists' like Perkins and Holland readily accepted that cunning-folk were capable of effecting cures, detecting stolen property and other such beneficial magical acts. Perkins, for example, believed that cunning-folk could identify witches, but argued that such evidence was inadmissible in court because during the process of divination the devil, displaying his usual wicked mischief making, might appear in the shape of someone who was perfectly innocent.[14] The point that such writers wanted to underline was that it was these abilities of cunning-folk that made them more dangerous than witches. This was most clearly evident with regards to healing. As James Mason conceded, 'there are diverse and sundry kinds of Maladies, which though a man do go to all the physitions that can be heard of, yet he shall find no remedy: wheras sometimes they are cured by those which are called cunning folkes'. The reason for their success, however, was because 'the sorcerers by the meanes of satan doe heale diseases ...

The which he is more apt and able naturally to bring to passe than man'.[15] In other words, the ability of cunning-folk to cure was proof that their power was satanic, since other than God only the devil possessed the requisite medical understanding to cure what no mortal could. It was widely accepted at the time that, despite his 'fall', Satan still possessed exceptional, superhuman intellectual powers, and an understanding of the natural world that no man could fathom. The London independent minister, Nathaniel Homes, described the devil as 'being a spirit of exceeding knowledge (for hee lost onely his goodnesse). He understanding better than men the Prophecies of the Old Testament, the secrets of nature, what nature may be heightened unto in being, or operation, both naturally and morally, oft times doth hitt right in Predictions.'[16] He could not perform miracles like God, but he could manipulate natural forces to make things appear miraculous. Cunning-folk were thought to tap Satan's skill in medicine and prognostication rather than actually being invested with such 'natural' powers themselves. In the words of Homes, Satan 'inableth them to tel many hidden things, he speaking in them or by them'.[17]

Critics were well aware of cunning-folks' popularity, and the various arguments that could be brought forward in their defence. The clergy in particular must have heard them on numerous occasions from the cunning-folk and their clients brought before the church courts. As a consequence, those against cunning-folk went to considerable lengths to explain why, although they might appear to do good, they were actually doing the opposite. A technique considered effective in this respect was to present the arguments in the form of a dialogue wherein the apparent benefits of cunning-folk were put forward only to be roundly demolished. In Henry Holland's *Treatise Against Witchcraft* we have Mysodaemon arguing with the learned Theophilus, the mouthpiece of Holland himself. Mysodaemon, for example, puts forward a defence that, 'such of these practitioners, as can and will cure the sicke, finde thinges loste, have a good neere gesse in praedictions, are not in any wise to be blamed ... they seeme to doe no harme, but much good, and they speake the very trueth often'; but Theophilus then demolishes this view by reference to the Bible and the demonological theories which have already been outlined.[18] As a didactic instrument George Gifford's *Dialogue Concerning Witches and Witchcraftes* was more skilfully rooted in the vernacular, the arguments for and against cunning-folk being laid out principally through the conversation between two peasants, Samuel and Daniel. Gifford, an Essex clergyman renowned for his qualities as a preacher, has been described as a 'Tudor Anthropologist' due to his understanding of the mentality of his parishioners and the reasons why they resorted to cunning-folk – all the better to provide explanations for their iniquity couched in their own idiom.[19]

Such texts were neither written nor produced in a format meant to instruct directly those who consulted cunning-folk, the majority of whom would have been illiterate. They were written, in part, to influence the ecclesiastic and legal authorities to proceed more ruthlessly against cunning-folk. Holland, for example, has Mysodaemon asking, 'may not the magistrate provide against this evill?' The answer being: 'The Almightie God chargeth him so to doe.'[20] But they were also presumably meant to help instruct the clergy and men of authority on how to counter, simply and effectively, the popular defence of cunning-folk on the frontline – in other words at the parish level. Although the evidence is minimal, it is probable that in churches up and down the country hundreds of sermons issued forth from the pulpit denouncing cunning-folk, explaining why resorting to them led to damnation. The iniquity of magical practitioners was also drilled into the laity through the catechism.[21] Catechising, which consisted of question and answer sessions in church, was an integral and compulsory aspect of Anglican worship. The aim was to ensure that everyone had an understanding of Protestant Christian tenets and understood the moral and religious conduct expected of them. Although the official Prayer Book catechism did not contain an explicit condemnation of cunning-folk, many other catechisms published for use by both clergy and lay folk did, including Gifford's own contribution, *A Briefe Catechisme* (1601). More influential, possibly, were the numerous editions of the catechism by Alexander Nowell, dean of St Paul's, in which pupils were instructed that amongst those who sinned against the First Commandment were 'soothsayers, conjurers, sorcerers, witches, charmers, and all that seeke unto them'.[22] What the catechisms did not do, though, was explain why cunning-folk and their like worked contrary to God's laws. This is where dialogues by men such as Gifford and Holland came into their own. They would have certainly helped clergymen and teachers to explain in an easily understood format why it was a sin to consult cunning-folk. As the church court records show, however, there was a gulf between providing such condemnation of cunning-folk and actually being successful in convincing the laity of their spiritual crimes.

Not all writers of the period saw cunning-folk with horns on their heads and the devil behind them, but rather as garbed in the capacious cloak and wearing the sly look of the trickster: more in the service of Mammon than Satan. The first English voice to debunk the reputation of cunning-folk in this respect was the Kentish gentleman Reginald Scot. In 1584, as the witch-trials were reaching their peak, Scot published a scathing attack not only on the prosecution of alleged witches but also on the whole basis of witchcraft and magic. In his *Discoverie of Witchcraft* Scot argued, like many since, that the witchcraft mentioned in the Scriptures bore little relation to that of his own time, and that the Hebraic terms relating to witchcraft had been mistranslated. For Scot the extraordinary powers ascribed to witches and other practitioners of magic were, as he believed the Bible implied, nothing but deceptions and delusions. Those who thought people possessed such abilities were blasphemers who denied the all-encompassing power of God. Scot had sympathy, therefore, for the unfortunate individuals who were being tried and hanged as witches, but utter contempt for cunning-folk who deliberately exploited and promoted blasphemous beliefs. He described as absolute 'cooseners' those who took 'upon them, either for glorie, fame, or gaine, to doo anie thing, which God or the divell can doo: either for foretelling of things to come, bewraieng of secrets, curing of maladies, or working of miracles'.[23] To further expose their cheating practices Scot provided a detailed exposition of such deceiving arts as juggling, legerdemain and illusion. He also presented the reader with a host of spells and conjurations in order to 'explode' their supposed efficacy and expose the whole dubious foundation of magic.

Although Scot argued his case brilliantly, he was swimming against the tide of contemporary thinking about cunning-folk. To deny that they possessed real diabolic powers was to undermine the theological orthodoxy of the time. Indeed, it was partly indignation at Scot's scepticism that motivated James I to write his *Daemonologie*, which laid out once again the diabolic nature of witchcraft and magic in the form of a dialogue. That is not to say that Scot's was a solitary voice. A pamphlet recording the trial of the cunning-woman Judith Philips in 1594/5 had no concern for her satanic influence, but was merely disgusted by the 'many cozening sleights and devices' with which she deceived 'the simpler sort of people in the country'. In a similar vein an anonymous witch-trial pamphleteer, writing in 1619, took the opportunity in his introduction to take a swipe at 'the conceit of wisemen or wisewomen', who were denounced as 'coseners and deceivers'.[24] In Thomas Heywood's play *The Wise Woman of Hogsdon*, first performed in the early years of the seventeenth century, the central character is portrayed as a clever manipulator rather than as a satanic conspirator. But it was not until the second half of the seventeenth century that Scot's opinions attracted wider sympathy. The sceptical views embodied in the writings of Thomas Ady and Robert Filmer were influenced by Scot, and later writers such as John Wagstaffe and John Webster pursued similar themes.[25] But no matter what side of the demonological debate intellectuals were on, they were all united in their loathing of cunning-folk: one side wanted them punished for satanic conspiracy, the other for fraud and promoting erroneous beliefs.

Another thing on which Protestant witchcraft writers could agree was the iniquity of the Catholic Church. This too helped shape attitudes towards cunning-folk. Following the Reformation, the Church of England and its courts set about suppressing all traces of what were denounced as popish 'superstitions'. It was not only the visible signs of Catholic worship that required effacing, but also a whole system of popular worship based around masses, sacraments, exorcisms, Latin prayers and the saints. Much of popular religion was concerned with the clerical and lay employment of these aspects of devotion to help cure and avert the misfortunes experienced by fellow parishioners. Holy water, consecrated candles, crosses, rosaries and other such trappings of Catholic worship were also imbued with magical powers, and were used in personal acts of folk magic as well as orthodox devotion.[26] From the 1540s onwards – with the exception of the brief reign of Queen Mary – it was the business of the church courts to ensure that no clergymen continued to offer such services, and also that no lay folk resorted to sinful Catholic 'relics' for personal succour. It was not just papist priests who were seen as agents in the perpetuation of Catholic worship, but cunning-folk as well. Protestant demonologists liked to portray priests and cunning-folk as representing some sort of infernal brotherhood. Both were labelled 'conjurors'. John Melton said of cunning-folk: 'you had your ceremonies from the Papists ... or they from you, for you both cousen the poore blinded people after one manner; first, of their soules, by drawing them to superstition; secondly, of their estates, by defrauding them of their money'.[27] A controversial Puritan exorcist, John Darrell, described a Lancashire wise-man, Edmund Hartlay, as using 'certaine popish charmes and hearbs by degrees'. The Wiltshire cunning-woman Anne Bodenham was accused of being 'much adicted to Popery, and to papistical fancies'.[28] Leaving aside such partisan criticisms and expressions of intolerance, there was an element of truth in the claimed association between cunning-folk and Catholicism. In their use of certain elements of prayer, exorcism and holy objects, cunning-folk borrowed from Catholic practices, not only at the time but also in subsequent centuries. Protestant suspicions were confirmed by the activities of people like Henry Clegate of Headcorn, brought before a Kent church court for curing bewitched people and cattle by repeating prayers and the creed. He confessed he had been taught to do so many years before by his mother and a neighbouring priest. In 1664–65 a Mrs Pepper was tried before the York assizes for using Catholic 'charms'. She had attempted to cure a pitman named Robert Pyle of witchcraft in the following manner:

> she did ... call for a bottle of holy water, and tooke the same, and sprinkled itt upon a redd hott spott which was upon the back of his right hand; and did take a silver crucifix out of her breast, and laid itt upon the said spott. And did then say that shee knewe by the said spott what his disease was, and did take the said crucifix and putt itt in his mouth.[29]

When not penning attacks on witches, cunning-folk and Catholics, some seventeenth-century theologians also turned their attention to another perceived threat from within – Quakers. The Society of Friends, which was how members of this lay Protestant movement referred to themselves, was accused of attracting converts by means of witchcraft and conjuration. The society's founder, George Fox, was labelled a sorcerer by some of his opponents, and it was said that he and others could 'fascinate' people with their stare. The trembling fits some members displayed when experiencing deep religious emotion, and which gave rise to the term 'Quaker', were considered by some to be a sign that they were under the control of the devil.[30] This helps explain the origin of a fulminating attack on cunning-folk by the Quaker activist, Richard Farnworth (d. 1666). Like most Quakers, Farnworth was troubled by the accusations of diabolism that were being made against his faith. When in 1654 an Independent minister, Nicholas Greaton of Tamworth, 'was there discovered to be a fortune teller, or an Inchanter, a Wizard that tells people lyes for mony', Farnworth decided to make a public issue of it by producing a condemnatory tract. By doing so he presumably aimed to distance the Friends from suspicions that they condoned or engaged in such magic.[31] In a raging attack, with words tumbling over each other to the point of incoherence, Farnworth tried to express his loathing for magical practitioners in general, and Greaton's 'wicked spirit' in particular. He gave general notice that 'all that are black artists, the Divel's wise men, witches or wizards, you are but in nicromancy, or the Devil's counsell and familiarity only, and knoweth not the counsell of God'. Such abominable people, he said, 'sought to harden the peoples heart against the truth'. For their customers he had equally harsh words: 'You that seek after wizards disobey the Lord, and turn from him, to enter into fellowship with the Divell, and take counsell of him in a wizard, and are defiled thereby'.[32] Farnworth's views were echoed by George Fox a couple of years later. Those who consulted wizards had 'gone a whoring', he declared, and God would 'cut them off from among his people'.[33] The Quaker position concerning cunning-folk and their clients was no different to that of the Anglican authorities, or that of the Catholic clergy for that matter.

The last years of the seventeenth and the dawn of the eighteenth century undoubtedly saw the intellectual perception of cunning-folk shift decidedly towards a position in which they were seen as pernicious fraudsters rather than Satan's servants. This was a view that came to shape the 1736 Witchcraft Act, and which was largely the result of increasing circumspection towards the whole basis of demonological witchcraft. The Anglican Church had long given up on trying to suppress popular magic at grassroots level, having pragmatically opted out of official censure in most dioceses by this time. A similar ecclesiastical trend is evident in its scholastic as well as judicial involvement with the laity. Around the same time catechisms also dropped any reference to those seeking out conjurors and charmers as committing a sin against the First Commandment.[34] It seems that as popular magic gradually became disassociated from diabolism, belief in the efficacy of magic no longer represented such a serious moral concern, and the Anglican Church distanced itself from its more interventionist past.

Although this tide of circumspection concerning the reality of witchcraft, magic and diabolic inspiration encroached more and more on the consciousness of the intellectual classes, there were many educated people who clung to belief in satanic contracts. In 1680 a gentleman named John Brinley of Brockton, Staffordshire, was so frustrated by the popularity of local cunning-folk that he decided to make it his 'business to undeceive the people, and to shew them that it is altogether unlawful to have recourse to such men, who practise unlawful Arts'. For Brinley, 'white witches' not only contravened the law of the land but also the word of God, though he accepted they did not always do so consciously: 'those that do such things are in a kind of league with the Devil, though ignorantly they think otherwise'.[35] In the following decade a periodical called the *Athenian Mercury*, which dealt with a wide variety of questions from readers on issues of the day, received a query concerning 'Whether magicians or conjurers can cause or force stolen goods, living creatures, etc. to be brought to their owners again'. The answer was couched firmly in demonological terms: 'Undoubtedly the Devil has power, by GOD's Permission, himself to perform all this – and may do it at the desire of his slaves, in order to enslave others, and take 'em the more off from their dependence on the divine being.'[36] Although the *Athenian Mercury* claimed to have a consultative board of learned men, there were in fact only three people involved, its publisher John Dunton, a mathematician and hack writer named Richard Sault, and the clergyman Samuel Wesley (father of John).[37] The author of the above response was almost certainly Wesley. We know from other sources that he was a great believer in the interventionist powers of Satan, and he also preached against cunning-folk on several occasions.[38] One wonders how far the urban professionals and tradespeople who read the *Athenian Mercury* would have accepted Wesley's belief in the diabolic powers of cunning-folk.

The issue was no doubt still contested enough to spark numerous coffee house debates as the seventeenth century came to a close.

In a similar vein, in 1707 an anonymous tract entitled *The Black Art Detected and Expos'd* condemned cunning-folk. Its author was induced to write this tirade against the 'Hellish impiety' of such people, and all those who consulted them, after he had been bound hand and foot by thieves and burgled. He was subsequently incensed to find that the local gossips reported he had not been particularly bothered about the thefts because his 'money, goods and plate' had been recovered thanks to the art of a cunning-man.[39] But the most outspoken attack during the early years of the eighteenth century was by a physician, Richard Boulton, an old school demonologist in the mould of Perkins, who defended the theory that witches and magical practitioners were part of a satanic conspiracy. His *Compleat History of Magick, Sorcery and Witchcraft*, published in 1715, was a last attempt to bolster a crumbling intellectual viewpoint, citing the weight of historical evidence provided by previous trial confessions as proof of the continued diabolical threat to Christendom. Although Boulton was far from being a leading light of the early eighteenth-century intelligentsia, the *Compleat History* was troublesome enough to sceptical intellectuals to require some sort of considered riposte. The man who responded was Francis Hutchinson, a clergyman and future bishop. In 1718 he wrote *A Historical Essay Concerning Witchcraft*, in which he largely repeated the arguments put forward by Scot nearly 140 years earlier. Just as Boulton had used published trial material to prove the existence of diabolic witchcraft, Hutchinson effectively used the same sources to demonstrate the fundamental flaws in the evidence brought against supposed witches. Boulton responded in splenetic fashion in *The Possibility and Reality of Magick*, attacking both witches and those who denied their continued existence. It should be remembered that, according to the old theological orthodoxy to which Boulton subscribed, cunning-folk were essentially viewed as witches. He undoubtedly had both 'bad' and 'good' in mind when he reiterated that 'the laws against such persons ought to be put in execution, lest we disobey God, and in excusing horrible crimes, suffer the world to be overrun with wickedness'.[40] Although Hutchinson bitterly opposed Boulton's views on witches, the two protagonists nevertheless found common cause when it came to cunning-folk. 'Not that I would have our cheating Fortunetellers, Jugglers, pretended Conjurers, Witch-Doctors, Gypsies, Calculators of Nativities ... or any real outward acts of sorcery, to be suffered unpunished', avowed Hutchinson. 'I am so far from that, that I heartily wish the grand-jury would present such misdemeanours, and have them punished more severely than they are.'[41] But to reinforce the argument that there was no conclusive evidence to confirm the continued existence of witches, it was essential for Hutchinson to remove cunning-folk and diviners from the witchcraft equation. It was crucial because, unlike witches, no one could deny that cunning-folk existed, or were practising what they were accused of (diabolism excepted) – there was ample evidence to prove it. Only by denouncing the former as a fraudulent reality could the latter be consigned as a historical chimera. Witches were a fact of the past but cunning-folk were very much a problem for the present.

In 1727 a book appeared with a title that deliberately aped that of Boulton's work, but which confirmed the position taken by Hutchinson. Its contents stoked anti-cunning-folk sentiment and may have influenced those who formulated the 1736 Witchcraft Act. *A Compleat System of Magick: or, The History of the Black-Art*, a work of over 400 pages, was published anonymously but can be firmly attributed to Daniel Defoe, one of the most prolific and influential authors of his time. Although we now know him for such literary masterpieces as *Moll Flanders* and *Robinson Crusoe*, much of Defoe's journalistic output was produced incognito. He was an opportunistic writer capable of generating heated political and social debates in the press by anonymously contending both sides of an argument. One could, therefore, question his scruples if not his prodigious abilities. This digression is relevant because the same fluidity of view is evident concerning the subject of magic. In 1711 Defoe wrote an article in a conservative periodical, *The Review*, in which he defended the reality of witchcraft by reference to Scripture and the weight of judicial evidence – the same proofs that Boulton's thesis depended on.[42] In the following decade, however, we find his views, like many others, moving over towards Hutchinson's position. Scepticism concerning the diabolic pact is evident in his 1726 publication, *The Political History of the Devil*, and a year later *A Compleat System of Magick* sealed the intellectual transition. From Defoe's now 'enlightened' viewpoint, witches were considered an anachronism, and cunning-folk were likewise to be discarded as relics of the past: 'The Black Art is at end ... so that you have now nothing left but a few Jugglers, Cunning Men, Gypsies and Fortune-tellers. In short the trade is decay'd'.[43] Decayed intellectually that was, not, he regretted, in terms of popularity. He decried both the deceits of cunning-folk and the conceits of those who continued to resort to them: 'tis not their cunning, but their clients want of cunning, that gives them the least appearance of common sense in all their practice'.[44] He thought about exposing 'the weak doings of those cunning men, and how they delude the poor people; but 'tis of no great use'.[45] Little could be achieved through denunciation he reckoned: popular credulity was too entrenched.

From the 1730s onwards, and particularly after the implementation of the 1736 Witchcraft Act, the clamour against cunning-folk subsided. Attacks had usually been tied up with the wider debate over witches, and as that became a redundant intellectual issue, in public at least, so the war of words against cunning-folk subsided too. Once separated from the witchcraft debate, writings about cunning-folk began to exhibit a more complex response to the continued existence of such people than just mere denunciation. Now that the strong fug of diabolism that clung around cunning-folk had largely dispersed, curiosity about them could be expressed in more diverse ways. An initial sign of this subtler intellectual engagement with the figure of the cunning-man was a pamphlet entitled *The Life and Character of Harvey, the Famous Conjurer of Dublin*, published in Dublin and London in 1728. Although the author remained anonymous, one surviving copy of this rare pamphlet has an old handwritten note on the frontispiece stating that it was by J. Swift. Familiarity with the works of the great satirist Jonathan Swift (1667–1745) leads one to suspect that this might have been from his pen. Over seventy-two pages the author builds up a portrait of Harvey, who is described as a tall, round-shouldered, pale-faced, ferret-eyed man who never laughed. He 'was pious; but then he never went to church. He talk'd often, of God, but much more of nature. He was a woman-hater, but then he was a mighty admirer of the stars.' No one knew from where he had come. Although widely read, the only books he owned were those concerned with the 'Black-art', otherwise he borrowed and hired what he wanted. His views were radical, and he swore that 'neither religion, justice, or health, would be the lot of mankind, till the orders of priest, lawyer, and physician were, utterly, abolished'.[46] Ultimately, Harvey is denounced as 'a mere farrago of a man' for espousing 'the power of witches and wizards, of conjurers and necromancers, over the minds, bodies and fortunes of man'.[47]

Like Defoe, much of Swift's writings were published anonymously or pseudonymously, and as a consequence work has wrongly been attributed to both of them. But if Harvey is one of Swift's creations, rather than one of his imitators, it was not the first time that he had focused on occult practitioners in such a fashion. Twenty years earlier he had published a mock almanac under the *nom de plume* Isaac Bickerstaff. The primary target of his satire was a successful astrologer and almanac maker, John Partridge. So subtly and skilfully written was the almanac that it was taken as a serious prophetic record both in England and abroad.[48] *The Life and Character of Harvey* displays the same subtlety as Swift's astrological deceptions, and it could quite reasonably be taken at face value as a biographical account of a real person. But there are a number of indicators to confirm that Harvey was Swiftian fiction rather than fact. Apart from the Dublin association – Swift was dean of St Patrick's in the city – Harvey's views also suspiciously echo those expressed by Swift elsewhere, particularly his dissatisfaction with organised religion. One can also detect Swiftian preoccupations in the content of several of Harvey's detailed prophecies. One of these harked back to the Lilliputians of *Gulliver's Travels*, for in it Harvey predicts that in the year 6000 the tallest man would only be five feet tall, diminishing to a mere two and a half feet in the year 8000, by which time most men would be eunuchs and the Apocalypse imminent.[49]

The fact that literary society of the early eighteenth century engaged with the subject of cunning-folk is surely a testament to the extent to which these magical practitioners continued to impinge upon the educated consciousness. They may not have received quite as much exposure as the astrological fraternity, but astrologers had their own literary mouthpiece in the almanac, which made them far more visible, and particularly irked 'enlightened' sensibilities concerning the role of print. It was also because of print that the critics could actually engage with astrologers, provoke them, and attempt to subvert their influence. Cunning-folk, on the other hand, did not engage in literary debate, and remained a largely silent and frustratingly diffuse target. On the rare occasion when satirist and cunning-person encountered one another in the flesh, the results could quite literally be explosive. One day in 1752 the eccentric Lancashire dialect author, artist and teacher John Collier (1708–1786) encountered a local wise-man named George Clegg. Collier, a renowned practical joker, thought Clegg a fitting victim for his next prank. Under the guise of his pen name Tim Bobbin, Collier subsequently wrote a humorous account of the experience entitled 'The Prickshaw witch blown up, or the conjuror out conjured'.[50] Here we have cunning-folk presented as figures of fun, condemned with mockery rather than censure, deflated by ridicule rather than argument. It was a technique Defoe had suggested as the only way to enlighten their 'foolish' clients. After all, nearly two centuries of preaching and judicial threat demonstrably had little or no effect. According to Defoe, 'The best course that I can think of to cure the people of this itch of their brain, the tarantula of the present age, in running to cunning men, as you call them, and the most likely to have success, is this, of laughing at them'.[51]

Clegg, a factory operative by trade, had originally practised in Whitworth, Lancashire, but subsequently resided in and around Rochdale.[52] It was at a book auction in that town one spring evening that Collier first caught sight of Clegg, 'an ancient man with one eye, a slouched hat, and very meagre countenance'. In response to a remark made about the cold weather, Clegg foretold the climatic conditions for the next week. Collier commented, 'you understand astrology, I perceive', to which Clegg replied that he had studied it since he was fifteen years old. 'Why then you can calculate nativities, tell fortunes, and find lost or stolen goods?' inquired Collier. Clegg informed him that he had done so for around forty years. To the question, 'Why, then you're a sort of conjurer?', Clegg answered with a smile, 'Eigh, I'm oft caw'd so'. Seeing an opportunity to play a trick on this 'kind of mungrel between fool and knave', Collier hatched a plan that began with his commissioning Clegg to draw up his young daughter's horoscope. They arranged to meet several days later. Meanwhile Collier, along with several companions, rented a room which they especially prepared for the meeting. They placed a pound of gunpowder under the chair destined for Clegg's posterior, and from the room above they intended to pour a quantity of 'well mixed t__d and p_ss' to dowse Clegg once the gunpowder had been ignited. After complaints from the landlord, however, they had to make do with plain water instead. The intention was quite simply to utterly humiliate the wise-man. On the fateful day, Clegg duly turned up and produced a sixteen-page account of the future life of Collier's daughter. After conversing in mock reverential tones about the wise-man's astrological handiwork, Collier ignited the gunpowder and ran out of the room, leaving behind a sooty, damp and dazed Clegg. That was the last Collier saw of Clegg, but cunning-folk did not take such set-backs lying down; months after the event Collier received the following letter:

> Sir, this comes to acquaint you, that if you do not pay me for the calculating your daughters nativity, I will make use of the law to get it, and then you may expect to pay dear for your pastime; for I do not find that ever you intend to pay me, for you have had time sufficient to pay me already the small sum of five shillings.
>
> Note – If you neglect to pay me, I will send the catchpoles in a few days: all from, Your abused servant, Geo. Clegg.

Collier replied in verse, concluding:

> No, no, good Faustus, 'twill not do,
> My teeth as soon as coin for you:
> And hope that this my flat denial,
> Will quickly bring it to a trial;
> When I don't doubt to make you pay
> For all your rogu'ries in this way;
> A cat with nine-tails, wooden stocks,
> And pillories, are for such folks;
> And sure there are some laws i' th' nation
> In force against your conjuration:
> Or, what deserves more ample scourging,
> Your cheating folks, with lies and forging.
> So if you squeak but in the gizzard,
> You're try'd by th' name of Prickshaw-Wizzard

In the last exchange we hear of the incident, Clegg had tried unsuccessfully to engage a local attorney, leaving Collier avowing to defend himself against 'the bedlamite'. Collier could not resist having the final word and wrote a subtler satirical swipe, 'A Codicil to the last Will and Testament of James Clegg, Conjurer', in which the wise-man asks that the following be engraved on his gravestone:

> Mourn all ye brewers of good ale,
> Sellers of books and news;
> But smile ye jolly priests, he's pale,
> Who grudg'd your pow'r, and dues.[53]

Clegg, himself, might not have begrudged such an epitaph.

Several decades after George Clegg's experience as a human rocket, an even more extraordinary event occurred in the annals of cunning-folk. For the very first time they were publicly defended as valued members of society. This message was transmitted in a biographical account of Richard Morris (1710–1793), a Derbyshire cunning-man who later set up a lucrative practice in Shropshire. A hundred years after his death, tales were still being told about his exploits in the Welsh borders.[54] The author, who once again decided to remain anonymous, obviously knew and liked Morris well, though he described himself as 'a critical observer of all his actions, for near fifty years'. The stated aim of publishing an account of his life was to explore 'whether good or evil has been the general result', with the outcome falling firmly in his favour.[55] The author, evidently of an anticlerical persuasion, thought 'that a country conjuror is more useful in the place he resides in, than the fat vicar, who only sleeps and stirs about his tythes'.[56] Although the author respected Morris's skills in astrology and medicine, he expressed some reservations about the validity and utility of his 'charms, and Spells and such Magic delusions, if they may be so called'. But in recognition of Morris's apparent successes he could not completely reject such matters:

> Yet how he had performed some notable cures, such as old inveterate agues, removed by burying three bits of paper sealed up, in a secret part of a field, and other disorders, by burning scraps without looking into the contents, is so unaccountable and extraordinary, that I am at a loss to account.[57]

Alongside the more usual portrayals of cunning-folk as charlatans and moral perverters, there persisted too the view that cunning-folk were a diabolically inspired evil. John Wesley was certainly no friend of cunning-folk, and like his father considered them to be Satan's servants. His Methodist followers expressed similar sentiments. When, in 1762, the mother of some supposedly bewitched girls asked the Wesleyan Bristol chemist Henry Durbin 'whether they should not go to those called *White Witches*, to have these troubles stopped', Durbin replied, 'if *they* could stop it, it must be done by the power of the devil; therefore I thought it not lawful to go to them'.[58] Despite this warning, the woman later repaired to a cunning-woman at Bedminster: there seemed no alternative. A similar case of child possession occurred in Plymouth in 1820. When some neighbours urged the child's mother, 'why don't you go to the white witch, he will soon cure him', the mother replied, 'I will not go to the devil for a cure'. As the Methodist chronicler of this case explained, 'Here then was a strong temptation; but the parents are Methodists, and they will not take any steps, or employ any means for relief, which are inconsistent with Christianity'.[59]

The late eighteenth century also saw the censure of popular belief in magic, tentatively coupled with its practical debunking. By demonstrating in relatively simple terms the deceptive and illusory nature of the magical arts, faith in cunning-folk and the like might be undermined. Education, entertainment and critique could be packaged together in true Enlightenment fashion. This was certainly the potential effect of *Breslaw's Last Legacy: or The Magical Companion*. The author, Philip Breslaw, expressed the hope that 'the knowledge which this book conveys, will wipe many ill-grounded notions which ignorant people have imbibed'.[60] The target audience was the 'great many of the sensible part of the world, that firmly hold the doctrine of magic', though he accepted that 'to such as will not be undeceived by the light of reason, I shall give full liberty to remain in the darkness of ignorance'.[61] But such claims were disingenuous since, although the *Last Legacy* explained in some detail the arts of legerdemain and illusion, it also included practical divinatory information on palmistry, cartomancy and the interpretation of moles. These were the staples of popular fortune-telling chapbooks. The author and publisher of the *Last Legacy* obviously felt it commercially necessary to pander to the thirst for divinatory knowledge, but in the process totally undermined the book's stated purpose. The author was well aware of this conflict of interest and attempted to absolve himself from the charge of hypocrisy. Regarding the exposition on cartomancy, for example, he explained, 'This method of telling fortunes is innocent, and much better than for a young woman to tell her secrets to a fortune-teller, who can inform her no better, if she pays her a shilling for it'.[62]

Reginald Scot had similarly attempted to 'explode' the popular faith in magic exactly two centuries before, as had the physician Thomas Ady in the mid seventeenth century,[63] but with the growth of literacy, printing presses and popular literature, there was more potential for spreading the message in the late eighteenth century than there had been at any other time. At least sixteen editions of Breslaw's book appeared in the forty years following its first publication.[64] Yet the original *Last Legacy*'s yielding to the popular demand for divinatory knowledge was, in itself, a tacit admission that attempts to undermine magical practitioners through practical demonstration were futile. People had no use for expositions showing that magic had no efficacy; they wanted knowledge of magic that *would* work for their benefit. Maybe if such publications had provided natural remedies for witchcraft, or detective techniques that led to a rate of success, they might have helped undermine cunning-folk. But they did not and could not. Besides, what cunning-folk professed to achieve in the field of magic went far beyond simple tricks and illusions.

On a more subtle level, though, publications like *Breslaw's Last Legacy* and Philip Astley's *Natural Magic: or Physical Amusements* (London, 1785) contributed to the very gradual process whereby the popular conception and terminology of magic and conjuring were sublimated. There had always been entertainers who practised professional sleight of hand of course, but there seems to have been a growth in their popularity and professionalism from the late eighteenth century onwards. There were men like Mr Moon, the 'celebrated conjuror', who from the late 1790s regularly toured Welsh border towns like Monmouth, Newport, Hereford and Gloucester. Although a fine tambourine player, most of his act consisted of 'Thaumaturgics, Mathematical Operations, and Magical Deceptions'.[65] One thinks too of the London street conjuror Henry Mayhew interviewed in the 1840s, who made respectable sums of money plying the West End, as well as performing in wax-work museums and at the Epsom races. He called himself a 'wizard' but was aware of its past connotations, commenting: 'I should think that wizard meant an astrologer, and more of a fortune-teller.'[66] Particularly with the rise of the music hall during the second half of the nineteenth century, the popularity and profile of stage magicians grew, in urban areas at least. If, two hundred years ago, a labourer had been asked, 'Who do you know who practises magic?', the likely response would have been a cunning-person. An urban labourer asked the same question one hundred years later would most likely have responded by referring to one of several well-known stage illusionists. As a result, those once potent titles of 'magician', 'wizard', and 'conjuror' increasingly became associated with the theatrical rather than the supernatural.

Such a shift in perception was slow, and particularly for those in rural areas magic and conjuration remained words associated with the world of cunning-folk, whose continued popularity is apparent from renewed denunciations of their trade during the early nineteenth century. In 1808 the Rev. Thomas Hawkins delivered two sermons in Warley Church, near Halifax, against the *Iniquity of Witchcraft*, and subsequently had them printed and sold for sixpence. The 'Iniquity' referred to was not witchcraft as in *maleficium*, but rather the magical activities of cunning-folk. A series of local incidents involving cunning-folk led to an eye-opening realisation that such people were as popular as ever, and operating with relative impunity. Prior to this, Hawkins, had, in his own words, 'smiled with contempt' at the popular resort to magic, but he became convinced that the religious and moral fabric of the people were under threat:

> Can it be right for Christians and Christian ministers to see their God blasphemed, and their fellow men duped and plundered, and pass it all off with a contemptuous smile at their weakness and folly? Is this to assert the honours of religion? Is this to vindicate the credit of Christianity and to protect the weak from the impositions of artful and designing men, who always make a prey of those weak persons, who (for want of better information) are but too strongly predisposed to confide in the solemn decisions and prognostications of certain 'cunning men?'[67]

Although the tone of Hawkins's sermons was redolent of those anti-magic tracts written by Perkins and the like two centuries before, they differed in context and in content to a considerable degree. Hawkins placed far less emphasis on cunning-folk's diabolic inspiration. There is no talk of pacts. Only occasionally does he allude to their relationship with the devil, and then usually in connection with the blasphemy committed by their clients, as when he asserted that submitting to their decisions was 'tacit obedience to Satan', a view which was backed up by reference to biblical passages.[68] This was, in a sense, diabolism without the devil.

By the nineteenth century Protestant orthodoxy had undoubtedly become more rationalistic. Over the previous century there had been considerable and often heated theological debate over the reality of miracles, spirits and demons, fuelled in part by the rise of Newtonian science and the philosophical writings of John Locke, David Hume and others.[69] The result was an increased distancing of religious reality and experience from the world of biblical supernaturalism. The once omnipresent devil became an abstract concept rather than a physical presence. Fear of direct satanic intervention in earthly affairs receded, except amongst some Methodists, Nonconformists and radical Protestant groups. The devil remained the embodiment of evil, but most Anglican clergymen no longer accepted that people successfully conspired directly with him to gain magical powers or earthly desires. With the demise of the view that cunning-folk played an integral part in a satanic plot to overthrow Christianity – a view that had so exercised sixteenth- and seventeenth-century minds – cunning-folk were only perceived as diabolic in the sense that they turned people away from placing their faith in God's beneficence. Considering that much of what cunning-folk did and said was infused with Christian terminology, this was still a difficult message to put across.

Instead of diabolism, Hawkins labelled the practices of cunning-folk as 'heathenish inventions', and described consulting them as 'giving countenance to the foolish superstitions and absurd practices of the pagans'.[70] In early modern attacks on popular magic such language was often linked in with anti-Catholic diatribes. Hawkins made no such denominational attacks, however, blaming neither England's Catholic past nor contemporary competitors like the Methodists for the continued popular resort to magic. The one comparison he did draw, which appears increasingly in nineteenth-century discourse on popular beliefs, was with 'The inhabitants of Africa, who are ignorant and depraved in a high degree'.[71] The expansion of British colonialism brought in its train missionaries who reported back to their colleagues on the 'heathens' and 'pagans' they encountered. It was only 'natural' then, that the English clergy should start to compare their own flocks with those newly converted ones in far-flung corners of the globe. The comparisons were uncomfortable. Many a parishioner in a country which had been Christian for more than a thousand years, and which boasted of being a beacon of Christian civilisation, was deemed to be no less 'benighted' than Africans and Asians who had only recently been introduced to the Bible. One exasperated newspaper editor, on hearing of the influence of a Yorkshire cunning-man, complained: 'We are sending missionaries and schoolmasters to the negro's of our West India Colonies to warn them against the atrocious deceptions of Mandrin, the Obeah-man, and are seeking, by the same excellent means, to guard the benighted Hindoo against the wizards in the far East', and yet the influence and popularity of such people in England was 'even more profound than that of the East, or the West'.[72] For Hawkins the situation required concerted and consistent action. He urged colleagues to prevent their flocks from being swayed by the 'muttering of a conjurer, a necromancer, a cunning man!' They must set their 'faces against such practices and every thing tending to countenance and encourage the same ... The church must be an example to the world. And church-members must shun the most distant approach to such diabolical practices.'[73]

The following year, authoritarian concern over magical practitioners was heightened further by the sensational trial and execution of Mary Bateman (1768–1809). This farmer's daughter from Asenby, Yorkshire, had turned to petty crime at an early age, being caught but not prosecuted for theft on several occasions. In her early twenties she moved to Leeds where she worked initially as a mantua-maker. It was at this time that she began to tell fortunes, and then branched out into practising love magic, curing witchcraft and a range of other magical services. She duped one poor woman, for example, by claiming that the guardians of the Leeds Benevolent Society could be magically 'screwed down' (her own terminology) to force them to give the poor woman more alms. Presumably as a potential line of legal defence, Bateman never actually claimed to have such powers herself, but rather pretended to be the assistant of a fictional wise-woman named Mrs Moore who, she said, was a seventh child of a seventh child. The concern over vagrancy at the time also surfaced in the case: it was stated that Bateman enjoyed the company of gypsies and other vagrants from whom she learnt some of her magical arts. Bateman's career, and that of Mrs Moore, came to an end after the death from arsenic poisoning of a client, Mrs Perigo, whom she was meant to be curing of an 'evil wish'. Bateman was convicted of murder and hanged. Her trial and execution were widely reported in the newspapers, and pamphlets and penny-books narrating her life and times sold for decades afterwards.[74] The story they told not only confirmed in the minds of some the pernicious influence of cunning-folk, but also served as a warning to the public of the moral and mortal dangers of resorting to cunning-folk and fortune-tellers. One pamphlet account of her life, published shortly after her execution, ended with the stark warning, 'those who trust in Diviners shall be confounded and perish'.[75] There was little sympathy for Mrs Perigo, the inference being that she was divinely punished for turning to a cunning-woman.

Ten years later the activities of the cunning-man, John Parkins, of Little Gonerby, Lincolnshire, were also the subject of a scathing attack, which was entitled *Ecce Homo*.[76] As with all those who had written about cunning-folk in the previous century, the author wished to remain anonymous and gave little away about himself apart from the fact that he lived near Parkins and was well acquainted with his activities and popularity. We can only speculate as to what incited him to castigate Parkins in print. He stated in his conclusion that he had 'written these remarks solely as a caution to the public', but one gets the impression that he was motivated as much by private considerations as public concern. As with Hawkins, the author's use of such terms as 'credulity' do not mark him out as an out-and-out sceptic in such matters. He subscribed to a common view of the time that witchcraft in its popular usage, that is harmful magic, had existed, but there was little contemporary evidence of its continued existence:

> I am rather inclined to doubt with the more enlightened part of mankind, the Existence of Witches and Witchcraft at all, – at least in the sense the Doctor represents it. But the testimony of the Bible, as to the Witch of Endor, is certainly conclusive evidence that there have been such; and perhaps there may be now – I cannot tell: such instances are very, very rare; and in all the cases I have heard of, the circumstances, when candidly and liberally

looked into, have always ended in a conviction, that no such charge was genuine.[77]

In this sense, Parkins could not be strictly condemned from the point of view that he was bolstering a deluded popular belief in witchcraft, but more precisely that what he identified as witchcraft was, on the evidence, no such thing. Furthermore, his professed ability to counter such witchcraft was denounced as a sham: 'I have no objection, however, to concede all my stoicism, and to allow, for once, the whole truth of the doctrine of witches and their craft: but against the power of Doctor Parkins to thwart or exterminate them, I solemnly protest.'[78] Having expressed his cautious belief in the possibility of witchcraft the author was consequently anxious to make clear that his views on the matter were not inspired by Nonconformist enthusiasm. While expressing great admiration for the Wesleyan writer Adam Clarke, the author noted, 'It may not be amiss by the way to acknowledge that the writer of these remarks is NO METHODIST'. Again, a number of pages later, he stressed that he was 'totally unconnected with every denomination of dissenting Christians.'[79] Although, at this time, such critiques of popular magic were primarily the work of clergymen or evangelicals, it would seem that the author of *Ecce Homo* was neither. Clergymen felt no need to hide behind anonymity. Just the opposite, they felt duty bound to set themselves up as beacons of moral light in order to demonstrate to the wider public that the church was ready to take action. *Ecce Homo*'s author was more likely a devout, respected citizen, incensed by Parkins's trade, but who may have had something to lose by openly criticising a man whose activities were so popular. Perhaps he was a prosperous tradesmen unwilling to offend his customers, or a licensed doctor in competition with the cunning-man. He certainly was not, as he put it, 'a prominent character on the stage of life'. There is little use of terms such as 'diabolic', and, for the author, Parkins's supposed 'crimes' were deception and the promotion of magical beliefs which had no credible basis, even if witchcraft itself may have had. Parkins was, in essence, 'a worthless adventurer' guilty of blowing 'into flame the slumbering embers of these superstitious notions'.[80]

From the mid nineteenth century onwards, there are no extant examples of the clergy – or anyone else for that matter – directly attacking cunning-folk in dedicated publications, although it is likely that the odd sermon was preached against consulting them.[81] The reason the religious voices of concern died down after the early decades of the nineteenth century certainly had little to do with any perception that the popular belief in magic was on the wane. Indeed, with the burgeoning of the local press from the 1850s onwards, regular newspaper reports concerning cunning-folk provided the clergy with ample evidence of their continued popularity. One likely explanation is that the issue of popular magic was overshadowed by the rise of spiritualism. Although some clergymen from all denominations embraced spiritualism, many others thought it a worrying recrudescence of 'superstition'. What made spiritualism of more direct concern was that it was popular amongst those pillars of organised religion, the middle classes. As a result, the focus on labouring-class beliefs was reduced. That is not to say the issue of popular magic was forgotten, but during the second half of the nineteenth century the clergy's interest in the subject was more likely to be expressed through a broader engagement with folklore.

The collection of popular customs and beliefs became a popular middle- and upper-class pastime, and was seen by many as an exercise in recording the vestiges of a more 'primitive' stage of human development. The clergy were ideally suited to the task, having close links with the 'common' people through their pastoral duties. The process of collection required a more informal dialogue with those who resorted to magic, which contrasted with the patronising, censorial tone that had characterised so many previous encounters. Engagement with folklore undoubtedly influenced the way in which at least some clergymen viewed cunning-folk. Hearing people explain in an informal, friendly manner why they felt they had no other choice but tread the path to the door of cunning-folk led some clergy to moderate their condemnation with a recognition that cunning-folk perhaps possessed some useful qualities. Take, for example, the Rev. John Atkinson, vicar of Danby, North Yorkshire, during the second half of the nineteenth century. The folklore of his parish was suffused with memories of the wise-man John Wrightson, who had practised in the village of Stokesley several decades before Atkinson's arrival.[82] Despite concluding from his many parochial conversations that Wrightson was 'to a given degree, a charlatan and an impostor', Atkinson admitted that he was also 'by no means an impostor *pur et simple*'. Atkinson recognised that 'he possessed, in common with many others then and since, wide and deep acquaintance with herbs and simples, and he used his knowledge with skill and judgement'. There was 'No doubt either that he possessed the power of influencing men's minds and imaginations, and knew it right well, and used it of set purpose and intention'. In conclusion, Atkinson stated, 'it must be admitted that he had much and effectual machinery available, other than what is implied when we style a man a "rank impostor"'.[83] One of Atkinson's contemporaries, the Rev. Elias Owen, went one step further by accepting that, at least with regard to their detective role, cunning-folk served a positive social function. Although he dismissed the idea that they possessed any real powers, he believed the popular respect for their magic acted as a useful deterrent against thieving. Accordingly, they 'occupied a well-defined and useful place in rural morality'.[84] A few other non-clerical folklorists echoed similar sentiments. The Somerset writer W. Willis Watson, who knew several cunning-men, recognised their positive psychological benefits. 'No doubt they practised a great deal of deception,' he observed, 'but they also gave some consolation to their clients.'[85] Such expressions hardly drowned out the continuing though muted chorus of disapproval. Hostile comments can be found in the work of folklorists such as the Dorset collector John Udal, who dismissed them as 'unscrupulous charlatans'.[86] The Rev. Sabine Baring-Gould wondered whether 'we are not too lenient with the professional white witch nowadays'.[87] Nevertheless, the engagement with folklore generally led to a more reflective understanding of who cunning-folk were and why people consulted them. From the mid nineteenth century onwards few clergymen, other than evangelicals, talked of those who consulted cunning-folk as people who had committed a sin. The negative aspects of cunning-folk still far outweighed the positive, but at least the positives were being more widely recognised.

With the clergy retiring from the battle against cunning-folk, the newspapers became their most vocal critics. From their inception in the early eighteenth century, newspapers had been heralded as the providers of rational knowledge, as educational conduits antithetical to popular 'superstition'. Their periodical reports of sensational instances of witchcraft and magic were primarily used as pieces of entertainment, but could also serve to highlight and condemn such popular beliefs.[88] Prosecutions involving cunning-folk and fortune-tellers were also occasionally reported, though usually in a casual manner: the fact they were on trial spoke for itself. Eighteenth- and early nineteenth- century newspapers also acted as a forum in which people could apologise to their communities for the criminal and anti-social acts they had committed. The *York Herald*, for instance, sporadically printed such confessions under the heading 'pardon asked',[89] and at least one cunning-man and his client were obliged to pay for such an advertisement. It appeared in the *Kentish Post* on 29 May 1754:

> Whereas I Sarah, the wife of Richard Bean, of Milton next Sittingborne, shopkeeper, some time ago, missed a gold ring, and suppos'd it to be sent to Mr James Green, of Milton aforesaid, coalmeter, in a pint of flour sold to his house; and for discovering the said ring apply'd myself to John Martin, of Milton aforesaid, tallow-chandler (a person said to be skill'd in the art or mystery of conjuration) who after making several trials of his art, declar'd, that Mahetabel, the daughter of the said James Green, had the ring; whereupon I challenged her with the ring, and called her a thief... Now I, the said Sarah Bean, declare myself heartily sorry for my weakness, and desire the said Mahetabel Green will forgive my error. And I the said John Martin, being truly sensible that by my means, the said Mahetabel Green was call'd thief, do declare myself heartily sorry for my weakness, in imposing, first on myself, then on others, and desire the said Mahetabel Green will forgive my folly; and I promise I will never more pretend to exercise the science of inchantment, conjuration, secondsightedness, or any such crafty science. I thought my skill was good, though it cost me nothing; but now I find it deceitful and vain, at the expence of five guineas. Sarah Bean, John Martin.

It was during the nineteenth century, with the rise of the regional and local press, that newspapers really began to aim their fire at cunning-folk. Local reporters and editors were acquainted with the people and places covered by their papers, and, members of the communities they reported on, many possessed a certain local pride. There was a desire in the provinces to be seen as enlightened and socially progressive as the major cities were perceived to be. The fact that people such as cunning-folk were able to practise, and, even worse, were widely resorted to, could be seen as a stain on an area's reputation. Some editors tried to ignore this uncomfortable reality by not deigning to report instances of cunning-folk's popular influence. Others followed a contrary policy, highlighting the activities of cunning-folk in order to expose their fraudulent practices, call for their suppression and thereby cleanse the fetid air of 'superstition' that they were thought to exhale. In 1819 the editor of the *Taunton Courier* published a letter roundly castigating those styled 'wizards' and 'cunning men', who were 'fattening on the silly prejudices of the weak-minded'. An account was given of the activities of one conjuror, Miller, in order 'to let the credulous see what miserable quackery they confide in, and to expose the unfeeling audacity of a man, who dares to impose on the simplicity of a poor invalid in such an awful manner'. Reporting on the trial of Sarah Roxborough in 1823, the *Staffordshire Advertiser* urged that the law 'should interfere and protect the public from the attempts of the designing'. Several decades later the *West Briton* described the renowned Cornish cunning-man James Thomas as a 'drunken, disgraceful, beastly fellow,' who 'ought to be sent to the treadmill', and demanded that 'the police, or some other higher authority, should take the matter up'. In 1856 the *Berkshire Chronicle* expressed its puzzlement that people were still consulting Maria Giles despite 'the repeated cautions which the public have had of this notorious woman'. Following her prosecution in 1871, the editor of the *Newbury Weekly News* also had some harsh words for her clients in an editorial entitled 'The "Cunning Woman" and her Dupes': 'while few will deny the justice of some punishment being meted out to such a notorious character, many will also be of opinion that the ignorance of her dupes would have richly deserved the pecuniary loss which they suffer from her.' He also endorsed the prosecution lawyer's singling out for vilification the place from which her clients had come: 'it was difficult to conceive that people could be so incredulous; but the fact might be accounted for that the parties came from Tadley, and they were unaccustomed to look for anything intellectual from that quarter'. The hope was, that by isolating Tadley, Newbury might be saved from the taint of rustic credulity and backwardness, despite the fact that Giles was based in the town.[90]

The interest in cunning-folk generated by the folklore movement and newspaper reports during the second half of the nineteenth century also prompted a number of Victorian novelists and fiction writers to explore the dramatic potential of such characters.[91] Charlotte Yonge's novel, *The Cunning Woman's Grandson*, was set in late eighteenth-century Somerset, and concerned the growing strains in the relationship between the eponymous cunning-woman, Granny Lake, and her orphaned grandson Robert, who attends one of the schools set up in the area by the evangelical reformer Hannah More. The novel's subtext concerns the moral and educational achievements of More in and around the Mendips. Lake is portrayed as a cave-dwelling, pipe-smoking old woman of 'gipsy cast', who ostensibly gains an income from spinning, knitting and parish relief. Yet as well as these humble means of support, 'there were sudden mysterious and uncertain gains through her repute as a cunning women'.[92] These gains came from telling fortunes, charming, herbalism and curing the bewitched. While Lake was a figure of fiction, the cunning-man in William Forfar's *The Wizard of West Penwith* was based on a notorious character who had practised in St Just, Cornwall, during the early nineteenth century. His fictional incarnation, named Freeman, plays a central and sinister role in this tale of murder and intrigue. Arthur Morrison also based his later novel *Cunning Murrell* on a deceased but real figure who had gained regional fame in and around Essex several decades before. Morrison had no time for pseudonyms, however, and took the liberty of using the man's name, James Murrell (1780–1860), to construct an entertaining but entirely fictitious drama of witchcraft and smuggling around him.[93] As well as appearing in central roles, cunning-folk also made a number of cameo appearances. Rudyard Kipling's light-hearted, Sussex-set story the 'Marklake Witches' was built around an episode involving Jerry, a 'white wizard' who cured people by 'herbs and charms', after the local doctor had failed to do so.[94] Thomas Hardy also wove cunning-men into several of his Dorset stories. In 'The Withered Arm' a couple of pages is devoted to a visit to 'Conjuror Trendle', who helps divine the identity of a supposed witch. In the *Mayor of Casterbridge* he describes a consultation with Conjuror Fall concerning weather prediction. Trendle's son and Fall are also mentioned in a dialogue in *Tess of the d'Urbervilles*, along with a long-deceased practitioner named 'Conjuror Mynterne'. It is possible that Hardy based Fall and Trendle on real characters, although there is no record of any practitioners of either name in the county. Conjuror Mynterne, however, seems to have been a real enough figure. In folklore sources mention is made of him practising in the isolated village of Batcombe sometime during the eighteenth century.[95]

While the cunning-folk represented in the works of Morrison, Kipling and Hardy were hardly treated with reverence, they were not portrayed as out-and-out charlatans. But Yonge felt duty bound to depict such people in the most negative of lights. Granny Lake is an unpleasant character who preys on the poor and ignorant, and, as is often the fate of such fictional types, she comes to a sticky end. Lake symbolises the pernicious, 'superstitious' state of the working classes before the growth of mass education. For conservative religious reformers like Hannah More and her admirer Yonge, cunning-folk were promoters of popular irreligion and degraded morality, and therefore inimical to the encouragement of virtue and piety.[96] No wonder, then, that Yonge has Lake expressing concern that her existence was being threatened by the spread of schooling. She commits the appalling sin of calling the saintly Patty More (sister of Hannah) a 'meddling, interfering upstart', and curses that her grandson's education has drawn him away from her world. His moral inculcation at the local Sunday School galls her all the more as she had only just 'broken him of all the Methody stuff he got from his mammy'. Her death is heavy with moral irony, for she is ducked for a witch and dies shortly after from the effects of her immersion. A search of her abode reveals a bag of coins amounting to £100, which the local vestry justly claims, 'since the old woman had lived on parish pay while she might have maintained herself'.[97] Although Forfar was less motivated than Yonge by personal religious considerations, Freeman was still portrayed as a base charlatan preying 'on the superstitious fears of the ignorant and weakminded'. Despite a supreme 'confidence in his own cunning and ability in frightening and deceiving his neighbours', he ultimately gets his just deserts and also dies an untimely death.[98]

As well as a dislike of cunning-folk, Yonge and Forfar shared the assumption that a social gulf existed between the 'progressive' later decades of the nineteenth century and the 'superstitious' dark ages of its dawn. Yonge talked of the incantations and charms that were 'universal in England till within the last fifty years', and Forfar referred to the throng of cunning-folk who 'received handsome incomes – not only from the illiterate and ignorant, but from people in the higher walks of life, so rife was the feeling of superstition which prevailed at that period'.[99] By setting their novels fifty to a hundred years in the past they were making a statement about the profound influence of popular education and enlightenment in the intervening years. Yonge and

Forfar believed that at the time of their writing the population of Western England had broken the spell of magic that had 'benighted' their ancestors. Yet the evidence suggests that the novelists' confidence was misplaced. Cunning-folk were still thriving in the mid nineteenth century and beyond. While Forfar and Yonge effectively consigned cunning-folk to the past, other more percipient writers showed awareness of their continued influence, and in the spirit of moral guidance wrote cautionary stories designed to undermine their existence. One such work was F. Bayford Harrison's novelette *A Wise Woman*, published as a cheap tract not for the novel reading middle-classes but for those who consulted cunning-folk.

Harrison's story concerns one Mother Pollard who implausibly combined cunning-trade with local jewellery thefts. She inveigles Ellen Warner, the young wife of a porcelain factory-worker, into believing she could conjure up a hidden treasure. Following Pollard's directions she does, indeed, find a treasure, though it consists of stolen jewellery. To cut a tedious story short, Ellen is arrested for theft, but then Pollard is forced to confess to the crime and is sentenced to eighteen months' hard labour. And the moral of the story? 'Ellen no longer had faith in Wise Women for she herself had become a wiser woman than before.' [100] The Society for the Promotion of Christian Knowledge pumped out huge numbers of similar cautionary tales at this period, and it is no surprise to find amongst them one directed at those who consulted cunning-folk. *Jane Lowe, the Wise Woman and the Seventh Son*, is set in southern England and tells the story of a labourer's daughter who seeks a cure for the king's evil (scrofula). First she goes to see a wise-woman, Widow Ranscombe, who gives her some green ointment made from herbs plucked by moonlight, and a written charm consisting of some biblical passages and the Lord's Prayer. Her condition fails to improve, so she then consults a local farmer, who is a seventh son of a seventh son. He too fails. Only then is the local doctor called in, who sends her to a local infirmary to make a full recovery. At various points in the story the ungodly nature of Jane's course of action is underlined. Of the wise-woman's use of the Lord's Prayer it is said, 'We have not warrant in the Bible for such a use of it, or of scripture words. It rather resembles the unlawful deeds of those witches and enchanters of old times, whom God has declared to be an abomination to Him.' [101] The aim of this tract was as much to promote popular confidence in orthodox medicine as to instil a sense of religious morality. The two were thought to go hand in hand. The tract's author, Susanna Warren, chided the common people for their lack of faith in doctors. While quacks came in for criticism, it was magical healers who were considered the most problematic. 'It is hard to believe' she sighed, 'that such practices prevail in a country which for so long has been a Christian one.' The story ends with Jane learning to lean on God and realising she should 'accept with thankfulness from His hands whatever help medical science can give'.[102]

Unfortunately, it is difficult to give a full account of clients' views of cunning-folk. The available source material hinders any lengthy consideration of the subject. Over the centuries the critics of cunning-folk far outnumbered any recorded expressions of goodwill towards them. The reason, of course, is that many of the satisfied clients of cunning-folk were illiterate, while those who were educated had little reason to publicise their involvement with people who lived on the edge of the law. The closest we get to the client's viewpoint is usually from the negative perspective of those who prosecuted them; in other words, when cunning-folk failed to satisfy their customers. Yet this, in itself, is revealing, indicating that cunning-folk were not always well regarded or even feared. Indeed, piecing together the fragmentary evidence from several centuries reveals a much more complex and ambiguous popular perception of cunning-folk, belying any crude characterisation in terms of white against black or good against evil.

First, however, it is instructive to examine what the critics of cunning-folk can tell us about the views of their clientele. As we have seen, most public critics were clergymen who often had occasion to hear their parishioners defending cunning-folk in person, either formally or informally. The seventeenth-century vicar John Gaule set out in some detail twelve different excuses people used to justify themselves, presumably gathered from personal experience. I have extracted them as follows:

1. 'I went for my owne satisfaction, and at my own hazard, and what has any body to do with it?'
2. 'It was not a witch that I went to, but a wizzard, a wise man, or a wise woman, as they call them.'

3. 'It was neither witch nor wizzard, but a juggling impostor.
4. 'I went to none but a good witch.'
5. 'I meant no body hurt in it.'
6. 'It was not I that went, but my wife, childe, servant.'
7. 'I medled with none of their witcheries, etc.'
8. 'I saw nothing, I found nothing but good.'
9. 'I was told nothing but truth.'
10. 'I went but to see if I might bee inform'd or finde what I had lost.'
11. 'What would you have me doe? I could not endure to see the poore thing so strangely handled, but seek out some remedy for it; and no body could tell what disease it was, all physick would do it no good, etc.'
12. 'I did it onely in an humour, because I had a mind, or fancy to know mine owne fate or fortune, etc.'[103]

These responses certainly sound like real reports of popular opinion, as they tally with the overall impression provided by other relevant sources. With regard to rebutting authoritarian criticism, the responses range from indignant ripostes to wheedling excuses. With regard to cunning-folk there are expressions of genuine respect moderated by doses of cynicism. The difference between theological and popular views comes through clearly with respondents maintaining the popular distinction between witches and cunning-folk in the face of clerical assertions that they were all in league with the devil. Gaule's list does not fully encapsulate popular attitudes, however, for it fails to mention one important justification of cunning-folk, recorded by several other authors of the period: that many people thought cunning-folk were doing God's work. This was a view that was obviously anathema to the clergy. In Gifford's *Discourse*, for example, one of his characters says, 'There be divers things which have persuaded me to thinke marvellous well of them, and even as of such as God hath given wisdome and skill unto, even for to doe much good.' James Mason similarly reported the argument that 'Often-times they use good and godly words and characters: and therefore their doings are not evil, nor wrought by Satan'.[104] As we shall see, cunning-folk did indeed employ biblical passages, names and characters in their charms and talismans, and made show of using the Bible in their consulting rooms. They often read out prayers and psalms, or required their customers to do so as an integral part of their magical rituals. People could not understand why cunning-folk should be condemned for putting their biblical knowledge to beneficial use. From a popular point of view, they were only doing what the Anglican Church should have been doing more of – using the power invested in the Bible for practical as well as spiritual purposes. As part of a cure for witchcraft, for instance, one Yorkshire cunning-man prescribed his patients to read Matthew 10: 4–42 and Psalm 70 at once, and then to read over Deuteronomy 28: 15–25 seven times at eleven o'clock at night.[105] This is exactly why some people saw cunning-men and -women as godly folk. As one of Gifford's rustic characters asserts, the local cunning-woman did 'more good in one year than all these scripture men will do so long as they live'.[106] John Parkins was cashing in on this perception when he avowed himself a 'servant of GOD'.[107] In the nineteenth century clergymen continued to complain that people considered the charms provided by cunning-folk and charmers as somehow holy. The Cornish vicar Richard Lyne noted that even 'well disposed persons' argued 'that only Scripture words, or only very good words, are used in their charms'.[108] That some people saw a halo above the heads of individual cunning-folk is further confirmed by comments from satisfied clients. To give a couple of nineteenth-century examples, a Surrey labourer interviewed by his local magistrate referred to a cunning-man he had consulted as that 'blessed man', and a Dorset man referred to another as 'a wise and a good man. What he told folk was always for their good.'[109]

Despite nice things being said about cunning-folk, most clients viewed them with circumspection rather than admiration, for anyone who had the power of magic could turn it to bad as well as good use. While few people would have had dealings with cunning-folk if they thought they would end up worse off as a consequence, or if they believed they were meddling with dark forces, some cunning-folk aroused a good deal of fear and apprehension. One such man was Peter Banks, who was tried before the mayor of Newcastle in 1673–74 for being an impostor. His 'cracks and boasts' of his 'inchantments, conjuracions, and magick arts; and, in perticuler, in conjureing evill and malitious spiritts' inspired more fear than respect. One witness stated, 'she trusts in God, and is not affraid of the devil, yet the said Banks by his strange stratagems affrights her'. Another woman deposed that, after falling out with Banks, 'she often in the night time was terrified and affrighted with visions and apparitions; and in such manner as she thought the said Banks was standing up in flames of fire'. In mitigation, she admitted that he had subsequently successfully cured her of witchcraft.[110] William Holland was felt by at least one of his former clients to be a master of dark powers. Holland, an iron moulder by trade, was prosecuted at the Oldham sessions in January 1848, where it was heard how an aged man came to believe that Holland was in league with evil spirits. His fears became so great that he would flee the instant he caught sight of Holland. On one such occasion he made for the local churchyard, believing that such hallowed ground would protect him.[111]

In both the above cases, and in other similar instances, those expressing fear of cunning-folk did not explicitly accuse them of diabolism or of having a pact with the devil. The talk was of evil spirits, which in popular discourse did not necessarily have overt satanic connotations. Witches were accused, for example, of sending evil spirits into people without the devil being directly involved in any way. So it would seem that the pulpit words of warning largely fell on deaf ears. Despite all the negative propaganda, the evidence suggests that few people in either the early modern or modern periods considered cunning-folk to be in league with the devil. The Rev. Atkinson found that in nineteenth-century Yorkshire, for instance, 'The Wise Man ... was scarcely credited with commerce with "T'au'd un", either personally or indirectly'.[112] The same statement could be applied to the rest of the country. There are always exceptions though. In the early modern period popular claims of diabolism were occasionally made against cunning-folk, but only *after* they had first been accused of witchcraft, which was a situation in which female practitioners were most likely to find themselves. Anne Bodenham, for instance, was accused by one of her former clients of drawing a magical circle and invoking 'Beelzebub, Tormentor, Lucifer, and Satan'.[113] In the nineteenth century the odd cunning-person who had a sinister character may have also attracted suspicions of diabolic relations, as distinct from suspicions of witchcraft. It was said of 'Wise Man' Wilkinson that, 'It was well known that he was in communication with the Devil. He never went to Church or Chapel ... Somebody who once saw him look on a cross by accident said that he was immediately twisted and torn as if in convulsions.' When a Somerset cunning-man was found dead with marks around his broken neck, some suggested the devil had come to claim him.[114] But such anecdotes sound like the type of legendary folklore that developed around such characters after their death rather than accurate reflections of how they were viewed in their lifetime.

The depth of popular scepticism concerning the abilities of cunning-folk is difficult to fathom. The fact they were prosecuted is no indication, since people did not necessarily resort to the law because they thought cunning-folk were unable to do what they promised. Rather, clients were dissatisfied because, for one reason or another, cunning-folk had not done their job properly or had not bothered to do it all. When the Somerset cunning-man Frederick Culliford was tried in 1876, his prosecutor, Emma Foot, expressed no lack of confidence in his magical abilities. Indeed, after the trial she continued to show faith in the power of a protective amulet he had supplied her. Foot's decision to prosecute was based on her belief that, rather than curing her mother of witchcraft, Culliford had tried to kill her using the same powers. As she said in court, 'I do not want to hurt the defendant. I only want my mother to get well.'[115] It would seem that Thomas Rendle's only aim in prosecuting Mary Murray in 1867 was to recover the money he had paid her, and thereby defray the costs of hiring another cunning-man. Murray's failure in no way dented his faith in cunning-folk in general.[116] Presumably, however, there had always been a significant number of people, not only amongst farmers, artisans and tradesmen but also the labouring classes, who were outright sceptical about the magical abilities of cunning-folk, and scorned their peers for consulting them. But whereas the expression of unbelief with regards to religion was for much of the period a criminal offence, and can therefore be traced in the archives, expressing scepticism about magic was largely acceptable and thus went unrecorded. One of the few pieces of evidence for popular incredulity are the stories collected by folklorists concerning tricks played on cunning-folk to explode their reputations. These usually concerned cunning-folk who failed to find their own goods, sometimes after pranksters had stolen items with the sole purpose of making fools of them.[117] What is not certain, however, is whether these stories circulated while the cunning-folk involved were alive, or whether they were generated decades after their death, when the potency of their reputations had dwindled. Yet for all the sceptical pranks, words of clerical condemnation, attempts at moral inculcation, bad press reports and literary denunciations, widespread faith in the power of cunning-folk was only undermined when people no longer required their services; and not because of a general acceptance that magic was a futile, empty or diabolic gesture.

# 3

## *Who and Why*

The general consensus amongst early modern commentators was that cunning-folk were so numerous they constituted a plague. According to Reginald Scot, 'some of the ministerie' affirmed there were as many as seventeen or eighteen witches of the cozening sort in their parishes. In the words of Thomas Cooper, 'Good witches' were 'rife almost in everie parish'.[1] Considering there were more than 15,000 parishes at the time, it could be reckoned from these statements that there were as many as a couple of hundred thousand cunning-folk operating in Elizabethan and Stuart England – rather more than William Wycherley's conservative estimate of five hundred. We will never be able to reach an accurate figure for the number of cunning-folk operating in any period, but it can be said with certainty that there were more than five hundred and less than one in every parish. The figures bandied about in the sixteenth and seventeenth centuries are so large because people like Cooper and Scot lumped together all those who practised any form of magic, fortune-telling or charming. On this basis, it is likely that there were indeed a handful of such people in many parishes. In terms of the distribution of cunning-folk, though, it is likely that one practitioner serviced a number of communities. It has been estimated that in early modern Essex no villager was more than ten miles from a known cunning-person. This was deduced from plotting thirty-four known practitioners consulted by Essex people between 1560–1603.[2] If we qualify this figure by realising that not all thirty-four would have been operating at the same time over the period, but then take into account the hidden number of cunning-folk who were never mentioned in court proceedings, the estimate appears most reasonable. It would seem that five or six miles was an average distance in any cases. Four clients of Thomas Harding, an Elizabethan cunning-man of Ickleford, Hertfordshire, travelled from places one, five, five and thirteen miles away as the crow flies, to consult him about a fever, a fairy changeling, stolen clothes, and horse rustling.[3] In the nineteenth century the known clients of Maria Giles came from Peasemore, Hampstead Norrey's, East Woodhay and Tadley, six, six, five and nine miles away respectively. It can be further calculated from the Essex figures that there was roughly one cunning-person for every 2500 to 3000 of the population in the county. When a similar process of deduction is applied to the evidence from nineteenth-century Somerset, the result is higher – one cunning-person per 6000 to 10,000 of the population at any one time.[4] Any comparisons have to take into account the fact that the population of the county by the end of the century was five times that of Elizabethan Essex. These are, of course, crude speculations, yet they do at least provide a more realistic impression of how many there were than that provided by anti-cunning-folk commentators. Up until the mid nineteenth century there may have been as many as several thousand working in England at any given time. They were certainly far fewer in number than clergymen.

Contrary to the modern notion that cunning-folk were mostly rural dwellers, there were repeated expressions of concern over the centuries about their widespread presence in towns and cities. In 1620 John Melton complained that 'many townes have been pestered with these wisemen', and London in particular. He noted some of those who had recently practised in the capital: 'the cunning man on the Bank side, Mother Broughton in Chicke-Lane, young Master Olive in Turnebole-street, the shag-hair'd wizard in Pepper-Alley, the chirurgion with the bag-pipe cheeke, Doctor Fore-man at Lambeth ... and many such impostors, that like the Birds of Wonder flye the light of the citie.'[5] Nearly a century later, the *Spectator* commented, 'It is not to be conceived how many wizards, gypsies and cunning men are dispersed through all the counties and market towns of Great Britain'. Another century on and Robert Southey was bemoaning that, 'A Cunning-Man, or a Cunning-Woman, as they are termed, is to be found near every town'.[6] Such observations were broadly correct. Cunning-folk were everywhere, but towns were their focal points, providing a concentrated customer base, and greater anonymity from the authorities.

Throughout the period covered by this book the general social profile of cunning-folk changed surprisingly little. The majority, roughly some two-thirds, were male. Evidence for the early modern period indicates that many were artisans, and a survey of eighteenth- and nineteenth-century cunning-men similarly reveals that over 80 per cent were craftsmen, tradesmen or farmers.[7] To put it in a broader context, cunning-folk came from a stratum of society that was at least semi-literate and which possessed a certain degree of authority in the community. Unpaid parish officials, such as constables and churchwardens, were usually drawn from this social group as well. It was also often people of this level who organised acts of popular justice, either contrary to or despite official authority. One practical reason why the profession was largely closed to the labouring classes was that, whereas craftsmen or tradesmen were often self-employed and could apportion their time between orthodox occupation and magical practice, labourers had little such freedom, making it difficult to provide the round-the-clock service that people expected from cunning-folk. Artisans and tradesmen could receive clients throughout the day in their shops and workshops, and it was no trouble to close their premises or get the wife or apprentice to carry on while they were out on occult business or in consultation. The hierarchical nature of social relations may also help explain the exclusion of the labouring classes from wielding magical power. Considering that a significant proportion of those who consulted cunning-folk were farmers, there might have also been a reluctance amongst this important customer base to consult and pay considerable sums to those deemed below them in the social pecking order.

Career prospects in the profession depended heavily on access to knowledge. People recognised that such arcane 'arts' as astrology, conjuration and the construction of charms and talismans were to a large extent acquired skills derived from books. It was access to these literary sources that further militated against the labouring classes becoming cunning-folk. They generally had neither the required literacy skills nor the financial wherewithal to purchase the necessary literature. That is not to say that all cunning-folk were fluent readers and writers: some clearly were not. After questioning an itinerant practitioner for nearly an hour in 1695 one Lincolnshire magistrate concluded, 'he understood no Lattin, nor no art or science, nor could scarce spell words right, nor write but indifferently with his pen'.[8] Yet, like most such characters, he possessed several almanacs and a book on mathematics, and the mere display of numeracy, literacy and literature was enough to convince many clients they were party to exclusive occult knowledge.

To a certain extent, magical ability was also held to be a natural or inherited gift. This was most evident when it came to healing. Seventh sons and daughters, for example, were believed to possess innate powers to cure certain conditions, and, not surprisingly, cunning-folk often claimed to be so blessed. But such hereditary abilities were usually related to specific fields of practice. They did not imbue the practitioner with comprehensive magical powers. Prior to the eighteenth century some cunning-folk and other healers also claimed to have gained powers from the fairies. In 1438 a Somerset fortune-teller and healer named Agnes Hancock was charged before an ecclesiastical court with communicating with fairies, and claiming that she 'sought their advice whenever she pleased'. The Dorset cunning-man John Walsh told an ecclesiastical court in 1566 that he would go up to the hills where there were 'great heapes of earth' at midday or midnight, and there he would speak with the fairies who would tell him which of his clients were bewitched and where stolen goods could be found. In later decades fairy associations were most likely to be claimed by female practitioners. Joan Willimott, a Leicestershire healer examined for witchcraft in 1618, said she obtained her abilities to help the sick after a man named William Berry 'willed her to open her mouth, and hee would blow into her a Fairy which should doe her good'. In 1645 Ann Jefferies of St Teath, Cornwall, was arrested and questioned about the healing touch she said she had gained from the fairies.[9] Interestingly, no examples of cunning-folk claiming fairy-acquired powers have been found after the early modern period, probably because in England (with the exception of Cornwall) there was a general popular disengagement from fairies during the eighteenth century, so relations with fairies carried less and less weight as sources of magical power.

Throughout the whole period, and particularly beyond the seventeenth century, cunning-folk had to deploy more than just birthright and fairy knowledge to demonstrate their abilities: they had to get their books out. For all the help he had from the fairies, John Walsh's statements suggest his magic book was as crucial to his work. The breadth of services offered by cunning-folk meant that more than a natural healing ability was required to generate a reputation. In Heywood's *Wise-Woman of*

*Hogsdon*, one of the characters complains, 'What can this witch, this wizard, or old trot, doe by inchantment, or by magicke spell? Such as professe that art should be deepe schollars. What reading can this simple woman have?' A similar sentiment was voiced nearly three hundred years later when a dissatisfied farm foreman remarked, after consulting the son of a respected cunning-woman, 'he was not scholar enuf' to help.[10] The restrictions placed on acquiring magical knowledge may also help to explain why women constituted only the minority of cunning-folk, yet made up the vast majority of fortune-tellers.[11] Until the eighteenth century few females were given the opportunity to learn to read and write, literacy rates amongst women only catching up with men during the second half of the nineteenth century. While the reputations of cunning-folk were built upon a combination of innate ability, natural prescience and acquired arcane knowledge, public expectations concerning the abilities of fortune-tellers were far more modest. Fortune-tellers professed limited skills, which required no display of literacy. They were thought to possess certain natural intuitive skills, which, when combined with relatively simple divinatory techniques such as palmistry, card reading, and the sieve and shears, enabled them to see into the future.

As with men, female access to education was related to social level. The daughters of artisans, tradesmen or small farmers were more likely to be literate than those of labourers, and most cunning-women were from this social level or at least attained it through marriage. The source materials, however, reveal frustratingly little about female status in this respect. For example, no mention of the social status of cunning-women can be found in the records for early modern Essex. What meagre evidence there is confirms that cunning-women were usually of a level above the common labourer, and possessed at least some degree of literacy. Judith Philips, who was whipped through the city of London in 1594 for cozening a Hampshire couple, was first married to an 'honest poor man' but later moved up the social scale by marrying a gunsmith. The Rye cunning-woman Anne Bennett, who was acquitted of consulting evil spirits in 1609, was the widow of a prosperous butcher, and her daughter who followed the same line of work was married to a minor gentleman. The Wiltshire cunning-woman Anne Bodenham, who was executed under the Witchcraft Act in 1653 for bewitching a maid, was married to a clothier, and was obviously literate as she ostensibly gained her livelihood by teaching children to read. Mary Bateman was the literate daughter of a modest farmer.[12] The notion that most cunning-women were midwives is not borne out by the sources, though some certainly counted midwifery amongst their medley of medical skills. Maria Giles, for instance, was described on one occasion as a midwife, and a Dorset cunning-woman, Mrs Bartlett (d. 1896), was an unofficial village midwife.[13] But it would be a mistake 'to blur the distinction between midwife and wise woman'.[14] As well as licensed midwives, many other women, some of them petty healers or 'doctresses' many others not, were recognised as having useful practical experience in childbirth. It would be highly surprising, therefore, if cunning-women had failed to practise midwifery, but they certainly not did make up a significant proportion of the profession at any time.

Many cunning-folk seem to have taught themselves the ins and outs of the business, amalgamating knowledge circulating orally with that obtained by reading. The early eighteenth-century conjuror Richard Walton, a former servant, confided that 'Altho' I was not brought up to physick yet by much studying and practice, God hath given to me great knowledge therein'. His astrological skills were likewise acquired through dedicated private study.[15] No doubt the close observance of other well-established cunning-folk also provided budding practitioners with ideas. As in any other trade, it was not unusual for the sons and daughters of cunning-folk to take over from their parents or other family members. Anne Bennett and her daughter have already been mentioned. Hannah Spence also took over from her more illustrious mother, Hannah Green, upon the latter's death at Yeadon, Yorkshire, in 1810. Richard Morris was trained in his youth by his fortune-telling aunt Deborah Heathcote. When the prosperous East Devon cunning-man Richard Baker died in 1819, his son immediately stepped into his shoes.[16] A few cunning-folk, aware of their own ambiguous social position, aspired to elevate the status of their sons by having them trained as orthodox medical men. The Lincolnshire cunning-man John Parkins sent his son away to live with and learn from a surgeon at Navenby, and the son of John Colmer, a high street herbalist and astrologer in Yeovil, gained a licence from the Royal College of Physicians of Edinburgh.[17] There are also a number of examples of budding cunning-folk who claimed to have learned their trade as servants or pupils of esteemed practitioners.

The Essex cunning-man William Hills, brought before the quarter sessions in 1651, was said to have been a pupil of the famed astrologer and almanac writer William Lilly. Anne Kingsbury, of Somerset, likewise said she had acquired treasure-seeking techniques from Lilly. Anne Bodenham learnt all about the business while a servant to the notorious London-based cunning-man John Lambe. John Walsh confessed that he had gained his knowledge of physic and magic from his former master, Sir Robert Drayton.[18] At a later period the Lincolnshire cunning-man John Parkins plausibly claimed to have been under the tutorship of the two most prominent London occultists of the period, Ebenezer Sibly and Francis Barrett. Indeed, Parkins claimed that he had lodged with Sibly for a time in 1796.[19]

It is worth focusing on Parkins a little more because we do gain some sense of his career progression. Just as Richard Morris began as a fortune-teller before expanding into the fields of magic and healing, so Parkins apparently developed his career in stages. According to his anonymous enemy, Parkins's first career move was to 'dignify himself with the title of Doctor', and then to commence as a 'Watercaster, Astrologer, and Fortuneteller'. His clientele initially consisted of 'silly servant girls, who wanted sweethearts, and brainsick lovers, pining after maids'.[20] He subsequently 'invented the system of Lamenism, or Spiritual Astrology', which consisted of charms that could be put to a range of uses, including the cure of witchcraft. These proved very popular, so Parkins 'by one bold stroke after another, arrived at his present pitch of worthless popularity'.[21] This progression was not unlike that of the infamous John Lambe two centuries earlier. Starting out as an English tutor amongst the gentry of Worcestershire, the 'first steppe that ever hee made' in the trade 'was the profession of that noble and deepe science of physicke'. Like Parkins, he also began to call himself doctor. It was only after setting himself up as a medical man that he then began to practise 'other mysteries, as telling of fortunes, helping of diverse [sic] to lost goods, shewing to young people the faces of their husbands or wives'. He also professed to be able to 'tell by the view of any person suspected for witchcraft, whether hee, or shee were a witch or not'.[22] As both the experience of Lambe and Parkins shows, assuming the title of 'Doctor' was an important step, and the evidence suggests it was a common practice throughout the period. Healing was central to their business and having an appropriate title generated social respect. This could obviously be seen as bogus and fraudulent, but only from our modern perspective or from that of licensed doctors at the time. In popular discourse before the twentieth century the title was not restricted to those with a university training. People also conferred it upon those who were thought to have a natural healing gift, seventh sons or daughters, or those who were skilled with herbs and magic. As a Shropshire woman commented about a folk-healer she had consulted, he 'wunna a regular doctor, and hadna bin through the colleges, still he could rule the planets'.[23] Under these criteria, most cunning-folk could legitimately lay claim to being doctors. For the historian, however, this broader usage throws up interpretational problems, particularly for the early modern period. When we find in witch-trial records someone deposing that they had been to a 'doctor' about their ill-health, was the medical man a doctor in the official sense or in the popular sense? One can only judge on the basis of what they practised.

Lamb, Morris and Parkins were in a minority in that most cunning-folk, once established, continued to maintain their other occupations. Even when magic alone made them prosperous, few completely gave up their usually less profitable occupations. However, although it is true that 'it was relatively unusual for a wizard to subsist entirely upon the proceeds of his magical activities',[24] it should not be inferred that many could *not* live off their occult earnings; this will become quite apparent a little further on when we come to talk about fees. The holding of dual occupations was not uncommon. Many people of the same class worked smallholdings or had secondary skills to supplement income or to provide a safety net during hard times. Even impecunious curates took up secondary trades. But we should not assume, because the records state they pursued a trade, that cunning-men actually followed them to any significant extent. It was said of Edward Savage (1759–1849), 'He was a small farmer, a herb doctor and gun-smith, but derived his chief source of income from his more superstitious fellow-mortals'. George Clegg was described 'as a factory operative by trade', though for many years he worked full-time as a wise-man. When the Somerset cunning-man James Stacey was examined in court in 1883 he was asked, 'What do you profess to be?' 'Well, I confess I'm a miller by trade', he replied. 'But you don't follow it?' inquired a magistrate. 'No, I do not.'[25] The sources in both the early modern and modern periods may give the impression that cunning-folk were only part-time magicians, but their other trades were often nominal or minor concerns. There were reasons other than finance why cunning-folk might want to maintain some semblance of a respectable occupation. For one, it kept them in the hub of the community. In their line of work it was important to be familiar with all the latest local gossip, and shops and workshops were focal points where such conversations took place. It is no surprise that a number of cunning-men ran drinking establishments, where alcohol loosened tongues and an attentive ear was bound to pick up useful information.[26] Cunning-folk also maintained their secondary trades as legitimate fronts behind which they could continue their illegitimate operations. As has already been made quite clear, one way or another the commercial practice of magic was a criminal act. To have no other visible means of occupation was bound to attract adverse attention from the authorities. In this respect, the national censuses of the nineteenth century presented a problem to cunning-folk, and consequently for historians. For obvious reasons, when interviewed by a census enumerator, cunning-folk were not going to have themselves put down as 'cunning-woman', 'wizard' or the like. Instead, those who maintained trades and crafts simply cited these occupations to the enumerator, while married cunning-women could describe themselves as wives. Only those who had no ostensible means of income had to think up other occupational aliases. Some, like James Stacey, just said they were labourers, while others could reasonably claim to be herbalists and cow doctors. What this means, of course, is that, unlike many other trades, cunning-craft cannot be identified from the census, which is only useful once cunning-folk are identified by other means.

When it comes to identifying cunning-folk higher up the social scale, amongst the educated classes, such as clergymen, physicians, surgeons, clerks and schoolmasters, classification is problematic. It is necessary to stick to the principle that cunning-folk are definable by what they practised. If we find clergymen and physicians offering the characteristic breadth of services – love magic, thief detection, astrology, fortune-telling, herbalism and unbewitching – they should be considered in the same way as other cunning-men who held down several jobs. It is rarely clear in the sources to what extent they did so. There were clergymen who practised astrology, but did not offer any magical services. There were also physicians who diagnosed and cured witchcraft, but did not resort to magic or divination in any way. These people cannot really be classed as cunning-folk.

At this point it is worth considering Macfarlane's occupational survey of Essex cunning-men, since it highlights this very problem. Of a sample of twenty-three practitioners, only a minority were artisans, tradesmen or farmers. The majority were professionals: seven were connected with the medical profession, three were probably clerics, two schoolmasters, two astrologers and one a churchwarden. This is rather at odds with the picture I have already constructed. However, the reason for this becomes clear when we look at the information on which the classification is based. The records used, mostly church court presentments, are not detailed enough to confirm that these professionals really were acting as cunning-folk. Thus one of the surgeons in the sample, reported to the archdeaconry court, was accused of 'practising sorcery under the service of surgery', and a physician was similarly accused of 'making a magic ointment'.[27] This does not necessarily indicate that they really were using magic, let alone that they were cunning-folk. Medical procedure at the time could quite easily be misinterpreted as magic. Similarly, when clergymen were charged with conjuration or witchcraft, they were sometimes actually being accused of practising Catholic rites and services, rather than curing witchcraft, detecting stolen property or the like.

It is probably fair to say that, until the mid seventeenth century at least, many trained medical men subscribed to the supernatural causation of illness, and attempted to cure the bewitched. The mid seventeenth-century physician Thomas Ady was well aware of this. Physicians, he said, were habitually being asked by their patients, '"Sir, do you not think the party is bewitched?", and to this many an ignorant physician will answer, "Yes, verily"'. Ady remarked that such diagnoses were 'a cloak for a physician's ignorance. When he cannot find the nature of the disease, he saith the party is bewitched.'[28] But highly intelligent and respected medical men, who could not be accused of ignorance within the context of their time, also held to a belief in witchcraft as a cause of illness, and were earnest in their diagnoses and cures. In 1662 three 'doctors of physick', wrote a book in which they declared that from the evidence of many 'credible authors', including such notorious continental demonologists as Jean Bodin and Nicholas Remy, it was 'manifest that diseases may come by witchcraft'. They accepted, though, that it was 'very hard to know these diseases, and we must be very industrious to discover them. This is because the Devil doth so warily get into natural causes, that it is not easily discerned what comes from natural causes and what from the Devil'.[29] In his treatise on *Sicknesses and Diseases from Witchcraft*, the respected Hitchin physician and apothecary William Drage listed a variety of herbs that he deemed effective against witchcraft once diagnosed, and described the manner in which fellow physicians successfully dealt with such cases. He mentioned one Dr Woodhouse of Berkhamsted, Hertfordshire, who was famed in the region for curing witchcraft, though there was nothing magical about his methods. In the case of one bewitched woman he 'prepared stinking suffumigations, over which she held her head, and sometimes did strain to vomit, and her distemper for some weekes seemed abated'. Another medical man similarly boiled herbs in a pot 'over which the bewitched do hold their heads'.[30]

The basis for such witchcraft cures was explained by the aforementioned triumvirate of physicians: 'The natural medicines are twofold, either such as evacuate foul humors, which the Devil useth to cause disease, or alterers and antidotes which are against the dispositions brought in by the Devil. For evacuation vomits are good ... But let the vomit be proper, and Purges must not be neglected.'[31] What distinguished such physicians from cunning-folk was that they did not recommend the use of charms or incantations. In fact they condemned them as superstitious and ungodly. Nevertheless, in offering to cure witchcraft, whether by natural means or otherwise, physicians laid themselves open to suspicions that they went beyond godly medicine. Those who consulted physicians about witchcraft could easily mistake an infusion or ointment, concocted on natural principles, as something magical. For many there was often no clear-cut boundary between magic and natural medicine. As a result, although some physicians did profess to cure witchcraft, many others undoubtedly refused to get involved in order to avoid ill-informed presentments before the ecclesiastical courts or worse. In 1682, during the trial of the so-called Bideford witches, it was heard how one of their supposed victims,

Dorcas Coleman, had been examined by Dr Beare, who cautiously concluded that 'it was past his skill to ease her of her said pains; for he told her that she was bewitch'd'. On many occasions this left cunning-folk as the only alternative source of help for the victims of witchcraft. Exactly one hundred years earlier, during the trial of the witches of St Osyth, it was revealed how Thomas Death, suspecting his daughter had been bewitched, brought some of her urine to an Ipswich physician named Bert. Death asked him whether witchcraft was responsible, but Bert was noncommittal and 'saide that hee woulde not deale so farre to tell him'. Death was 'not satisfied to his minde'; when he met an acquaintance shortly after he 'asked him where hee might go to a cunning man'.[32]

Those brought before the ecclesiastical courts for practising astrology cannot necessarily be considered as cunning-folk either. The church hierarchy frowned upon astrology, some theologians considering it blasphemous, others seeing it as outright diabolic. Yet for many, including not a few clergymen, astrology was a legitimate pursuit not at all at odds with Christianity. This was certainly the case John Vaux, curate of St Helen Aukland, made in 1633 when brought before the diocese of Durham High Commission for practising astrology. Vaux supplemented his stipend by selling almanacs and casting figures to detect thieves and stolen property, and was in the habit of making his astrological calculations on the communion table. This may have just been an act of bravado, but it seems more likely that he thought his work would be better guided on such a hallowed surface. He considered he was doing nothing contrary to either the laws of the realm or of God. When reproved by a local gentleman for his figure-casting, Vaux answered, 'I will prove it by scripture to be lawfull. Did not Samuell tell Saul what was becomen of his father's asses?' When asked if, like the prophet Samuel, he believed he was inspired by the spirit of God, he replied 'he hoped he had the same Spiritt'.[33] In all the witness statements against Vaux there is no mention of his providing any other occult services beyond figure-casting, and no one accused him of being a wise-man or conjuror. While the puritanically minded condemned astrology as the Devil's work, there were those, medical men included, who considered it as mere vanity and falsity. Astrology was incompatible with true science and medicine, and those who claimed to be learned in both were more conceited than the common cunning-man. 'A Quack Astrologer', wrote one scornful critic, was:

> a gypsy of the upper form, a wizzard unfledg'd, Doctor Faustus in swadling clouts, the fagg end of a soothsayer, or the cubb of a conjurer, not lick'd into perfection; one that hath heard of the Black Art, and his fingers itch to be dabbling in't; but ... contents himself to deal with him [the Devil] obliquely by way of a cheat'.[34]

Despite such harsh words, astrology remained an integral aspect of medical orthodoxy until the eighteenth century, and continued as a key element of folk medicine well beyond that. The most obvious proof of this being the continued popularity of Nicholas Culpeper's, *The English Physician or Herball*, first published in 1653, in which the astrological government of each medicinal plant is described.

The attacks on astrology were threatening enough to require numerous defences. In another of his medical publications, William Drage upheld the astrological component of medicine from accusations of magic and diabolism:

> it is possible some men may be instigated by their curiosity to contract with the Devil, to make them capable of telling Fortunes, and fore-knowing things, seeing Astrology is oft so uncertain; but of such we must judge what may be, by what hath been; they have seldom been Astrologers; and few Witches have any judgement in Astrology, if any; nor doth the Devil will them to learn any thing thereof.[35]

Richard Napier would certainly have concurred. This respected Anglican rector of Great Linford, Buckinghamshire, handed over most of his clerical duties to a curate, and until his death in 1634 dedicated himself to the private study of natural magic and the public practice of astrological physic.[36] His motivation for pursuing this alternative occupation was not financial. He saw himself as reinforcing his Christian duties by soothing the bodies and minds of the laity as well as their souls. As his meticulously kept casebooks demonstrate, he dealt with hundreds of cases of suspected witchcraft amongst the many thousands of patients he received over the years, and he supplied not only natural remedies but also astrological amulets. Although a believer in witchcraft, he rarely confirmed his clients' suspicions of bewitchment, usually interpreting their symptoms as the result of natural physical ailments or spiritual turmoil. The famed astrologer-physician William Lilly acted in a similar way.[37] Cunning-folk by contrast nearly always diagnosed witchcraft. Whether Napier's patients saw him as a cunning-man we do not know. Some probably did, but many probably did not. People went to Napier as a clergyman and a physician, and both professions were thought to have the ability to cure witchcraft as well as cunning-folk. There is a danger of underestimating popular perspicacity. People were quite capable of distinguishing between a clergyman who cured witchcraft and a cunning-person who cured witchcraft. In fact several people went to Napier *after* concluding they had been bewitched by cunning-folk. When a malevolent neighbour once called him a conjuror, he responded with alarm: the inference being that he was not usually described in such terms. Cunning-folk and astrologer-physicians were seen differently in terms of social position and skills, and consequently people would have interacted differently with each type. Furthermore, a sizeable minority of cunning-folk were women, who were obviously never represented in the clergy, and were excluded from the ranks of licensed physicians and surgeons. We have to be careful, then, of accepting descriptive labels at face value. Under the title, 'sorcerer', 'conjuror' or 'doctor', court documents and contemporary commentators lumped a diverse range of people who in a number of respects had little in common.

There were, nevertheless, clergymen and physicians who to all intents and purposes practised as cunning-folk; who, in other words, offered the same broad range of commercial services to boost their incomes. They are difficult to identify with any certainty. The vocal anti-witch clergyman, Joseph Glanvill (1636–80), met one likely candidate while investigating a haunted house. The man, a Somerset physician named Compton, was described by Glanvill as 'a very odd Person'. They met at the house in which the supernatural activity was centred. Compton, obviously on the look out for lucrative business, asserted that the disturbances were the work of witches, and offered to sort them out for a £100. He also practised scrying, and impressed one of Glanvill's acquaintances by showing him an image of his wife in a looking-glass.[38] The clearest example is Joseph Blagrave, a Reading-based astrologer-physician, who laid bare the whole of his trade in an extraordinary book published in 1671. Blagrave would certainly have rejected any imputation that he was a common cunning-man. He stated, for example, 'The curing of such who are bewitched, is not done only by such, who are called white Witches (as many foolish do imagine) for the white Witch and the black Witch are all one ... they are but confederate Witches'.[39] Yet, with the exception of producing written charms, he did everything that people expected of cunning-folk. He cured the bewitched with plants chosen and applied according to their astrological aspects. He also used herbs as talismans, making his patients 'wear a select number of solary herbs gathered at the hour of the Sun'.[40] Importantly, he also detected witches, and employed rituals of sympathetic magic such as witch bottles to torment them, though he gave a pseudo-scientific explanation for their efficacy. He was prepared to answer any question whatsoever using horary astrology, including those concerning thefts, strays and fugitives. Even the casting out of devils was part of his repertoire, and in his book he provided a detailed account of how he had exorcised the daughter of a Basingstoke turner, using prayers, adjurations and herbs. Such a versatile practitioner must have been considered a cunning-man in his neighbourhood.

By the mid eighteenth century the well-educated gentleman wizard, like Blagrave, was on the verge of extinction. Conjuring clergy and witch-doctoring physicians died out partly due to a new intellectual climate, and partly because of commercial and professional developments. Although during the eighteenth century the medical profession was far from the highly regulated body it became in the Victorian period, a distancing process was going on between licensed and unlicensed practitioners, and between apothecaries, surgeons and physicians. The medical market place was extremely diverse, but boundaries between orthodox and unorthodox medical behaviour were slowly hardening. Social propriety was increasingly becoming a commercial issue, so for practitioners wishing to distinguish themselves from the 'common herd' and maintain their appeal with the wealthy and expanding middling-sort, a display of outward respectability became paramount. Physicians had to find their niche in the market, and the practice of astrology, let alone magic, was not conducive to a respectable reputation. Even those denounced as 'quacks' by licensed medical men tried to vaunt their scientific credentials in order to distance themselves from a medical past perceived as 'superstitious'.

For some clergymen, particularly curates, making a comfortable living was still difficult, although, in general, the prospects were better than they had been in the previous century. So the temptation was still there to exploit their spiritual position, not only out of cynical cupidity, but also out of a charitable Christian sense that they were helping their parishioners. Nevertheless, there is little evidence of the continued existence of true cunning-clergy at this time, though a few clergymen continued to practise astrology, even if it was increasingly frowned upon by 'respectable' society. One of the last astrologising clergymen proffered his skills to north Devonians during the early nineteenth century. His popular name was Parson Joe, and as his notebook, seen a hundred years after his death, showed, he drew up horary calculations for people in his local area.[41] But, in general, the opportunity to indulge in such moonlighting enterprises was increasingly restricted during the eighteenth century. Despite the waning influence of the church courts, concerns over the growth of Methodism led the church to maintain a close eye on its representatives. This, coupled with the social distance the expanding middling classes were putting between themselves and what was deemed the 'vulgar' beliefs and practices of the lower orders, worked against the pursuance of magical services. Amongst the lower social ranks of the well educated, namely clerks, excise officers, schoolmasters and the like, cunning-trade continued longer. During the first half of the eighteenth century, Timothy Crowther, a Yorkshire parish clerk whose brother became a master at Clerk's School, Skipton, practised as a cunning-man. Later in the century a Lincolnshire schoolmaster named Fynes did likewise. Writing in 1826, the Reverend Polwhele wrote that within his memory there had been 'cunning' clerks.[42] But by the early nineteenth century similar social and professional developments meant that this class too gave up the trade. As a consequence, by the mid nineteenth century artisans, tradesmen and small farmers had the business to themselves.

Having argued that many people distinguished between cunning-folk, dog-collared astrologers, astrologer physicians, and physicians who cured witchcraft, we shall now continue to define who and what cunning-folk were by highlighting the differences between cunning-folk and other groups of magical practitioners of a similar social rank. This process of definition is necessary because cunning-folk have often been clumsily lumped together with these other practitioners, giving the impression of an undifferentiated mass of magical healers. There were no hard and fast boundaries indeed, but there were significant differences between distinct groups of practitioners who had their own defining social and practical characteristics. To heap all these people together, as the demonologists did and as some historians and folklorists have done, is to imply that those who consulted them also saw little difference between them. To resort to an analogy, many common folk had only a dim understanding of the doctrinal differences represented by the various Christian churches and denominations, but they were nevertheless conscious of the practical differences, and consequently viewed the churches differently.

The conflation of cunning-folk with charmers has caused the most significant confusion in the history of popular magic. This mistake is quite understandable, since they were mostly from the same social group, and they both proffered supernatural healing. But charming was a distinct tradition, based on either the possession of an innate healing touch, ownership of a healing object, or most commonly the possession of one or more simple verse charms usually based on extracts from the New Testament or apocryphal biblical stories.[43] Knowledge of these charms was passed down secretly from one generation to the next, sometimes only on the charmer's deathbed. Charmers generally, though not always, respected the tradition of gratuity. They did not demand money and many would not even accept any words of appreciation, though gifts in kind were accepted if freely given. In many areas charms could only remain efficacious if they were transmitted to someone of the opposite sex. Charmers rarely practised any other forms of magic, though some complemented their 'gift' with herbal medicine. In general the tradition of charming did not extend to healing the bewitched or the possessed. The charms were concerned with a well-defined range of natural ailments, such as ague, bleeding, burns, bruising, snakebites, toothache, jaundice, and scrofula. There was no ambiguity about what charmers did. They were merely custodians of a God-given gift, not masters of equivocal magical forces. Consequently, people did not prosecute charmers as they did cunning-folk: there was little to accuse them of, as they imposed no charges and they did not provide faulty diagnoses since they did not diagnose. That does not mean that charmers were immune from legal interference. In the early modern period they were frequently presented before ecclesiastical courts by clergymen and churchwardens (not their clients) and charged with sorcery. Hence some of the confusion in the historiography. During the modern period they were also occasionally called to account at inquests, usually in relation to burns victims who had first been taken to a charmer rather than a doctor, and who had died shortly after.

Charmers and cunning-folk had distinct identities, and represented different branches of folk medicine, though some cunning-folk did offer to charm for money. To these two groups can be added a range of other healers providing supernatural cures who neither offered the array of services provided by cunning-folk nor were bound by the traditions of charming. Girdle-measurers, for example, claimed to be able to determine whether someone was bewitched or troubled by fairies by measuring the fluctuating length of their belts or girdles.[44] These specialists seem to have died out by the eighteenth century. More resilient were the toad doctors of western England, who continued to ply their trade until the end of the nineteenth century. They cured primarily scrofula, though their charms were also thought efficacious against other ailments, including bewitchment. Their mode of cure consisted of putting the leg of a live toad in a muslin bag and placing it round the sick person's neck.[45]

There are a number of reasons why people may have wanted to become cunning-folk. The desire for money, power or social prestige, and even to do good, all undoubtedly played their part. Based on a reading of the early modern source material, it has been suggested that cunning-folk were primarily motivated by the desire for prestige rather than payment.[46] Some of them certainly paid considerable attention to cultivating social prestige, in the sense of earning respect from their communities. They courted public attention, appeared at social functions, and joined local associations. The Newton Abbot cunning-man John Collander was a member of the Oddfellows, for example. William Brewer, of Taunton, was a prominent invitee at club feasts in surrounding villages. John Wrightson courted public recognition and maintained the respect of many; the Rev. Atkinson 'never once heard him spoken of as a man of mischief, or as an evil-liver, or as extortionate'. Richard Morris, too, 'was well spoken of by the generality, as a good sort of a man. He was charitable to the poor, and neer meddled in any political dispute.' He owned several properties in Frankwell, Shrewsbury, including the White Horse Inn, which he left in trust to the newly founded Manchester and Salford Lying-in Hospital (1790).[47]

In contrast, though, there were others who cared little about social respect, and had few qualms about soiling their characters in public. The evidence suggests that cunning-folk could prosper even with a poor reputation, and some knew it. We have already seen that the Newbury cunning-woman Mariah Giles was unlikely to have won any popularity contests. The nineteenth-century Devon cunning-man William Salter, known locally as the 'Bideford White Witch', might have equally been described as the 'Bad Boy of Bideford'. In March 1846 he was found carousing in the streets with several prostitutes, and a couple of months later he was fined a total of eighteen shillings for being drunk and disorderly on two separate occasions after nights out on the town.[48] The thirst for power outweighed the motive of prestige it would seem. It was the aura of power that allowed people like Salter to discard any semblance of social propriety, live unorthodox lifestyles, and yet still be accepted. This was of course power only in limited terms and in local contexts. It was based purely upon the popular recognition of their magical abilities, and once their abilities were widely called into question it drained away, and so too did toleration of disreputable social and private behaviour. William Dawson, who tried and failed to assume the mantle of his uncle John Wrightson, 'died a wretched death, that of a drunken, miserable, beggarly outcast, "like a dog by the roadside"'.[49]

While recognising the incentives of prestige and power in the motivation of cunning-folk, money was surely paramount. The point was rather well put by the eponymous cunning-man in Charles Burney's eighteenth-century musical, adapted from a Rousseau play:

> But when folks have been at our dwelling,
> And to us have their secrets betray'd,
> We for hearing their tale – and then telling,
> Are sure to be very well paid.
> And this is the plan
> Of a true Cunning-Man.[50]

In confusing cunning-folk with charmers, historians have underplayed the lucrative nature of the business. The following observation from the seventeenth-century clergyman Richard Bernard has been ascribed to cunning-folk: 'some have professed, that if they should take any thing they could doe no good.'[51] However, this statement clearly concerns charmers and the tradition of gratuity that bound them. I have not come across any case where cunning-folk did not request or expect some form of payment either in kind or cash. When they did decline cash payment it was usually as part of a strategy to counter possible criminal charges. For this reason a Cheltenham cunning-man, mentioned in a case of false arrest in 1829, did not accept money directly from clients, but told them to hand it to his child instead.[52] There is plenty of evidence over the period that considerable sums of money could be made, substantially more than any of their secondary occupations could bring in. Circumstantial corroboration comes from Bernard again, who knew a Cambridgeshire cunning-man who reckoned he could have earned as much as £200 a year if he had wanted.[53] This figure was perhaps an inflated boast, but at a time when few craftsmen or small tradesmen were likely to earn more than £20, cunning-trade could realistically bring in double that, particularly if they were fortunate enough to attract wealthy clients as well as the lower orders.[54] Anne Bodenham, a former servant, earned enough to own her own house and before her execution made a will in which she left legacies to her friends. During a long career spanning the second half of the eighteenth century, Hannah Green was estimated to have amassed savings worth as much as £1000. A Yorkshire contemporary, Susanna Gore (1736–1826), of Driffield, was said to have 'accumulated a considerable amount of property'. The Dorset cunning-man James Baker (b. 1777) was able to buy a house and accumulate a few acres of land from his earnings. Early in the nineteenth century Thomas Atkinson, whose wife also ran a sweet shop in Kirkby Lonsdale, was described as leaving 'quite a fortune'. In 1806 the *Leeds Mercury* disapprovingly reported that a cunning-man known locally as Rough Robin earned eighteen shillings for just one morning's work, which was as much as an artisan might earn in one week.[55] At the time of his arrest in 1863, John Collander was earning between five and six pounds a week, and had no qualms about flaunting his prosperity. He was well known for his profuse expenditure, and 'made himself very conspicuous when walking through the streets by the gold chains and the medals he wore, and by his luxuriant feminine ringlets'.[56]

The amount cunning-folk charged usually varied according to the nature of the job. Simple fortune-telling was generally the cheapest service, and whether in the seventeenth or the nineteenth century typically only cost a few pence. When the London practitioners Joseph Haynes, James Domingo and his pretended wife, who dressed as a man, went on a commercial tour of Hertfordshire in 1676, they charged variously 3d. and 6d. a client. In the 1840s William Holland was still only charging two to three pence a session.[57] It has to be remembered, of course, that cunning-folk vied with numerous petty fortune-tellers in the prediction market, and this competition kept fees low. Theft detection was a more restricted practice and as a result cost significantly more. In 1651 a Chelmsford cunning-man named William Hills charged two clients 8d. and 10d. respectively for detecting stolen goods.[58] In 1672 the Somerset cunning-man William Vowles charged one shilling to detect the whereabouts of some stolen cloth and to reveal the identity of the thief. Fees could also rise depending on the value of the stolen goods. Thus Anne Bodenham only charged 12d. and a jug of beer to restore a stolen spoon, but required seven shillings to detect the whereabouts of three gold pieces.[59] Two hundred years later similar sums were still changing hands for the same service. Maria Giles extracted sums of between 6d. and a shilling from several clients, but earned £2 8s. on one occasion; and in 1858 a Wells cunning woman, Martha Miles, demanded four shillings to recover £10 worth of stolen bacon, but eventually accepted half a crown.[60]

Curing the bewitched was generally the most expensive exercise. During the nineteenth century the average price for unbewitching was around a pound. In 1838 a Lincoln wise-man charged a guinea to cure a bewitched man. In 1875 a Devon cunning-man charged a pound to unbewitch a labourer, though he accepted payment in instalments. Ann Fare, of Tiverton, Devon, lightened the pockets of a sixteen-year-old labourer of twenty shillings. Seven years later, Joseph Butler, of Dudley Port, charged £1 14s. 6d. to take off a spell. William Cotton of Rolvenden, extracted a total of twenty-five shillings to drive evil spirits out of an elderly woman. William Brewer, however, charged somewhat less. He told one client that he usually charged eleven shillings, but was in the habit of returning a shilling to prompt payers.[61] As with thief detection, fees usually varied according to the worth of the bewitched, with humans being valued more than livestock. So in 1858 James Baker of Morden, Dorset, charged seventeen shillings to cure one customer of witchcraft, but only five shillings to cure another client's bewitched pig. James Tunnicliff billed a Staffordshire dairy farmer, Thomas Charlesworth, five shillings for each member of the household, the same sum to take the spell off his cheese kettle, but only 3s. 6d. for each cow, calf, sheep, pig and stirk (heifer) on the farm.[62]

Although a pound was still a lot of money to a poor labourer, it could be argued that such charges were competitive. Similar sums were often paid out to qualified doctors and veterinarians without positive results. Furthermore, the curing of witchcraft required an outlay on goods as well as services. Parchment for charms, herbal and chemical ingredients for medicines, and bottles and pots all had to be purchased by the cunning-person. But the thinking of some callous and unscrupulous cunning-folk, of which there were undoubtedly many, was 'why take a pound when more could be extorted?'. The smell of desperation excited the senses of such people, and they apparently had few qualms about enticing the life savings from others who were at their wits' end with worry and suffering. Maria Giles accumulated a total of £3 16s. 4½d. in payment for the treatment of a bewitched man named Joseph Gunter, of Aldermaston, Berkshire. As his wife stated in court, 'I was in hopes she would cure my husband, and I would part with everything if I could get him better'. He did not. Giles said he was 'double bewitched'. When she demanded a further £3, Gunter's niece went to her aunt's sister in Reading and five other places to try and raise the money, but none was forthcoming. In 1867 Mary Murray obtained £4 10s. to cure the wife of Thomas Rendle, who suffered from paralysis attributed to witchcraft. These were very substantial sums to a labourer like Rendle. He earned only ten shillings a week, and had scraped together a few pounds savings over the years. It should be said in mitigation that Murray offered to return all fees if she failed to cure Mrs Rendle. However, an offer was all it turned out to be. She failed either to cure her or return the money, and so Rendle brought the case to court. In 1876 the Norfolk cunning-man James Stagg informed the labouring parents of a bewitched girl, of Carbrooke, that it would cost 'between £6, £7 or £8 if I get your daughter well'. They did not have such a sum in the house, but the sick girl said to her mother, 'See what money I have got in my work-box'. She counted out a total of £5. 'Well, mother', said the girl, 'let him have the £5, for if he gets me well I can go to service and soon get it up again.' Stagg was not satisfied though. He looked around the room, and, on seeing some shell ornaments on the table he said, 'Let me have these large shells'. Mrs Read, the girl's mother, replied 'No, you will not have them. My sister sent me them as a present from Yarmouth.' 'I must have these', demanded Stagg. He then took a fancy to some more ornaments because they were the 'right colour'. Mrs Read exclaimed 'Good God! What will my husband say if you take all of them?' 'Oh, he will not say anything if I get your daughter well', answered Stagg, and off he went with them tied up in his handkerchief. But the award for cynical audacity should, perhaps, go to James Tunnicliff, whose initial modest charges gradually mounted up to a huge £30. By the time Tunnicliff had finished with him, Charlesworth was a wreck, worse off not only financially but also physically and psychologically. Tunnicliff strung him along for weeks, and there is good evidence that he deliberately poisoned Charlesworth to reaffirm and prolong the idea that he was bewitched.[63]

As these examples show, avarice was not an uncommon vice amongst cunning-folk, but the whole profession cannot be tarred with the same brush. For every Tunnicliff there was a Brewer, who, the usually hostile newspapers admitted, 'had none of that grasping, sordid greed for lucre which is so grave a defect in the character of your average sorcerer'.[64] The cunning-trade could be highly profitable or merely provide a modest living combined with some other occupation. It depended on a variety of factors. If you had no conscience about defrauding people money could pour in. The risk of course was that the greater the fee the more the expectation of results, and the bigger the disappointment the more chance that a client might prosecute. This leads on to the next point. Profitability also depended on avoiding prison. Incarceration for any considerable length of time not only meant an instant loss of income but also provided the opportunity for a competitor to establish him or herself in the meantime.

A question that inevitably arises when considering cunning-folk concerns the extent to which they believed in the powers they professed to possess. There really is no answer to this. Cunning-folk may have shared the same trade, but they exhibited a wide range of characters and motivations. Nevertheless, it has been suggested that, 'so far as one can tell, self-confessed impostors were only a minority amongst the large fraternity of practising wizards', and that cunning-folk 'generally believed in their own powers'.[65] It really is impossible to prove the sincerity of any cunning-person. Maybe Maria Giles earnestly thought she could cure Joseph Gunter, and maybe James Stagg felt he had earned his money, but the evidence is highly doubtful. Stagg claimed, for instance, that the medicine he gave the Read girl cost him £4 13s., though he provided no proof that it had. Protestations of probity have to be taken with a pinch of salt, for they were usually made in legal situations where people were obviously going to have to defend their integrity. There are a few instances, though, of cunning-folk confessing to their frauds. An early sixteenth-century Knaresborough cunning-man, John Steward, admitted that he duped his clients, and 'could no thing do, but some tyme it happened as he said, and that was as the blynde man cast his staff'. Some three hundred years later a wise-man of Stalybridge, Lancashire, made a similar death-bed confession to a Methodist minister, James Brooks. Brooks 'found him very penitent. He acknowledged that he knew no more than other persons, and repented of the deceptions he had practised'.[66] Richard Walton also acknowledged the deceptions he had practised upon his clients. He admitted to 'putting too large a Price upon my Drugs, when I had an opportunity for it, or when I really might have afforded them cheaper'. He also confessed to making up astrological predictions, and selling anti-witchcraft charms to people when he was 'sure they had no need of it'. He was particularly regretful of the deceit he practised upon a man named Guest, who had two valuable mares stolen from his property. He had paid for an advertisement to be distributed offering two guineas to anyone who could secure their return. Having received no response to this handbill, he went to see Walton. Walton had also recently been consulted by the two thieves, and so knew where the horses were. Although Walton gave Guest correct information leading to the recovery of his mares, and was consequently rewarded with the two guineas, he felt very guilty about having pretended to divine their whereabouts by astrological means.[67] Yet, the fact that cunning-folk like Walton unscrupulously imposed upon their clients is still no proof that they were completely cynical about the powers they professed. Walton evidently believed in the veracity of astrology, believed in witchcraft and the power of charms, and considered himself capable of achieving results in both areas; but to save time and effort, and also to satisfy the convictions of his clients, he cut corners and pandered to them rather than correcting their false suspicions.

# 4

## *Services*

People consulted cunning-folk because they provided explanations and solutions for the many misfortunes that occurred in their daily lives, as well as holding out the prospect of a better future through the attainment of love and money. People came to them with requests ranging from the obscure and petty – one man asked Billy Brewer to reverse magically the yellowing of his best clothes – to matters of life and death, when cunning-folk were called in to cure the terminally ill or assassinate suspected witches. No job was too small and few jobs were too big, short of resurrecting the dead. To the romantically inclined they held out the promise of ideal husbands, to the greedy small fortunes, to the sick a last resort, to the farmer salvation from financial ruin, to the sailor protection from the elements, to the thief agonising pain, and to his victim the recovery of property. An examination of what cunning-folk practised tells us far more than just what they, as individuals, got up to. It provides an insight into the anxieties and fears of much of the population at large, and a window onto their private hopes and personal aspirations. And if there is one desire that people dreamed of as much in the past as now it was the prospect of obtaining sudden wealth. Today hopes are pinned on the lottery but for many people in the early modern period such a dream could only be realised by the discovery of buried treasure.

Throughout early modern Europe many people, from the cash-strapped nobility and clergy down to the humble labourer, were seduced by the prospect of discovering fabulous, hidden hordes of money and precious metals by occult means. England was no exception. In 1527, for instance, the Lincoln episcopal visitation heard how John Curson convinced some men that several thousand gold and silver coins lay hidden in a mound besides a cross near Kettering. The treasure was apparently contained in pots guarded by 'a man sprite and a woman sprite'. Curson told his accomplices that he had handsomely paid a 'cunnying man' to help him detect this marvellous cache. A year later William Stapleton, a monk of St Bennett's Abbey, Norfolk, admitted conjuring spirits to help find a treasure that would enable him to pay for a dispensation to leave holy orders. He was aided in his search by 'two cunning men'.[1] Treasure-seeking was one of those trades that led people to the doors of cunning-folk, people who in other circumstances would never have consulted them. In particular, cupidity brought together cunning-folk and the clergy, two groups who were otherwise in direct competition. Thus in 1510 a cunning-man and ex-schoolmaster named John Steward, of Knaresborough, teamed up with three clergymen and a former lord mayor of Halifax to uncover by conjurations a chest full of treasure at Mixindale Head near Halifax. They agreed to meet at the appointed spot on the 28 January, armed with three huge magical circles made of virgin parchment, but they got lost in a thick fog and the project was abandoned in farcical fashion. Local gossip about the adventure subsequently led to their prosecution before an ecclesiastical court at York.[2] Before being called to account, a London cunning-man, William Wycherley, had also planned to team up with a priest and two others for a treasure expedition somewhere between Newbury and Reading. He had previously attempted to conjure up treasure near Fulham, but had failed dismally, so Fulham's riches remain hidden to this day. He put his lack of success on that occasion down to the use of a ceremonial sword which had not been consecrated.[3] Conjurations like those performed by Wycherley had two main aims. In those cases where treasure was believed to be guarded by spirits or demons, conjurations were employed to command them to give it up. But spirits and demons did not always play an obstructive role, and could be conjured up to help detect the whereabouts of hidden caches of precious goods. Instructions on how to perform such operations were to be found in grimoires such as the *Key of Solomon*, which will be discussed in the next chapter.

Spirit conjuration was a valuable though not an essential tool for the treasure-seeker. As one seventeenth-century manual of practical magic affirmed, it was not necessary to use any 'ceremonies, nor to draw any circles, or to use any inchantments; onely those that dig must be of a cheerfull minde'.[4] Some merry seekers merely dug at sites where treasure was traditionally meant to lie hidden, such as barrows, ruins and wayside crosses – no intellectual barriers there then. On a more erudite level, the stars could also be employed. The renowned sixteenth-century astrologer Simon Forman was an enthusiastic astrological detector of hidden riches, though he admitted he usually 'digged for treasure in vain'.[5] But for those cunning-folk who did not have access to the requisite magic books, or sufficient knowledge of astrology, there were other methods of magical detection they could employ on behalf of their clients. The Somerset cunning-woman Anne Kingsbury used enchanted dowsing rods, described as being half an ell in length (22.5 inches), to find a treasure hidden in a house in St Mary's Street, Bridgwater. Under examination she said that she had learned how to use them from William Lilly. This may not have been an idle claim. In 1634 the famed astrologer had publicly demonstrated the use of such 'Mosaical Rods', made of hazel, during a treasure-hunt in the cloisters of Westminster Abbey organised by the king's clockmaker, David Ramsey.[6] While learned conjurors with their grimoires commanded demons, spirits and angels to come to their aid, the more humble could, instead, call upon the services of the fairies – or at least claim to do so. In 1594 Judith Philips convinced a Hampshire couple that a great treasure lay hidden under a hollow holly tree next to their house. Their wits befuddled by the prospect of untold wealth, she inveigled them into undergoing a demeaning ritual, devised by Philips for her own cruel pleasure, in which she saddled and bridled the man and rode him back and forth between the tree and the house. After riding him in this fashion, she told him and his wife to grovel on their bellies under the tree, while she went to consult the queen of the fairies about the treasure. She subsequently cozened a wealthy, widowed London tripe-wife, telling her 'your husband in his life hid about your house great store of treasure, for which cause there are sprites now that haunt your house'.[7] A rather more earnest attempt to consult the fairies was made by the cunning-woman Anne Bennett, and her tenant Susan Swapper. In 1607 Susan was 'troubled' by fairies who told her a pot of gold was hidden in a field outside Rye, which had formerly been the property of Anne. She went out to find it one day but failed. She did meet the queen of the fairies, however, who told her that if she knelt in obeisance to her she would not want for money.[8]

Treasure-seeking was a dangerous enterprise for cunning-folk to get involved in. With the exception of those who dug into Bronze Age barrows, the chances of finding buried treasure using magic were exceedingly poor. As a result, many cunning-folk refrained from getting involved. The wisest course of action when a client came to consult about treasure was that adopted by a cunning-man named 'Old Leigh'. When Richard Kitch came to him concerning the reputed treasure in Bridgwater, Leigh confirmed the report but recommended Anne Kingsbury as the best person to find it. Those, like Kingsbury, who took up the challenge were presumably either sincere in their quests and had faith in their magic, or were merely itinerant rogues who could disappear from the scene when the inevitable happened and nothing was found. The latter reason explains why gipsies continued to gull people with tales of riches long after cunning-folk had withdrawn from the business.

While the discovery of treasure was never an important aspect of cunning-trade, another form of detection, that of thieves and lost property, was integral to their existence. Next to unbewitching it was the most lucrative aspect of their business. It has been suggested that cunning-folk were only consulted about theft in 'special circumstances', but the evidence suggests it was, in fact, a commonplace response.[9] There were several types of request that people asked of cunning-folk. Most simply wanted to know where their stolen or lost property could be found. Some further paid to have the goods magically returned to them. Others also desired to know the identity of the thieves, so that they could seek private retribution or publicly denounce and prosecute them. Cunning-folk responded to these queries in a number of ways, depending on the specific details of the case, the extent of their familiarity with each client and where he or she lived, and their own level of prudence or lack of it. The latter point is important because there were numerous pitfalls in the detective business. Joseph Blagrave found to his personal cost that it 'oft times brings trouble', leading to accusations that 'we do but cozen and cheat people of their mony'.[10] Those who displayed a lack of caution or misjudged the situation not only embarrassed themselves but also threatened their own reputations and careers.

When queries concerned the whereabouts of stolen or lost property there were three main strategies cunning-folk could pursue. First, they could simply confirm that the property was indeed lost or stolen, and inform the client that nothing could be done; their goods were gone for good. This option was most likely to be put into action when clients came from places too far away for the cunning-person to have any background knowledge of the facts. Not surprisingly, though, some clients did not deem this response very satisfactory. They had basically paid to hear what they already feared. Furthermore, lost objects sometimes have a knack of turning up unexpectedly. In such an event the cunning-person was made to look a complete fool. The mid seventeenth-century Tamworth cunning-man Nicholas Greaton found himself in just such an awkward position. Thomas Taylor had consulted Greaton about two mares which were believed to have been stolen from his father and a neighbour on the same night. Greaton regretfully informed Taylor that 'it was impossible for them to have them again, for he said they were gone northward, but that proved false, for they were gone westward, and they had them both again.'[11]

The second option was to temporise. The cunning-person held out the possibility of being able to return the goods without actually promising anything. Such work, the cunning-person would say, required considerable time and effort, and there was no guarantee of success. Nevertheless, such words were enough to tantalise clients, who would make several return visits to see how the process of restoration was progressing, each time leaving with their purses a little lighter. When, in 1827, a woman named Mary Davis had £10 stolen, she went to consult a Cheltenham cunning-man. On her second visit, he told Davis that 'it would be very hard to recover' because it had been 'removed' from its original location by the thief. She continued to see how he was getting on, but he never quite managed to bring the case to a successful conclusion.[12]

The third strategy was to promise the restoration of stolen goods, usually by offering to torment the thief into submission. The secret hope was that knowledge of the victim's visit to the cunning-person would reach the ears of the thief, who would be frightened into clandestinely returning the goods. The deterrent effect of their reputations was, in fact, the most important asset cunning-folk had in this respect. The evidence suggests that on many occasions purloined items were indeed returned, to the general satisfaction of all except the thieves. When, in

April 1807, John Lupton of Bedlington had his pocket-book and a small leather bag, containing a total of £15 17s. 6d., stolen from his house, he immediately told his neighbours that he intended to visit a cunning-woman in Shields. He did so a couple of days later, and was told by her that he would find the money and bag lying at his backdoor on his return home. The fearful thief returned the pocket-book as the wise-woman had foretold, though it was still short of some £5. It was a successful resolution nevertheless.[13] The local constable could have done no better, and Lupton presumably had little faith in him. Fear of retribution from cunning-folk, however, was only likely to influence the petty, opportunistic thief rather than the hardened criminal, and in most recorded instances of successfully returned goods the thieves were servants, hired labourers or neighbours.

The risk inherent in this option was that the thief either had no fear of magic, or never got to hear that a cunning-person was involved. In such instances, cunning-folk were guilty of making empty promises and dashing the hopes of their client, and it was often after such an experience that dissatisfied clients prosecuted. Who better to demonstrate this than our old friend Maria Giles. In October 1871 Hannah Long, of Pamber, Hampshire, was coming back from Reading with her cart when a pair of watertight boots, a quarter-pound of tea, and a half-pound of sugar went missing from the back. Several days later she travelled to Newbury to see if Giles could restore the lost or stolen goods. After consulting her book, Giles confidently asserted that they would be brought and laid in front of Long's house the following day or the day after, between six and seven in the morning. As Long told the court, 'when I left home it was in the belief that the prisoner could bring back my things, and when she told me so I was pleased, and still believed she could. But for that belief and statement I should not have parted with my money'. Giles had similarly been prosecuted eighteen years earlier after charging a carter's boy £2 8s. for the return of goods stolen from his stable. She said she would achieve this by tormenting the supposed thief, 'an old miser – whom she would make pay for it'. It was Giles who ended up paying for it with a prison sentence.[14]

When it came to the identification of thieves there were two further options. The more risky of the two was to name the guilty party explicitly. In some instances cunning-folk probably knew the identity of the culprit or heard local gossip about who was suspected. Some took a chance, perhaps, and named local people with well-known criminal reputations. In other instances cunning-folk probably reiterated the name of someone whom the client had already mentioned as a suspect during the consultation. Whatever the scenario, taking the step of denouncing an individual in this manner risked being brought before the courts. As we have seen, some of those so named, and sometimes subsequently arrested, sued for defamation, or made complaints that led to prosecutions under the various Witchcraft Acts. In August 1614 Elizabeth Gibson of Whitechapel, London, was committed 'as a wizard for charging Walter Jones and Jane Grey that they robbed the Lord Ivors'. Later in the century, William Vowles, a cunning-man of Blagdon, Somerset, was hauled before the quarter sessions after having given an impressively detailed account of the theft of some cloth from the local miller William Allen. Vowles's detective work told him that the wife of James Thatcher had 'tempted her husband to steale it and that about eleven of the clocke on the same Sunday night the said Thatcher pulled the said cloth out the said Allen's mill with a long pole having a crooke or hooke in the end of it through an open plate in the wall and boards behind the water wheels and carried the same to his owne house'.[15]

The alternative, less risky strategy was to employ some divinatory ritual in which clients confirmed their own suspicions without cunning-folk having to name someone explicitly. This usually involved the client looking into a reflective surface of some sort, such as a mirror, crystal ball, piece of glass, bowl of water, cup of ink, or even a polished thumbnail. A cunning-man of Fivehead, prosecuted before the Somerset quarter sessions in 1669, showed 'ye people in a glass' the image of some sheep-rustlers.[16] Two hundred years later Maria Giles also used a simple piece of glass with a black background. One of her clients, a hawker named Emma Gregory, gave the Newbury borough magistrates the following account of her and her friend Ford's experience of looking into the glass:

> It was the man who followed behind my cart whom I suspected, and she pretended she had brought him in the glass. I heard she could bring any man to the glass, and she showed us the glass and we looked in but could not see my things. I asked her to let Ford see the man first. Ford looked in

the glass, and said he could see himself and could discern someone else, but he could not say who. I wanted to see, and looked in the glass ... Did you see the thief? – I could see nothing but myself. I didn't feel satisfied as I couldn't see anything and wanted to go.[17]

Gregory was obviously not as receptive to auto-suggestion as many other clients who apparently did see images of those they suspected. Perhaps Gregory's experience explains why some cunning-folk, rather than aiding clients to realise their own images, provided vague delineations of the appearance of the thief or thieves. These were usually verbal descriptions, such as the one James Wheeler of Instow, Devon, gave a client in 1836, which merely concerned a 'dark haired man and a sandy haired woman'.[18] Less common but more impressive was the production of sketches showing the physical appearance of the culprits. On one occasion, a Stamford wise-man drew an exact likeness of the thief of a flitch of bacon, from which the client immediately recognised someone he knew.[19]

Some of the divinatory methods used in thief detection have already been mentioned but there were numerous others. Astrology was one of the most common techniques employed for finding lost property, identifying thieves and locating where they lived. In 1613, for instance, John Wheeler, who ran an apothecary shop in Grub Street, London, was charged twice for being a 'wissard' and for seducing the king's subjects by making them believe that 'by erecting a figure he cann helpe them to [find] stolen goods'.[20] As Richard Walton's confession and other cases indicate, however, cunning-folk often only made a pretence of drawing up astrological calculations, either out of laziness or because they did not have the necessary skills. The sieve and shears was another less sophisticated technique that was widely used by cunning-folk and the general public. This consisted of either sticking the sharp end of some shears into the wooden rind of a sieve or balancing the sieve on some shears. Next, an appeal was made to the Holy Trinity or to St Peter and St Paul, the names of those suspected were called out, and the sieve would turn at the mention of the guilty party. Intriguingly, this divinatory tradition had died out by the nineteenth century. The more enduring Bible and key ritual, of which there were several variations, followed a similar procedure. William Wycherley's description of his own technique should suffice. He asked one client to put 'the names in writing of such persons as she had in suspicion. Which names he put severally into the pipe of a kay'. He then took a psalter and laid the key upon the eighteenth verse of the first psalm. 'When this verse was said over one of the names, which was a woman, the book and key turned rounde'. He admitted frankly that 'he hath used this practise so often that he cannot express how many the times'.[21] The illiterate version of the technique required that the names of the suspects be called out. As well as these two popular methods, written charms were also used to afflict thieves and thereby force them into returning goods, and spirits could also be conjured up to do likewise.

Much of cunning-folk's work in the field of love and sexual relationships was concerned with simple fortune-telling, providing clients with information about whom they were to marry. This was usually done by means of palmistry, scrying or astrology, but there was plenty of scope for invention. One of John Parkins lamens or charms, for example, ensured that 'any lady may have a clear, full, and most perfect sight of the gentleman she will marry, so as to perfectly know him by a vision or dream in the night'. He also sold another that 'a lady may marry the gentleman she loves', though only 'if agreeable to the will of God'.[22] More lucrative was the business of rekindling love between married partners, an ever-present and often insurmountable source of anguish in the days before legal divorce. One of the charges brought against the Newcastle wise-man, Peter Banks, in 1673–74, was that he offered to compel 'ill husbands to be good to their wifes'. He achieved this by drawing up magic leases binding the husband to good behaviour. One customer, Jane Crossby, obtained one of these leases for ten shillings and two new shirts, and was delighted to find that for a year 'her husband was loveing and kind; but the yeare expireing, and she not renewing her lease, her said husband was ill and untoward againe'. When Sarah Ann Tomlinson, of Oldham, went to Clayton Chaffer to have her fortune told, the 'doctor' told her the shocking news that her husband had been carrying on with another woman for over six years. Tomlinson proposed to leave him, but Chaffer dissuaded her, saying that her husband would sell all her furniture. He proposed instead to 'make him one of the best of husbands', a service he had provided for 'scores who had lived happily ever after'. To this end he sold her for seven shillings a written charm sealed with different coloured wafers, which she had to place next to her heart under her stays. She also had to put some herbs in his tea, and burn his urine in the fire while saying the Lord's Prayer and reading certain parts of the Bible.[23] Cunning-folk further claimed to be able to draw back absconded wives, husbands and lovers. Mary Bateman dealt with many cases of 'love-sick girls, and nervous women', one of whom was a pregnant young woman abandoned by her lover. For a guinea she offered to 'screw' the man down and make him marry her. One of Maria Giles's many brushes with the law was a consequence of promising a woman named Mary Ann Fisher that she could drag her absent husband back 'over hedges and ditches'. After several fruitless visits to Giles, costing a dress and twelve pence, Fisher eventually found her husband two months later in Winchester, where he had been with the Militia.[24] John Parkins, displaying his usual commercial acumen, not only dealt in bringing men and women together but also in keeping them apart. His fourth lamen was constructed to 'most powerfully protect and defend any lady against all the various powers of seduction, insult, etc. and also from the malignant grasp of the most atrocious and abandoned libertine, at all times and places whatsoever'.[25]

There is little evidence that cunning-folk dealt with explicit sexual problems such as venereal diseases and impotency. This was probably because the symptoms of the former could be fairly easily identified as having a natural cause, while witchcraft-inspired impotency, although a significant source of accusations in some parts of Europe, was rarely heard of in English courts. A number of cunning-folk did, however, act as abortionists. Mary Bateman convinced the young woman mentioned above that her unborn child was impeding attempts to draw her errant lover. She gave her 'certain medicines' which successfully aborted the foetus but ruined the health of the woman. This was a very risky business for both the patient and the practitioner. Herbal and chemical abortifacients were often highly toxic, there was no guarantee of success and death was a distinct possibility. The Norwich cunning-woman Sarah Whisker was transported for life in 1846 after giving an irritant, white hellebore, to a pregnant servant, who subsequently fell badly ill.[26]

There were numerous other minor services cunning-folk provided. In fishing communities, for instance, there was a market for charms to ensure successful voyages. Peter Banks sold protective leases to 'diverse seamen' for the sum of twenty shillings. The contents of one read as follows: 'I charge you and all of you, in the high sword name, to assist and blesse Cuthbert Burrell belonging to [name of ship omitted] from all rocks and sands, storms and tempests thereunto belonging, for this yeare.' During times of war there must have been increased demand from soldiers and sailors for such protection. Towards the end of the Napoleonic Wars the ever-helpful John Parkins heavily promoted his tenth lamen for military and naval officers. It was a most impressive charm, which would 'not only protect and defend the British Army and Navy in all those times of the greatest danger, but also give them a most complete victory over all their enemies, both foreign and domestic'. John Parkins's role in the downfall of Napoleon perhaps deserves more recognition.[27] On the other hand, some cunning-folk were less supportive of the war effort, in that they offered to influence the militia ballot for men reluctant to enter military service. Cunning-folk also dealt in predicting and influencing the outcomes of wagers, lawsuits, and contests, as well as making debtors pay up.[28]

While detective work, love magic and the other services already mentioned were the bread and butter of any cunning-person's business, healing the bewitched was their speciality. They were not the only unbewitchers around. In the early modern period, as has been shown, some physicians and surgeons also offered the service, as did gypsies, and lay and clerical exorcists. But cunning-folk were undoubtedly the most available and flexible, and possessed a wider arsenal of tools. They were, moreover, the principal dealers in preventative charms against witchcraft, and, unlike most physicians, also identified witches. They were, therefore, the only healers to offer a comprehensive package of anti-witch measures. From the late seventeenth century onwards, with the withdrawal of orthodox medicine from the cure and diagnosis of witchcraft, this aspect of cunning-trade must have assumed an even greater importance. With the exception of gypsies, they became the only occupational unbewitchers left in business, and with a rapidly expanding population there was no let-up in the number of people seeking remedies for witchcraft. There is no need to doubt John Parkins when he observed, 'I have had a great number of cases of witchcraft in my hands since I have been in business'. 'If I was to attempt to give you a full account of all the different cases of this nature', he continued, 'I suppose it would make a large volume of itself.'[29]

The evidence suggests that, even in the seventeenth century, most people did not run off to cunning-folk as soon as they fell ill. Unless the sick or their families had already experienced other forms of misfortune, witchcraft was not suspected at first, and home remedies were applied or trained physicians were called in. During the trial of three women for witchcraft in 1682, one of their alleged victims testified that she had 'been very much pain'd and tormented in her body these many years last past'. She told the court that 'she hath sought out for remedy far and neer, and never had any suspition that she had had any magical art or witchcraft used upon her body, until it was about a year and a half ago'.[30] For this woman and many like her, it was the failure to find a diagnosis let alone a cure that set in motion the often long drawn-out process from private suspicions of witchcraft, to consultation on the matter with family and friends, to identification of the culprit, and finally to prosecution or assault of the suspected witch.

The clergyman Richard Bernard urged those who suspected themselves bewitched to 'enquire not of a devilish wizard, but of learned and judicious physicians to know their disease'. Many followed his advice, and it was only after the 'learned' members had obviously failed that people then sought out cunning-folk.[31] Until the mid nineteenth century many ailments were unknown or difficult to diagnose correctly, and even for those that were identifiable and understood there was often no effective treatment. Before the advent of pharmaceutical analgesics, anaesthetics and antibiotics, general practitioners could provide little relief, let alone successful treatment for many of those who consulted them. Over and over again we hear in the sources how people went to cunning-folk as a last resort, after having spent considerable sums of money on orthodox doctors, to no avail. One of Joan Peterson's clients, who suffered from terrible headaches, 'made tryal of many doctors, but could have no redress'. His condition improved, however, after Peterson gave him a special drink. The father of a bewitched girl exorcised by Joseph Blagrave told that 'he had spent much money upon several doctors and others but they could do her no good'. The local minister's best efforts also came to nothing. The Yorkshire clergyman Thomas Hawkins, writing in 1808, knew of several parishioners who had only resorted to cunning-folk after orthodox medicine had failed to cure what were originally thought to be natural ailments. One man, 'applied first to the faculty, but obtained little or no relief', and 'his wife suspected that he might have had "hurt done" him' – in other words that he was bewitched. A local cunning-man was then consulted who guided the man back to good health. In 1857 a Surrey labourer told a local magistrate how a cunning-man had cured his sick wife of witchcraft after 'all the doctors had tried and I had spent my last shilling on 'em'. When Sophia Read's daughter fell ill in 1876, she spent six weeks under the supervision of the local general practitioner, Dr Ewart of Watton, Norfolk, but to no effect. She subsequently told a cunning-man, James Stagg, 'Well, if you can do my daughter any good I shall be thankful, for it seems more than the doctor can do'.[32]

Could cunning-folk do more than the licensed doctors? This is a very difficult question to answer. As the above examples show, some clients were obviously happy with the treatment provided. On the other hand, the prosecution evidence supplies numerous cases to the contrary. But merely providing a concrete diagnosis of witchcraft could have a beneficial, psychosomatic effect. An orthodox doctor could often only provide a vague description of the problem like 'softening of the brain', 'hardening of the heart', or 'noxious humours', and they were unable convincingly to explain the cause. This understandably created doubts in the minds of their patients. Lack of recovery led to further suspicions that the doctor had misdiagnosed and was useless. This contrasted with a cunning-man, who after a perfunctory examination immediately provided both a firm diagnosis, witchcraft, and a cause, a witch. With the nature and source of the problem thus identified sufferers were given renewed hope that a cure was possible and maybe even certain. The power of positive thinking has been proven to have physiological benefits, and so, in this sense at least, magic may have worked; but those accused of witchcraft often paid the price.

The diagnosis of witchcraft could be reached by examining the patient's urine. The wife of the sick Yorkshireman mentioned by Thomas Hawkins took a bottle of her husband's water to a cunning-man who 'skilled it', confirmed he was bewitched, and observed that he 'had suffered extremely, but that by God's help he could do him good'. When, in 1876, Emma Foot gave some of her sick mother's urine to Frederick Culliford and asked if there was an 'ill wish' upon her, the cunning-man 'took the bottle in his hand and shook it and looked at it and said "Yes

I know there is"'. James Haywood, who was convicted for murdering Ann Tennant in 1875, had his suspicions that she had bewitched him confirmed by a 'cunning-man' and 'water doctor' named Manning of Coughton. Manning told him that if he filled a glass bottle or phial with his urine, turned it upside down, and bubbles rose to the top, then he was certainly under a spell. In a variation of this practice a cunning-woman of Bedminster, who in 1762 was consulted by the mother of some possessed children, bid her 'take the two children's first water in the morning, and put it in a pipkin on the fire; and if, when it boiled, all colours of the rainbow came out of it visibly, she could cure it'.[33] Another form of diagnosis, condemned by several physicians, was to wash the patient in a decoction of vervain. If the resulting run-off changed colour or contained many hairs, which it must have done on most occasions, then witchcraft was at work.[34] In many cases, though, cunning-folk automatically pointed the finger at witchcraft without any pseudo-medical examination of either patients or their urine. People seemed to have accepted that cunning-folk were skilled enough to recognise witchcraft simply from the symptoms described by the patient or from their physical appearance. When, in 1604, John Wendore of Newbury was called in to treat Anne Gunter, he had only to look at her to see she 'was not sick, but rather ... bewitched by some evil neighbour'.[35]

The cure of witchcraft could be effected in three main ways: by going straight to the source and tackling the witch either physically or through the law courts; by breaking the spell at a distance via magical rituals; or by using a mix of herbs and charms to expel the witchcraft from the patient's body. Cunning-folk were instrumental in facilitating all these methods, and they sometimes employed a combination of all three. Those who chose or were advised to tackle the witch directly first had to know his or her identity, and the same divinatory methods were used as were employed for thief detection. In 1616 a cunning-man used a looking-glass to show Edward Drake of King's Lynn the woman who had bewitched his daughter. A Plymouth cunning-woman, Mary Catherine Murray, employed a simple glass of water to the same effect. She told one client to look into the glass and he 'saw some shadows', which Murray assured him were the figures of the man and woman who had bewitched his wife. Joan Peterson adopted the following combination of urine-scrying and divination to identify the bewitcher of a cow-keeper's cow:

> she desired the woman to save her water [urine], and bring it to her, which she did; then taking the water, shee set it on the fire, and it had not been on long, but the water rose up in bubbles, in one of the which she shewed her the face of the woman which the Cow-keeper's wife suspected to have bewitched it.[36]

As this account clearly indicates, the client saw what they wanted to see; in other words, the person they already suspected. The process was one of confirmation rather than detection.

Not all clients had prior suspicions about who had bewitched them though. Some could think of no one who might have wished them harm, and so went to cunning-folk in the hope of getting an initial lead. In such instances, as with thief detection, cunning-folk often provided a vague account of the culprit, and left the client to try and match the description to anyone he or she knew amongst their family, friends or neighbours. Another common strategy was to tell the client that the next person they encountered in the street or who came onto their property was the witch. When, in 1890, the horse of a dairyman of Longbredy, Dorset, died, the dairyman went to consult Mrs Bartlett, who told him that the person who had 'overlooked' the animal would shortly try and borrow something from him. Not long after, a neighbouring dairyman asked to borrow some harness equipment. He was consequently accused of witchcraft, and the former friends became bitter enemies.[37] An equally arbitrary, anti-social practice employed by a few reckless members of the profession was to pick on someone out of the blue. In 1858, for instance, James Baker called at the cottage of a labourer, William Lattimer of Kinson Pottery, Dorset, to determine who had bewitched his pig to death. During the inspection another of Baker's clients, a woman who had recently paid him seventeen shillings to relieve her mind of some 'weight', came to visit Lattimer, who was her neighbour. At this point, Baker suddenly announced, 'That is the witch that killed thy pig'. When the facts of the case came to the attention of Lattimer's employer, Baker was arrested. On being searched, the police found an old-fashioned spoon that he claimed was charmed, and which was essential to his unbewitching rituals.[38]

Once the witch was identified, the victim could, prior to 1736, bring the accused to court, or, as occurred frequently throughout the centuries, attempt to scratch the witch. The act of drawing blood was the strongest form of counter-magic that could be employed, and sometimes people were drawn to commit such an assault on the advice of cunning-folk. In the 1570s, for example, an ostler of Windsor, who 'at the last' consulted a local cunning-man named Father Rosimond about a 'great ache in his limbs', was told he was bewitched and was advised, 'if you can meete her, and all to scratche her, so that you drawe blood of her, you shall presently mende'.[39] Occasionally, cunning-folk took the bold step of directly confronting witches in person. In 1596 a Staffordshire 'cunning man' instigated a bit of extra-legal torture, when he attempted to confirm the guilt of Alice Gooderidge by putting a new pair of shoes on her feet, and then placing them close to a fire 'till the shooes being extreame hot' she would confess. She did not, however, and the pamphleteer who recorded the case mocked the cunning-man's 'ridiculous practise', though he accepted the proof of her testimony when 'threatened more sharply'. Several other confrontations between cunning-folk and witches are known from the nineteenth century.[40]

A less risky policy was to tackle the witch at a distance. By conducting various rituals of sympathetic magic, witches could be physically tormented into removing the spells they had cast on their victims. Perhaps the most potent of these was the fabrication of a witch bottle. A nineteenth-century Norfolk farmer explained the process: 'She [the cunning-woman] came and told us to take some particular liquid and put it in a bottle with some of the hairs out of the noddle of my wife's neck, and the parings of her finger nails and toe nails (these we cut quite close) and some old horseshoe nails.'[41] The 'particular liquid' was the patient's urine, and other sharp objects like thorns and pins could also be added. The vessel was then sealed, and either boiled over a fire or buried, often under the hearthstone. The vessel was symbolic of the witch's bladder, and the sharp objects would cause him or her to experience excruciating pain. Thus when a Londoner named Chamblet boiled a witch bottle on the instructions of a Spittlefields' 'doctor', he swore he heard the witch's voice at his door, 'and that she Screimed out as if she were Murdered, and that the next day she appeared to be much swelled and bloated'.[42] Burning some of the thatch from the cottage of the suspected witch or items of the bewitched's clothing had a similar effect. In 1682 the parents of a bewitched girl named Mary Farmer were advised by 'Dr Bourn' to burn her clothes. He assured them 'that then the witch which had done her the hurt, would come in'. The parents testified in court that, having done this, a neighbour, Joan Buts entered their house, 'and tumbled down, wallowing on the ground, making a fearful and dismal noise'.43 To cure livestock it was fairly common to remove the heart of one of the dead animals and either roast it or stick it full of pins or thorns and hang it up the chimney. Again, the magic was based on sympathetic association. Piercing or burning the victim's heart caused that of the witch to suffer terribly. There were other variations on the same theme. An early nineteenth-century Yorkshire cunning-man instructed a client to make a 'thing composed of hair having sixteen tails or more, with a seal fixed to each tail'. When this was burned in a fire, along with some special paste, a poor widow who lived in an adjoining apartment was observed to 'have been violently agitated and affected all the night during the performance'.44 These types of what might be called distance magic were popular with clients not only because of their powerful imagery but also because of the perceived immediacy of their effect. Indeed, Joseph Blagrave was 'credibly informed by some who have gon to these cunning women or white witches, that their cattle, or the patient afflicted have been perfectly well before they have gotten home'.45

Some of the most revealing evidence we have concerning unbewitching practices concerns the attempts by cunning-folk to tackle the consequences rather than the sources of witchcraft. Most cunning-folk employed a multi-pronged approach to curing witchcraft, using a combination of written charms, magic rituals, prayers and herbal medicines, thereby appealing to the physical, psychological and spiritual needs of the sick. An initial example of this approach comes from early seventeenth-century King's Lynn, where a cunning-man told the father of a bewitched girl to 'make a cake' consisting of baker's flour and the girl's urine. He was told to cook the mixture 'on the harth, wherof the one halfe was to be applied and laid to the region of the heart, the other halfe to the back directly opposit; and further, gave a box of ointment like treacle, which must be spread upon that cake, and a powder to be cast upon the same, and certain words written in a paper, to be layd on likewise'.[46] But the most common solution was to prescribe a treatment comprising of written charms and herbal remedies. Richard Bernard noted a good example of this dualistic approach:

> the wizard prescribed ... a certaine medicine of divers hearbes, which I had from the man himselfe: but over the head, and before he began to prescribe the medicine, these words must bee written, as they were taken from his owne mouth: *Onguint Manera Iaiaanquint Manera*, words senseless; but in these words were hidden the power of the medicine.[47]

John Parkins likewise advertised that those who bought his lamens and amulets would have 'the virtues of all their said medicines so much increased and augmented that the sick and the diseased will be most speedily restored to their former good state of health'.[48] So while physicians believed that herbal medicines alone could cure witchcraft, cunning-folk worked on the basis that an additional magical component was required. In practice this undoubtedly gave cunning-folk an edge in the unbewitching market: physicians only applied themselves to the patients' bodies while cunning-folk sought to assuage their psychological needs as well.

The content of the charms provided by cunning-folk is the subject of a later chapter, so we need only focus now on the ingredients of the potions they prescribed, though the evidence is admittedly meagre. Some witch-doctoring physicians recommended the plants true-love and St John's wort for internal cures, while fumigants of bay, rue, sage and rosemary were also considered effective. Joseph Blagrave used distillations of marigold, rosemary and angelica.[49] Cunning-folk seem to have employed a similar range of ingredients. After all, they borrowed from the same oral and literary fund of knowledge about herbs. Nicholas Culpeper's, *The English Physician or Herball*, first published in 1653, was one widely used source. It went through numerous editions over the years; the cunning-man John Parkins even published his own version with an index reference to 'witchcraft'. According to Culpeper, the best herb was bay, as it 'resisteth witchcraft very potently, as also all the evils old Satan can do to the body of man'.[50] Ursula Kemp recommended three leaves each of sage and St John's wort steeped in ale, while William Brewer made a decoction of dried bay leaves and peppermint. Amongst the eighteen ingredients an Exeter cunning-woman claimed her medicine was made from were liquorice, alder and rum.[51] Such herbal ingredients were thought to have their own anti-witchcraft properties, but in practice they might also have acted as beneficial tonics and emollients for the natural ailments afflicting the supposedly bewitched. When the herbal remedy James Stacey prescribed for one patient in 1892 was analysed by a doctor, he concluded that it was a 'slight tonic'. Such remedies were certainly as good as anything many doctors prescribed at the time. During an inquest in Somerset in 1854, for example, it was heard how a cunning-man gave the deceased (who suffered from fits) an ointment composed of sage, wormwood, jack-in-the-hedge and lard, which the patient had to rub on the back of her ear. A local doctor, who was also consulted, similarly prescribed that a mustard plaster be applied to the back of her neck. In terms of efficacy, the cunning-man's remedy was probably the better of the two, although ultimately neither was of much use.

The sinister side of unbewitching was bewitching. There was a fine line between using magic to torment witches and using the same magic to torment 'normal' people. We have already seen how cunning-women were occasionally prosecuted as witches, usually after disputes with clients led to the uttering of threats. But cunning-folk were also popularly thought to trade in witchcraft: to act as mercenary witches. It was said of Father Rosimond, for instance, that 'he can help any manne so bewitched to his health againe, as well as to bewitche'.[52] The extent to which cunning-folk were employed to bewitch is, however, very difficult to assess. People certainly believed the trade was going on. In 1746 a woman told John Wesley that a man she had offended had paid a conjuror fourteen shillings to bewitch her. The family of a young woman, who was exorcised by a Catholic priest in 1815, believed her illness 'arose solely from the malice of a rejected admirer, who, they said, had employed the assistance of a reputed wizard at Dudley, to do her a mischief'.[53] But such examples are no proof that cunning-folk had really been so employed. After all, this was obviously dangerous commercial territory. If a cunning-person's reputation for bewitching came to overshadow their unbewitching abilities it threatened their career. Although there is little evidence of cunning-folk actually being paid for such work, some at least pretended they had been so employed in order to extort money from clients. This is exactly what Joseph Butler (aged fifty-two) did in 1882 to get £1 14s. 6d. from the wife of a locksmith named Thomas Starkey. As was heard at his trial in May of that year, Butler, a chain-maker and tobacconist in Dudley Port, was consulted by Mrs Starkey, who told him she believed there was a 'spell of voices put upon her', and that one voice sounded like his. Mrs Starkey, who one suspects was suffering from schizophrenia, said she was troubled day and night by the voices, and asked Butler if he could remove the spell. Butler replied that it was he who had put the spell upon her and could just as easily take it off. He said that ten of her neighbours had paid him to work the spell, the names of two of whom he mentioned along with a description of a 'little sallow-faced woman'. He further informed her that 'it was fortunate she had gone to see him or she would have been in the cemetery'.[54] Cunning-folk also promoted the notion that they traded in witchcraft by accusing other, usually unnamed and fictitious, practitioners of being responsible for their client's bewitchment. When, for example, a Mrs Giles consulted a cunning-woman of Bedminster about the witchcraft that plagued her family, she was told that 'a man in Bristol had given many pieces of gold to a woman in Gloucestershire to do it'.[55] James Tunnicliff spun several stories to Thomas Charlesworth about how his mother had at different times paid various men to cast a spell over him and his farm. Tunnicliff extorted money out of him under the pretence that he had to go and do battle with these mercenary witches. On one occasion, he was paid £3 to counter a tormentor named Wilson at Derby. Tunnicliff reported that 'Wilson had been very stubborn but that he would be stubborn with him and would finish him in three days'.[56] But the resort to such ruses was fairly uncommon, and there is little evidence that bewitching was anything more than a very minor trade. Gossip and rumour about such practices was far greater than the reality. The Rev. Hawkins even knew of a spiteful man who went to a cunning-man to ask him to afflict some enemies, and was disappointed when the latter replied, 'I can do nothing against them, they are *saints*'.[57]

Having outlined what cunning-folk did, it is also important to consider how they promoted both themselves and what they had to offer. Cunning-folk operated in a competitive market where reputations and first impressions were very important. People did not necessarily choose cunning-folk on the pragmatic basis of nearness and cost: they were quite prepared to travel many miles on foot or by horse to see the one who was considered the best. A Lincolnshire servant whose savings had been stolen travelled nearly twenty miles to see a Stamford wise-man, and there are several cases of people in nineteenth-century Somerset bypassing one cunning-person on their way to see another more reputed.[58] To generate such reputations cunning-folk had to display a considerable level of customer care, while the successful employment of various tricks of the trade also enhanced the impression of magical powers.

Compared to orthodox doctors, some cunning-folk provided exceptional client care. They often travelled considerable distances to see their clients, were prepared to make night calls and even offered to stay for days at a time, though such personal treatment obviously came at a cost. One cunning-man travelled ten or twelve miles to see an elderly patient, sat up with him all night and even went to prayer with him. Another practitioner visited a client on four occasions, charging half a guinea each time, and eventually had her move into his own house so that he could more effectually treat her.[59] When a famed Isle of Man wise-man, Mr Teare, was interviewed by Joseph Train in the mid nineteenth century, he confided to him that 'he was required by his professional business to travel more than any person in the Island, and when I expressed my surprise at a person of his advanced years enduring such fatigue, he replied "the crab that lies always in its hole is never fat"'.[60] A more delightfully apt metaphor could not be found. But while such pragmatically solicitous treatment was obviously important, so too was the need to make a strong visual impression. This could be achieved by wearing extraordinary and outlandish garb, and adorning consulting rooms with unusual objects and decorations. One nineteenth-century Yorkshire wise-woman was described as having 'some eye to stage effect, and possessed some stage properties'. These included a stuffed and dried lizard, while papers and herbs were strung from the ceiling. During consultations she wore a conical hat and robed herself in a sheet scrawled with magical signs.[61] But such theatricality was not to everyone's taste. Mr Teare, for instance, dressed soberly in old-fashioned, undyed woollen breeches, vest and coat, topped with a broad-brimmed, low-crowned slouched hat too big for his head.

There were other ways to impress. As early as 1370, a Cheshire man employed the following imaginative ruse during an investigation into the theft of some money. He dug a deep pit in his barn, in which he hid an accomplice dressed in black garments, disguised to represent the devil. He then called in a number of his neighbours and pretended to conjure up the evil one to name the thief. This was somewhat exceptional, and most deceptions were rather more prosaic. When she wanted to convince a client that her house was haunted by spirits, Judith Philips got two henchmen to beat on the walls during the night. Reputations for detecting stolen property could be boosted by organising a theft in the expectation that the victim would turn up for a consultation on the matter. Reginald Scot described the 'confederacie' of 'Steeven Tailor and one Pope' in just such a scam. Tailor hid his neighbours' horses and goods, and then recommended that they consult Pope to find them.[62] Success was guaranteed. One of the most widespread of deceptions was to eavesdrop on clients while they waited for a consultation. The wives and husbands of cunning-folk, or paid stooges, would greet the clients, inform them that the cunning-man or –woman was not in at present but was expected to return shortly. In the meantime, they coaxed out of the clients the nature of their problems, while the cunning-folk, who were concealed close by, overheard the conversations. The Exeter conjuror James Tuckett listened through a papered-over hole in the wall. Another nineteenth-century Devon cunning-man had his reception room walled on one side with folding doors. His wife would engage the customers in conversation, and after thirty minutes he would enter through the front door having made a show of passing up the main street in full view of the room's window. He would then amaze his customers by divining the reason for their visit. George Clegg used the very same ploy.[63] As a character says of the wise-woman of Hogsdon, who had her own secret cabinet for the same purpose, 'neither hath she her name for nothing, who ... can foole so many that thinke themselves wise'.[64]

Word of mouth was obviously sufficient to build a widespread following, but the process was slow. The quickest and most effective means of promotion over large areas was to advertise in the printed media. In seventeenth-century London astrologer-physicians vied for trade in a very competitive market and many resorted to distributing flyers to draw in custom. The reputations of numerous eighteenth-century quack doctors were built on the basis of handbills and newspaper advertisements. Yet cunning-folk rarely availed themselves of this influential media. In the early modern period this was quite understandable, as access to the presses was limited. Before 1695 print shops were legally restricted to London, Cambridge, Oxford and York, and the costs involved in the printing, delivery and distribution of material were prohibitive. Besides such practical factors, cunning-folk were surely also aware that many of their potential clientele were illiterate, which obviously reduced the commercial impact of print. But with the expansion of the printing industry, and the rise in literacy from the eighteenth century onwards, it might have been expected that cunning-folk would have followed the quacks in exploiting print. Some did, of course, but not many. In 1795 James Hallett of Chichester, a 'mathematician and astrologer', 'the original curer of all diseases', who cast nativities 'for the cure of witchcraft', produced an imaginative handbill with an engraving of himself seated in a consulting room surrounded by paraphernalia of his trade. John Wrightson also distributed a trade card that began, 'J. Wrightson, Cow doctor, a seventh son, Stokesley, begs leave to acquaint the public that those who are afflicted with any kinds of inward disorders ... may be relieved by sending their water'.[65] Significantly, no mention was made of witchcraft. Like many of those who were also herbalists, Wrightson was careful to present a 'respectable' public façade. This is most evident from examining the advertising columns of newspapers. While astrology, herbalism and quack medicines were all deemed appropriate services to mention, unbewitching certainly was not. I have examined many newspapers from the eighteenth and nineteenth centuries and never found anyone advertising that aspect of cunning-trade. Even the greatest exploiter of print, John Parkins, shied away from proclaiming his witch-doctoring services in the papers. Newspapers had too wide a readership, and there was no control over distribution. While many potential clients might be attracted, so too might magistrates and clergymen. Cunning-folk were not secretive individuals but their profession required them to exercise some caution.

Parkins may not have divulged all his business practices in the newspapers, but he was quite open about his experience of witchcraft in his tracts and pamphlets, and in this respect he was unique. Parkins had set up his Temple of Wisdom in the village of Little Gonerby sometime during the first decade of the nineteenth century, but it was in 1810 that there came a turning point in his career when he began an impressive programme of publication and self-promotion. Parkins was evidently a fluent writer and skilled astrologer. Unlike his Lincolnshire contemporary, the high-minded astrologer John Worsdale (1777-c. 1828), who published several learned astrological disquisitions,[66] Parkins's publications were quite deliberately targeted at a popular audience, in other words his pool of potential customers. His first major foray in the world of publishing was heralded in the local press on 11 May 1810, with an advert in the *Lincoln, Rutland and Stamford Mercury* announcing that on that very day 'A new fortune-telling book, by Dr Parkins' had been published by Tegg's of Cheapside. The following week the same advert also appeared in the *Lincoln and Hull Chronicle*. The book in question was *The Universal Fortune-Teller*, which Parkins described as 'a treasure of immense value'. It cost 2s. 6d. and was 'illustrated by curious wood cuts, of signs, figures, planets, etc.', just the sort of thing to catch the eye of the chapbook-reading public. A copy preserved in the British Library shows, however, that there was actually little 'curious' about the woodcuts. Numerous popular fortune-telling publications of the period contained similar images, while the contents too concerned the usual chapbook mix of information on divination by cards, palmistry, physiognomy, moles, as well as basic astrological information. It was, nevertheless, a well-constructed guide carefully pitched at its target audience, and went through several editions in subsequent years. It also had a national distribution, being stocked by a number of booksellers around the midlands and the north, namely those in Babbington, Boston, Brigg, Derby, Leicester, Lincoln, Louth, Manchester, Newark, Preston, Sleaford and Stamford. Later in the same year *Drakard's Stamford and General Advertiser* announced another of the cunning-man's popular publications, *Culpeper's English Herbal, Corrected and Enlarged by Dr Parkins of Grantham*. This was just one of many editions of Culpeper's *Herbal*, but it included colour plates and an additional section by Parkins containing medical receipts for 'eye-water', various salves and oils, as well as recipes for cheesecake, custard, mince pies and the like.[67] In the following decade Parkin went on to develop his marketing strategy, broadening his appeal beyond herbalism, fortune-telling and pudding-making. A series of brief publications soon ensued, such as the

*Celestial Monitor*, a *Dissertation on Villany* and the *Wise Man's Crown*, but in 1812 he made his boldest stroke by openly publicising the utility and power of his magical lamens in several circulars and booklets, which were distributed around the region by pedlars. He also had agents in Herefordshire, including Mr Price, the proprietor of an umbrella shop in Hereford, Mr H. Griffiths of Burghill and Dr Farmer of Preston Wynn. The first such publication was a twenty-four page tract entitled *The Cabinet of Wealth: or The Temple of Wisdom*, in which he described the virtues of his various lamens. The powers he vaunted were extraordinary by any standards. He claimed, for instance, that for one guinea he could 'teach any person how to make one single grain or corn of wheat produce more than half a bushel of the same grain in one year (proved), so that the poor man who has a garden may get as much bread from the same, as will support his family'.[68]

In a subsequent publication, *The Book of Miracles: or Celestial Museum*, published in London in 1817, Parkins provided a lengthy account of his views on the nature of his business, recounting his many successes, backed up by copies of letters from satisfied clients. It is a wonderful piece of puffery, written in a fluent style, but would not have proved particularly effective in publicising his services to a semi-literate audience. Maybe this was a deliberate strategy; perhaps Parkins was deliberately targeting a more sophisticated readership consisting of artisans, tradesmen and farmers. People from these groups made up a significant portion of cunning-folk's custom, and several of his case studies concerned people from this level of society who sought good marriages, good health, lost property, or relief from witchcraft. One of the most striking aspects of this publication was Parkins's complete openness about the reality and danger of witchcraft. He observed, for example, how:

> sometimes whole families will be thus afflicted, their cattle, and all that they have (when not timely prevented), have fallen victims to these minions of darkness, which have brought them to their ruin and death; while you now know where to obtain a never failing remedy for the same, if you apply to me for that purpose, before it is too late.

To illustrate this point he went on to recount the story of the first case of witchcraft he had ever dealt with, which concerned a farmer whose house, family, cattle and dairy were all bewitched by an old woman. Other successes included a woman of Ludborough who was 'grievously afflicted by witchcraft'. He was paid by her overseer of the poor to effect a cure 'at near fifty miles distance'. The cost to the parish was one guinea.[69] Just in case any reader might have thought him a mercenary charlatan, Parkins strained to establish his honourable intentions, urging all to 'Fear God, honour the King, and frequent the Church'.[70]

Few cunning-folk went to the lengths of Parkins in advertising their business, few possessed such literary acumen, and few were so open about witchcraft. Parkins was to all intents and purposes a cunning-man, yet he out-quacked the quacks when it came to exploiting print. He may not have been representative of cunning-trade in this respect, but his publications provide us with a unique insight into the wise-man's world. His publications were a potent mix of studious explanation, magical exposition, wild boasts and pious reflection; a heady brew that most cunning-folk never expressed in print but which many demonstrated everyday in their actions.

# 5

# *Books*

In popular cultures where most information was transmitted orally, and only a minority were able to read and write, literacy meant power. It comes as no surprise, then, to find that cunning-folk made a great show of the fact that they possessed and used books and manuscripts. Not just any books, however, but ones that would impress. Size mattered, as did the appearance of antiquity. It also looked good to display volumes in foreign languages so as to enhance the impression of erudition in the eyes of those who could read a little. In this chapter the nature of these mysterious books and texts, and how they were used, will be examined. For it was through cunning-folk that the literary and oral traditions of magic merged, and via them that learned magic was diffused more widely. This was part of a phenomenon which has been referred to as the 'democratisation' of high magic. The evidence for it can be found in the books and manuscripts owned by cunning-folk, and the charms they produced for their clients.

Although manuscript books of ceremonial and astral magic, usually written in Greek, Latin or Arabic, circulated throughout western Europe during the medieval period, access to them, both physical and linguistic, was restricted to a narrow elite of nobles, monks, priests, and physicians.[1] Several dozen pre-1500 magical manuscripts of British origin have survived, which is impressive considering that they were condemned by the papacy. Inquisitions did not operate in England, but on the Continent an unknown but probably large quantity were burned by inquisitors. Yet this atmosphere of prohibition was also the reason significant numbers of manuscripts have survived: their owners were very careful about preserving and concealing them. As one thirteenth-century book collector remarked, 'a secure place ought to be set aside for them, which no one can enter save their proper owner'.[2] The most influential sources of ritual magic in pre-Reformation England seem to have been the *Liber sacer*, also known as the *Sworn Book of Honorius*, and what historians describe as pseudo-Solomonic works, most notably the *Ars notoria*. The former was probably an original Latin composition first appearing sometime in the thirteenth or early fourteenth century. As with most such magical texts, it was given a venerable pseudo-authorship, being purportedly written by Honorius, son of Euclid. The *Ars notoria* also appeared around the same time, and was ascribed to the biblical Solomon, son of King David, ruler of Israel. It was concerned neither with demonic magic nor with practical conjurations to fulfil base desires, but rather consisted of a series of prayers and invocations to the angels to help the operator gain mastery of the 'liberal' arts – in other words to improve his wisdom, knowledge, and intellect. It contained holy orations on how to obtain good memory rather than good money.

During the fifteenth and early sixteenth centuries, however, another, less high-minded, pseudo-Solomonic work of uncertain origin, the *Clavicule* or *Key of Solomon*, began to achieve a wider popularity and notoriety across Europe precisely because it *did* provide information on how to gain wealth, love and power. It listed the principal demons, detailed their signs and seals, and described the conjurations and rituals required to command these in order to find great treasures, detect thieves, procure the love of women and curse one's enemies. This was information of far more use to cunning-folk and their clients than that provided in the *Ars notoria*. But few cunning-folk would have been able to read these early manuscript copies of the *Clavicule*, *Sworn Book* and their variants because they were in Latin. Those who could were often schoolmasters. John Steward, who in 1510 employed what sounds like a Solomonic circle to conjure up treasure, was an ex-schoolmaster, as was another treasure conjurer investigated in 1521 by the mayor of Norwich. Another example is John Lamkyn of Holbeach who was cited in a defamation case a couple of decades later. But knowledge of conjurations could be learned through practical demonstration as well as reading, and one suspects that other less educated magical practitioners gained instruction on the conjurations contained in the *Clavicule* from erudite acquaintances. In 1538 a London scrivener named Pole, rumoured to be a skilled treasure-seeker, said he had friends in the country who possessed 'books enough for all purposes'. Before his arrest he was about to take a treasure trip to Yarmouth. One wonders whether his destination was the house of Thomas Owldring. A contemporary of Pole, the London cunning-man William Wycherley, mentioned Owldring as being 'a conjurer' who had 'very good bookes of conjuring, and that a great number'. Wycherley's own knowledge of the *Circulus Salamonis*, as he called it, probably derived from some such acquaintance.[3] Judging from the surviving manuscripts, it was only from the mid sixteenth century that such influential texts as those attributed to Honorius and Solomon began to be transcribed into English, and so made more accessible to those lower down the educational ladder. Surviving examples from this early period are very rare, and one of the few still intact can be found in the British Library. It is entitled *Sepher Raziel*, and contains information on the influence of the stars, the magical properties of stones and herbs, the operations of angels and acts of ritual suffumigation which bear resemblance to material in the *Sworn Book*.[4]

The rise of printing was a crucial facilitator in the spread of occult works. From the early sixteenth century onwards, Latin magical textbooks printed on the Continent began to circulate in Britain. The key development for cunning-folk, though, was the publication of major texts in English. The first significant translations were of Albertus Magnus's *Book of Secrets* in the mid sixteenth century, which described the magical properties of stones, herbs and beasts.[5] It was not until over a century later, however, in that period of fervid publication during the Interregnum, that translations of the most important source books of magic began to appear. The sudden bloom of magical and astrological books in this period caused concern in some quarters that such translations would lead to the expansion of deleterious, sinful knowledge down the social scale. The Huntingdonshire clergyman John Gaule was quick to query, 'Whether the superstitions of Sorcery and Witchcraft be not taught and promoted, countenanced, and encouraged by the Printing, and permitting such multitudes of Magical books? Especially the translating of them (by way of Vindication, and Apologie) into the vulgar tongue?'[6] His fears of magical democracy were probably triggered by the landmark translation and publication of Cornelius Agrippa's *Three Books of Occult Philosophy* the previous year. Its translator was James Freake, a man about whom we know very little, but whose decision to work on the *Three Books* sealed his place in the history of occultism.[7] The Latin original had first been printed in Antwerp in 1531, and other reprints and editions followed, ensuring that it was accessible and widely considered by English intellectuals during the sixteenth and early seventeenth centuries. Although Agrippa did little to deserve it, after his death in 1535 his name attracted the glamour of Faustian reputation. Despite the fact that the *Three Books* were largely lacking in the practical spells and talismans of use to cunning-folk, its publication must have generated a good deal of interest amongst them and other less well-educated magical practitioners at the time. Similar interest probably greeted the appearance in 1658 of another long recognised occult classic, *Magiae naturalis*, by Giambattista della Porta (1535–1615).[8] This had first been published in Naples in 1558, and it was not long before it found its way into the hands of English magicians. In 1570, for instance, it was confiscated from the Oxford student and budding alchemist John Buckley, who was investigated for invoking wicked spirits. It emerged that Buckley had also translated passages from the book for a less well-educated client.[9] The 1658 English publication was a fine translation of an expanded edition that had been published in Naples in 1584. Demand for the translation led to a reprint in 1669. However, like the *Three Books*, this was a learned disquisition on occult philosophy, and it is probable that the title and reputation of the book, more than its contents, would have attracted the interest of cunning-folk.

The most important figure in the translation of magical texts in this period, and a man to whom later cunning-folk owed a considerable debt, was Robert Turner, a Cambridge-educated astrologer, occultist and botanist. He was the author of at least two medical works, *The Brittish Physician: or The Nature and Vertue of English Plants* (London, 1664), and the *Compleat Bone-Setter* (London, 1656). The latter was purportedly based on the writings of the friar Thomas Moulton, but it actually bears little relation to Moulton's work. Some of Turner's translations of continental books were similarly dubiously ascribed. But this was of little consequence to a target audience thirsting after vernacular magical enlightenment. In 1656 he 'Englished' *Paracelsus of the Supreme Mysteries of Nature*, which divulged 'the rare secrets of Alchymy, and the miraculous cures of Diseases by Sigils and Lamens', otherwise described as 'celestial medicines' for healing such ailments as witchcraft, leprosy, vertigo, gout and painful menstruation. A year later he produced a companion Paracelsian volume entitled *Paracelsus of the Chymical Transmutation*, which was devoted to issues more philosophical than practical. In a similar vein, he also brought out the first printed translation of that key occult text the *Ars notoria* or *Notory Art of Solomon*. It was dedicated to a fellow physician and astrologer William Ryves of St Saviours, Southwark, and included a cabalistic key of magical operations and an exposition on judicial astrology. The most likely source for this translation was another printed version – probably an edition of Agrippa's *Opera* published in Lyons in 1620 – rather than one of the manuscript versions which had circulated for several centuries.[10]

Turner's most influential and lasting contribution, however, was a translation of the *Fourth Book of Occult Philosophy*, which appeared in 1655. This key textbook of practical demonic magic was spuriously attributed to Agrippa. A Latin version had first been published on the Continent in 1567. Despite being denounced as a fake by Johann Weyer (Wierus), one of Agrippa's former pupils, it soon became one of the most notorious magical textbooks in western Europe. England was no exception: in the preface to his *Daemonologie*, James I noted that those 'who would know what are the particular rites and curiosities of these black arts (which is both unnecessary and perilous) he will find it in the fourth book of Cornelius Agrippa, and in Wierus'.[11] The original *Fourth Book* is actually a rather slim volume, so Turner also included translations of other influential magical texts, including the *Heptameron: or Magical Elements*, which was spuriously attributed to the Paduan physician Peter de Abano (*c.* 1250–1315), and the *Arbatel of Magick*. The *Arbatel* had initially been published at Basle; but, although the first edition bears the date 1575, it is likely that it was actually printed in the early seventeenth century. It is not a large work, claiming to be first tome of nine, though there is no evidence the following eight ever appeared. Turner's edition proved very popular amongst contemporary occultists, and a reprint appeared in 1665.[12]

It is important to stress that Turner was publishing translations of continental printed works rather than of the earlier manuscripts I have already mentioned. Thus the tradition of ceremonial magic as practised over the next two centuries was not a continuation of some semi-indigenous magical inheritance but a printed one, based largely on foreign sources. There is little evidence to suggest that cunning-folk possessed either manuscripts earlier than the sixteenth century, or later copies of medieval manuscripts. Those early manuscripts that had survived were eagerly sought out and bought by wealthy early modern collectors of occult literature. We know, for example, that one surviving fourteenth-century manuscript of the *Sworn Book* was once the property of the Elizabethan mage John Dee (1527–1608), and subsequently of the dramatist Ben Jonson (1572–1637).[13] Those in the manuscript collection of the eminent physician and naturalist Hans Sloane (1660–1753) formed the basis of the British Museum's collection, while those acquired by Elias Ashmole (1617–92), a founding member of the Royal Society, are now part of the Bodleian Library's unique collection of occult manuscripts. Thus the rarity of medieval magical texts, the high price put on them and the barrier of language continued to preclude their ownership by all but a few learned and wealthy individuals.

As well as the aforementioned key texts, the 1650s and 1660s also heralded a stream of other publications via which knowledge of ritual magic was disseminated in English.[14] In 1660 Dr R. Read published an enlarged edition of John Wecker's *Eighteen Books of the Secrets of Art and Nature*, of which book sixteen was partly concerned with explaining magic. English occultists also published their own discourses, which were usually based on the Latin works of the Renaissance mages. The well-known astrologer and self-styled Rosicrucian John Heydon wrote his influential *Theomagia: or The Temple of Wisdome* in 1664. This was a very long disquisition on geomancy and astronomy, setting forth the occult powers of angels, and was not concerned with conjurations and spells. However, cunning-folk would certainly have appreciated its detailed practical guide to astromantic and geomantic divination, and the diagrams showing the various signs and characters of the planets and their angels. One of the book's publishers, Thomas Rooks, also published Turner's translation of the *Fourth Book*, and was a significant contributor to the democratisation of high magic in this period. The method of invoking spirits was also laid bare in great detail in Meric Casaubon's *True and Faithful Relation of What Passed for Many Years between Dr John Dee ... and Some Spirits*.

Although these texts found their way into the hands of some cunning-folk, it is surely one of the greatest ironies in the history of magic that, apart from the *Fourth Book*, the most influential vehicle for the dissemination of high magic to a wider audience was, in fact, Reginald Scot's *Discoverie of Witchcraft*. As has already been seen, for Scot, cunning-folk and priests alike were 'couseners, liers, and witchmongers'.[15] In order to expose their fraudulent activities and show 'what notorious blasphemie' necromancers and conjurors committed, Scot elucidated in great detail a wide range of charms, talismans and rituals. These included an inventory of the names, shapes and powers of the principal devils and spirits used in conjurations, which he compiled from Johann Weyer's critique of magic *De praestigiis daemonum (On the Wiles of Devils)*. Weyer, a physician to the duke of Cleves, almost certainly obtained his information, in turn, from a manuscript of the *Clavicule of Solomon*. Scot further provided directions on how to call up spirits, and illustrated these with diagrams of magic circles and the characters and seals of the angels.

According to Scot, one of his main sources of knowledge on ceremonial magic was a manuscript called '*Secretum secretorum*, The secret of secrets', which was the work of one T. R. 'written in faire letters of red & blacke upon parchment, and made by him, Ann. 1570'. He also mentions another man, John Cokars, in relation to the manuscript. According to Scot, 'in the beginning of their booke of conjuration' it was stated that it was 'invented and devised for the augmentation and maintainance of their living, for the edifieng of the poore, and for the propagating and inlarging of Gods glorie'.[16] Judging from these words, T. R.'s use of magic was not restricted to private occult experimentation, but was rather a matter of public service for financial gain. We can speculate, then, that T. R. was no more or less than a cunning-man. His manuscript was in English, but where T. R. obtained his information from, and how Scot came by it, is unknown, though it certainly did not derive from any work printed in English. Scot, however, did mention some of the works that he believed conjurors were using at the time:

> these conjurors carrie about at this daie, bookes intituled under the names of Adam, Abel, Tobie, & Enoch ... They have also among them bookes that they saie Abraham, Aaron, and Salomon made. Item they have bookes of Zacharie, Paule, Honorius, Cyprian, Jerome, Jeremie, Albert, and Thomas: also of the angels, Riziel, Razael, and Raphael.[17]

Although the title *Secretum secretorum* had long been ascribed to a well-known, medieval pseudo-Aristotle concerning medicine, astrology, alchemy and geomancy, it was also given to books of conjuration.[18] When, for example, William Stapleton hatched his plan to find treasure in 1528, he obtained two books that contained the necessary invocations and instructions, one called *Thesaurus spirituum* and the other *Secreta secretorum*.[19] T. R.'s 'Secret of Secrets' was one of a family of English versions of the *Clavicule of Solomon* that began to circulate several decades later. This can be said with certainty because a couple of late sixteenth-century English manuscripts of the *Clavicule* exist, with which the content of T. R.'s grimoire can be compared. These surviving texts show us just what T. R.'s grimoire would have looked like. A substantial but incomplete version of about the same date is also written in red and black ink, and contains a similar range of material as that presented by Scot, including a comparable variation of the 'The forme of adjuring or citing of the spirits'.[20] The original owner of the manuscript is unknown, though it seems to have been copied from a manuscript owned by Thomas Clarke 'in Divinitie', and was subsequently owned and tinkered with in the following century. Although of undoubted value for experimental magicians, its content suggests that its early owners, like T. R., used it to offer commercial services. As well as conjurations, and illustrations of the various sigils found in most *Clavicules*, the manuscript also contains simple charms against the ague and for detecting thieves, and also a charm against witchcraft, which a later owner obviously found of particular interest as he transcribed several obscure words into clearer English.

What Scot was inadvertently providing was important information on practical magic, which had never before been available in English print, having only been accessible to a privileged few in manuscript. It would be no surprise, therefore, if the *Discoverie* was being consulted by cunning-folk very soon after its publication. But this was by no means the end of the story. Two new editions of the *Discoverie* appeared in 1651 and 1665. The motive behind the production of these reprints, after a gap of over sixty years, was possibly less to do with growing interest in Scot's sceptical views, and more to do with the occult interest generated by the publication of Agrippa's *Three Books* and Turner's various translations. The 1665 edition of the *Discoverie* was made even more attractive to the practical occultist by the inclusion of an anonymously written second text entitled the 'Discourse on Devils and Spirits'. This second 'Discourse' was an additional disquisition on ritual magic, some of it supposedly borrowed from the 'Manuscript of Nagar the Indian', which contained further information on how to conjure up spirits, and detailed the consecration of various ceremonial paraphernalia. The very fact that someone chose the *Discoverie* as a vehicle for disseminating such valuable occult information further suggests that Scot's work was already being used as a grimoire. It is unlikely that learned metropolitan occult philosophers, who could read and had access to all the continental works in Latin, would have bothered with the purely practical information provided by Scot. It was primarily cunning-folk who most benefited. One piece of evidence in support of this proposition is provided by the prosecution in 1687 of Ann Watts, described as a fortune-teller. Although she usually resided on the outskirts of London, she obviously made forays into rural Essex looking for custom. Thus it was that she was caught one day sleeping rough in a wood, and was brought before the local petty sessions. Watts had brought her books with her and these were confiscated and later burned. The books in question were two works by Cornelius Agrippa (presumably Freake's *Three Books* and Turner's *Fourth Book*), one of John Gadbury's almanacs, and Reginald Scot's *Discoverie of Witchcraft* (probably the 1665 edition). Watts may have valued Scot's work for its elucidation of illusionist tricks.[21] It is just as likely, however, that she valued it for the practical information it provided on spells and conjurations. Along with Turner's translation of the *Fourth Book*, the *Discoverie* was not only the most accessible work on magic because it was in English, but also because it went through several editions and consequently there were more copies available.

After the flood of occult publications during the 1650s and 1660s a drought set in. Neoplatonism fell out of favour, and so natural magic and occult experimentation declined in intellectual circles. The flow of publications may have dried up, but there undoubtedly remained considerable interest in high magic, and not only amongst cunning-folk. Private magical experimentation continued in an unknown number of studies and private rooms up and down the country. One such occult explorer was the respectable Gloucestershire farmer Peter Drinkwater, who died at his Sandhurst farm in 1839. A self-taught scholar of considerable intelligence, it was said that 'Nature had endowed him with considerable literary talent', and that there was 'scarcely a book collector in the kingdom who had not served him with rare works'. As an obituary records, astrology was his chief interest but 'he had a belief too in magic to a certain extent, and confidently thought he should become gifted with talismanic power. His increasing anxiety on this subject amounted to monomania, and caused much regret to his friends, by whom he was much beloved.'[22] Ritual magic also remained a subject of curiosity amongst members of the educated 'middling sort', particularly teenage males, who occasionally sought out folk magicians to further their knowledge in this respect. Let us look, for example, at the youthful experience of the Methodist preacher and theologian Adam Clarke (1762–1832). As children, Clarke and his brother spent all their money on popular chapbooks, immersing themselves in the fantastic tales of Thomas Hickathrift, Jack the Giant Killer and the like. They also read cheap fortune-telling books: they certainly owned a copy of the popular *A Groat's Worth of Wit for a Penny*. As a result, the young Adam, 'heard and read much of enchantments and enchanters ... Whether there were any thing real in their pretended science he could not tell: but his curiosity prompted him strongly to enquire'. He came to hear of Cornelius Agrippa's *Occult Philosophy*, a book about which his schoolfellows apparently told 'wonderful tales'. This led him to try to obtain a copy. On learning that a schoolmaster living several miles away had one, he begged his father to write a letter requesting the loan of the book for a few days. The schoolmaster refused, but not long after Clarke found a more obliging owner. A family of travelling tinkers settled nearby and it was soon reported around the countryside that they were conjurors and possessed mysterious books. Clarke visited the head of the family, who entertained him 'with strange relations of what might be done by spells; figures, diagrams, letters fumigations, etc.' The following day the tinker produced a copy of the *Three Books of Occult Philosophy*, and Clarke spent the next few days making copious notes. Before moving camp, however, the tinker confided 'that there was a fourth book of the incomparable Cornelius Agrippa, without which, as it contained the practice of the art, it would be useless to attempt any operations'. From what he had heard and read Clarke was, at first, persuaded that ceremonial magic 'was innocent, for everything seemed to be done with a reference to, and dependence upon, God'. Yet, after reading a condemnation of magic in *The Athenian Oracle*, he never tried any conjurations, and as his religious sensibilities developed he distanced himself from the occult sciences altogether.[23]

John Cannon (1684–1742), a one-time excise officer and writing master in Somerset, also recorded in his memoirs how as a nineteen-year-old he had befriended a certain John Read, a self-educated shepherd and farm servant, who was well read in astronomy and the occult sciences. Over the years Read had accumulated a good store of valuable books, yet when he moved to a new position in Dorset he left behind most of them save 'two books of ye Magick art one of wch was Intitled Cornelius Agryppas Occult Philosophy Y another ye title I never knew'. These two works Read hid, like some cautious medieval mage, 'in a certain place made for ye purpose on a down where he used to keep sheep called Milbern [Milborne] down on ye borders of Dorsetshire and gave me a token to distinghuish ye place where he had hid them'. Cannon was undoubtedly impressed by Read's occult power. On one occasion, as they walked together across a field, Read made:

> a circle on ye ground wth a pick he had in his hand having ordered me to abide in ye center and having also drawn some figures or characters in ye dust and use words the air suddenly changed and grew darkish and became like a mist with a jostling wind and even lightening and thunder at a distance that it surprized me insomuch I requested him not to proceed any further for I believed it diabolical and me thought he look'd terrified and began to undoe what he had done and suddenly ye air appear'd serene and clear as before.

This brush with what he perceived to be dark forces was enough to put Cannon off the occult for good, and, like Clarke, he later wrote that he 'utterly despised any thing sounding of magick or occult sciences'. No surprise, then, that he never sought to recover Read's books despite being in the area frequently. He further urged 'all persons not only to detest such books but sacrifice them in the flames as ye men of Ephesus did by Pauls preaching'. Read's books may still lie buried somewhere in the hills above Milborne Port.[24]

These cases present an interesting reversal of the notion that during the eighteenth century, as never before, the flow of rational knowledge cascaded down the social scale washing away unenlightened and 'superstitious' beliefs amongst the uneducated. There were obviously hidden channels that ran counter to the prevailing flow via which magical knowledge flowed up the social scale. We find abstruse, erudite knowledge of the occult sciences being held by autodidact working men, who carried on a rural tradition of solitary magical experimentation, largely divorced from the middle-class urban occultism of the time. It was to their social inferiors that the educated, rural middling sort turned in their search for magical enlightenment, particularly if they wanted to keep knowledge of their interests from the ears of their parents and peers. Outside the major towns, the libraries of cunning-folk were one of the few places during the eighteenth century where rare texts of occult philosophy could be consulted.

It is instructive to switch our attention to the Continent for a moment. While in England the printing of magic texts went into decline during the late seventeenth century, in much of the rest of Europe, by contrast, printers were beginning to disgorge extraordinarily huge numbers of grimoires for the popular market. By 1854, for example, it was estimated that in the Ardennes region as many as 400,000 chapbook grimoires were in circulation.[25] This is surely an exaggerated figure, but it is still indicative of the huge sales of such literature. In Germany the *Sixth and Seventh Books of Moses* was the grimoire supreme. Although it had circulated in manuscript form under the title of *Magia divino-mosaica* during the early modern period, we only find it in popular print from around 1797. Although it purported to be a record of the messages received from God by Moses, it in fact contained numerous magical seals and rituals of conjuration, including information on how to call up the dead.[26] Throughout Scandinavia *The Book of Cyprianus* or *Liber Cyprianus*, said to have been the work of St Cyprian of Antioch, who was put to death in the year 304, was the most popular magical text. His name was also used to market a number of common dream books, and in this context his reputation was as great as that of Mother Shipton in Britain.[27] The mass dissemination of magical texts was most impressive in France, where chapbooks of ritual and inventive magic, belonging to the popular literary tradition of the *Bibliothèque Bleue*, competed with almanacs for valuable space in the pedlar's pack. It is not only the sheer numbers of chapbook grimoires produced by French printers that surprises, but also the variety of texts produced. Once closely guarded codices treasured by a learned elite were now available to labourers for a few pence. The most popular were *Le grand Albert* and *Le petit Albert*. The former work was largely based on Albertus Magnus's *Book of Secrets*, concerning the magical properties of plants, animals and minerals, while the latter contained numerous further spells and conjurations. More concerned with demonic magic was *Le dragon rouge*, which borrowed from the *Clavicule of Solomon*. It contained information on commanding spirits, finding hidden treasure, and even contained a spell to make women dance naked. There was also the *Grimoire du Pape Honorius*, a version of the *Liber sacer*, which instructed how and when to conjure up demons, including Lucifer himself. The *Enchiridion Leonis Papae*, attributed to Leo III and fabled to have been presented to Charlemagne on being crowned emperor, also contained prayers, exorcisms and charms for practical purposes. Other similar titles peddled around France during the eighteenth and nineteenth centuries included, *Le véritable dragon noir, La chouette noire, La poule noire, Oeuvres magiques d'Henri Corneille Agrippa, Le grand grimoire, Cyprien mago ante conversionem*, and *Abracadabra monumentissima diabolica*.[28] Most of these works tend to carry much the same information, and include numerous woodcuts of talismans and occult characters to excite the imagination.

In Britain tens of thousands of fortune-telling guides and dream books were sold during the eighteenth and early nineteenth centuries, but in contrast to France, there were hardly any popular guides on learned magic.[29] Some chapbooks contained the odd magical receipt, usually concerning theft or love, but their publishers generally steered clear of providing details of demonic or ceremonial magic.[30] The one major exception was an anonymous work entitled *Witchcraft Detected and Prevented: or The School of Black Art Newly Opened*, which was published in Peterhead by P. Buchan, and was reprinted at least three times during the 1820s. It is small in size, but over a hundred pages long, and from its appearance was undoubtedly targeted at the popular market. I will let the learned 'member of the School of Black Art' introduce his work in his own words:

> The greater part of this highly curious little volume is selected from the ancient and scarce works of the principal writers on these subjects, particularly

from SCOTT'S *Discovery of Witchcraft* ... It also contains a variety of the most approved *CHARMS* in *Magic; RECEIPTS* in *Medicine, Natural Philosophy,* and Chemistry etc.[31]

In the preface its editor commented that 'the learned, or rather more selfish part of the modern community, has endeavoured to banish from the minds of the public a belief in magic and witchcraft', and it was to counter this tendency that *Witchcraft Detected* was printed. The people should not be denied access to such knowledge, he thought, and they should be left to make up their own mind as to whether magic worked.[32] Yet it was still felt necessary to deflect potential criticism by stating that the book was published:

> more with a view to amuse than to be put in practice: but, if there be a reality in these terrific names of *magic* and *witchcraft,* and if any one fear the evil of those who practice these diabolical arts, there are antidotes, remedies, and a catholicon given here. If there is not a reality in these things, then this volume can tend to no evil purpose.

In the editor's opinion there was no inherent conflict between magic and Christianity. Unlike the moral reformers, he believed the resort to magic need not lead to moral degradation as long as one's purpose was honourable. He did, however, advise his 'youthful readers to beware of meddling too much with those things that have a tendency to alienate or estrange the mind from God'.[33]

After the preface, the reader was treated to a 'General Essay on Magic' the main thrust of which was a defence of astrology. In it reference was made to the mystical writings of Emmanuel Swedenborg (1688–1772), which at least proves that the 'General Essay' was not purely regurgitation from some seventeenth-century source. There followed a list of the divine and demonic names for use in magic, the 'Secrets of Nature, Extracted from Albertus Magnus', and 'Choice Secrets in Astrology on Several Useful Occasions'. The black artist also divulged large amounts of weather lore, and lists of lucky, evil and perilous days. Much of the book otherwise consisted of magical receipts, such as how 'to make the Sympathetic Powder, from Sir Kenelm Digby; for curing wounds at a distance'.[34] Significantly, most of the conjurations had been extracted from Scot's *Discoverie,* including 'The form of adjuring or citing of Spirits to arise and appear'; how to 'dissolve bewitched love', 'ointments for the transportation, etc. of witches', charms 'To help a person under an ill tongue, and make the witch appear, or the ill effect cease', and, to 'find her that bewitched your cattle'. By the early nineteenth century editions of the *Discoverie* were undoubtedly hard to come by on the second-hand market, so what *Witchcraft Detected and Prevented* provided were some of the most useful charms and magical remedies from Scot, in a cheap and accessible format.

*Witchcraft Detected* apart, it is puzzling why British publishers, unlike their French counterparts, failed to cash in on the 'Black Arts'. The *Fourth Book, Arbatatel of Magick, Magical Elements* by Peter de Abano and Albertus Magnus's *Book of Secrets* were all available in English and waiting to be plundered for the popular market. Some chapbook writers were certainly aware of them. In the popular fortune-teller *Mother Bunch*, for example, there is a passing reference to Agrippa. Considering the popularity of such divinatory chapbooks, grimoires would surely have sold just as well in this country as elsewhere, particularly of course amongst cunning-folk. Although little research has been done on the censorship and suppression of chapbook publishers in the period, the fact that they did not produce books of conjuration suggests that they deemed the subject too sensitive, and were fearful of attracting adverse scrutiny from moral reformers and the state. A similar sense of caution and self-censorship is also discernable concerning sexual matters, creating an underground market for French publications on the subject.

If the classic texts of ritual magic were not available in a cheap and easily obtainable format in Britain, where could eighteenth- and nineteenth-century cunning-folk obtain information on learned magic? We know that some possessed impressive libraries. The Essex cunning-man James Murrell owned various works on astrology and astronomy, many seventeenth-century medical books and several unbound manuscripts on conjuration and astrology. A cunning-man who lived near Llanidloes 'had, for a man of his position and education, a valuable library'. The books of 'Wise Man Wilkinson' were seen by J. S. Fletcher, and were 'most of them old Latin works on the black art, or medicine, or mathematics, or the distilling of herbs'.[35] Fortunately, from various sources we can piece together the book collections of several such cunning-men. The most complete account we have is that of the Harries of Cwrt-y-Cadno. Their library at Pantcoy farm was by all accounts considerable, but unfortunately it was broken up after the death of Henry Harries in 1849. From two men who saw the library before it had been completely denuded, we gain a good idea of its contents.[36] There were Bibles in various languages, books dealing with magical charms, and 'various old works on occultism, numerous medical works and magazines, various devotional and other books'. The following is a list of those books still left in the library by the end of the century, accompanied by my own additional notes where useful:

1. Culpeper, *Astrological Judgement of Diseases*. First published in 1651 as *Semeiotica Uranica: or An Astrological Judgement of Diseases*, it went through several editions over the next couple of decades. Its author, Nicholas Culpeper, is now more famous for his much published herbal. This would have been a very useful publication for cunning-folk as it provided comprehensive instructions concerning, amongst other things, the 'cause and end of disease', and whether the 'sick be likely to live or die', all judged from 'the good or evil position of the moon at the time of the patient lying down, or demanding the question'. It also contained a treatise on urine-scrying.

2. John Baptista Porta, *Natural Magic* (London, 1658).

3. Reginald Scot, *The Discovery of Witchcraft* (London, 1665).

4. *Synopsis Medicinae*. This was an edition of William Salmon's *Synopsis Medicinae: A Compendium of Physick, Chirurgery and Anatomy*, which was intended as a self-help medical work to aid the poor. It was first published in 1671. As Salmon (1644–1713) was one of the leading astrologers of his time, it has a strong astrological content. It is obvious why it appealed to later cunning-folk, having been written primarily for the non-trained reader, and for its espousal of astrological medicine.

5. Middleton, *Practical Astrology* (1679). John Middleton's astrological guidebook was divided into two parts. The first was an 'introduction to the whole art of astrology', while the second dealt with horary questions concerning 'the life of man, his estate, brethren, or short journeys'. A useful guide for astrologising cunning-folk.

6. Butler, *Astrologer a Sacred Science* (1683); first published 1680. John Butler was an Oxford divine, and this book was aimed at defending astrology from accusations that it was a diabolic activity. It was also a rebuttal of an attack on astrology by the Cambridge divine Henry More.[37]

7. Beveridge, *Private Thoughts on Religion*. This was presumably one of

numerous eighteenth-century editions of *Private Thoughts* by William Beveridge (1637–1708). It has no occult value, and one of the Harrieses either bought it for serious theological contemplation or to pad out the shelves with eye-catching old tomes.

8. *Prophecies of Michael Nostradamus*. Although the prophecies of Nostradamus were published in English as early as the mid sixteenth century, and several editions appeared during the late seventeenth century, the only extant publication I have found with the exact title of *The Prophecies of Michael Nostradamus* was published by J. Roberts of London in 1715, so I believe that this was the edition in the Harries's library.

9. *The Secrets of the Invisible World: or A General History of Apparitions* (London, 1770). As its title suggests, this was a general exposition of the nature of ghosts and apparitions, and was largely based on Daniel Defoe's work, *An Essay on the History and Reality of Apparitions* (London, 1727).

10. Ebenezer Sibly, *A Complete Illustration of the Celestial Science of Astrology: or The Art of Foretelling Future Events* (1788). This huge tome of over a thousand pages was first published in four parts between 1784 and 1788. It is an erudite but popular blend of judicial astrology, divination and some magic. It obviously sold well, for by 1812 it was already in its eleventh edition. Like other publications on the occult sciences at the time, it was hardly an original work though, much of it being compiled from well-known seventeenth-century publications by Lilly, Gadbury and the like.[38] Sibly's large work would have been a fine adornment in any bookshelf, and provided valuable, practical occult information. It comes as no surprise to find a nineteenth-century Cornish folklorist remarking that 'Here much of such lore has been learnt from Sibley's [sic] "Treatise on the Occult Sciences", which is the oracle of our western astrologers'.[39]

11. Heydon, *Astrology* (1792). This was most likely a reprint of *The New Astrology, or The Art of Predicting ... Future Events*, which had been published under the dubious authorship of 'Christopher Heydon Jr' in 1785, and reprinted the following year. The real Christopher Heydon was a respected astrologer who had died in 1623. He published one work on astrology in 1603, while a book based on his work was published posthumously in 1650 and reprinted in 1690.[40] For cunning-folk, the pseudonymous work would certainly have proved to be of more accessible and practical use.

12. *Astrologer's Magazine* (1793). This was a short-lived periodical which ran from 1791 to 1794. For the first couple of years of its existence it was

called the *Conjurer's Magazine*. Its contents consisted of a mish-mash of horoscopes, items on occult philosophy, prophecy, conjuring tricks, and explanations of simple chemical experiments. It is possible that the first of the Harries cunning-men, Henry Jones (1739–1805), bought the magazine at the time of its publication, but it is just as likely that it was bought second-hand years later by one of his sons. The cunning-man Richard Morris was apparently a great admirer of and correspondent to the magazine.[41]

13. Cooper, *Primum mobile*. This was the first English translation of an influential book by the seventeenth-century Italian astrologer Placido Titi (Placidus de Titus). It was first published as *Tabulae primi mobilis* (Padua, 1657), and caused a good deal of heated debate amongst English astrologers at the time. Surprisingly, it was not until the nineteenth century that it was translated in its entirety by John Cooper and published in London in 1814.

14. *The Straggling Astrologer* (1824). This weekly periodical struggled to make an impact and only ran from June to October 1824. It initially cost 4*d*., though the price was soon reduced to 3*d*. Even after this reduction the circulation was still too poor to make it a viable concern.

The only other detailed account we have of a cunning-man's library is that of 'Owd Rollison', a nineteenth-century cunning-man of Roe Green, Worsley, Lancashire.[42] His books included:

1. Cornelius Agrippa, *The Three Books of Occult Philosophy* (London, 1651).

2. Lilly, *Christian Astrology* (London, 1659). First published in 1647, William Lilly's populist guide to astrological practice must have been a valuable tool for astrologising cunning-folk. It was, as Lilly claimed, 'a most easie introduction to the whole art of astrology', providing clear instruction on how to use an ephemeris, erect a scheme of the heavens and interpret the signs of the Zodiac. It would help cunning-folk 'judge or resolve all manner of questions contingent unto man, viz., of health, sicknesse, riches, marriage'.

3. John Gadbury, *Thesaurus astrologiae* (London, 1674). Gadbury was a prolific author who consequently became the target of literary attacks accusing him of being a 'Quack-Astrologer'.[43] His *Thesaurus* would have been a useful acquisition for anyone interested in astrological medicine, as it contained the 'choicest mysteries relating to physick'.

4. Ebn Shemaya, *The Star* (London, 1839). Ebn Shemaya was the pseudonym

of the astrologer David Parkes. This rare book provided 'a complete system of theoretical and practical astrology'.[44]

5. Zadkiel, *Grammar of Astrology* (London, 1849); first published in 1833. One of several serious but accessible works by Richard Morrison, the famed nineteenth-century astrologer, best known for his *Almanac*.

6. Zadkiel, *Tables for Calculating Nativities* (London, 1850). Obviously a useful tool for those cunning-folk who had the ability to draw up horoscopes.

7. Christopher Cooke, *A Plea for Urania* (London, 1854). Cooke, a London solicitor, wrote this 338-page contemplation on the history, utility and legal position of astrology as a defence of what he considered a noble science. It would not have helped Rollison with astrological calculations, though it would have proved useful in constructing a defence case if ever he was prosecuted under the Vagrancy Act.

We also know that George Wales of Barmby, Yorkshire, and James Morris of Cwmbelan, Montgomeryshire, possessed copies of Agrippa's works, though it is not stated whether they were the *Three Books*, the *Fourth Book*, or both. During the early nineteenth century Thomas Light of Walton, Shropshire, cherished a rare copy of Heydon's *Theomagia*. After his death it was sold to a Birmingham bookseller. When John Rhodes of Salford was arrested for fortune-telling in 1865, the police confiscated a large number of books including what was referred to as Agrippa's *Occult Philosophy* in manuscript, William Lilly's, *An Introduction to Astrology* and Raphael's *Prophetic Alphabet*. Joseph Railey, who was arrested in 1857, owned *Napoleon's Book of Fate, A Manual of Astrology: or The Book of Stars*, one of W. J. Simmonite's *Astrological Ephemeris*, Zadkiel's Bohn's Library edition of William Lilly's, *Introduction to Astrology, Philosophy Reformed and Improved* (presumably Henry Pinnell's translation of Paracelsian and other such work, published in 1657), Raphael's *Prophetic Messenger*, a book on the elements of chemistry, and 'a book dedicated to Sir Walter Scott', probably Raphael's *Astrologer of the Nineteenth Century*. In the same year, police raiding the premises of Clayton Chaffer found 'books and papers of necromancy', though, disappointingly only Raphael's *Prophetic Almanac* (1857), Good's *New Universal Fortune-Teller* and *Raphael's Witch or Oracle of the Future* were specifically mentioned.[45] Raphael's various publications seem to have proved particularly popular with cunning-folk and astrologers around the country. They were lively, easy to read, and contained lots of practical knowledge on various forms of divination, as well as a dash of magic. His compendious *Astrologer of the Nineteenth Century*, with its section on spells and charms, would have been particularly useful.

Judging from the evidence of these libraries, it seems that in the nineteenth century there was a lively trade in rare seventeenth-century works on astrology and magic. Nearly two hundred years after many of these books were written we find them continuing to be read, or at least *used*, as guides and manuals of the occult arts. Those who were now consulting them were no longer learned gentlemen patronised by the ruling elite, however, but occultists and cunning-folk persecuted as 'rogues and vagabonds' by the state. The scarcity of some these books led to the circulation of manuscript copies. As already seen, John Rhodes owned a manuscript of Agrippa's *Occult Philosophy*, and another, earlier, part-translated and adapted manuscript of the *Fourth Book* can be found in the National Library of Wales.[46] Frederick Hockley, one of a close group of London occultists practising in the first half of the nineteenth century, possessed numerous manuscripts including *Solomon's Key*, which, as he explained in a note at the beginning, was 'found in the Chaldee and Hebrew tongue by a Jewish Rabbi at Jerusalem and by him translated into Greek and from thence into Latin and transcribed by Fredk Hockley the first day of Marche 1828'. During his early adult life Hockley actually made a living copying out magical manuscripts for the London occult bookseller John Denley. From one of Hockley's letters written in 1874 we learn, for example, that in 1822 Denley had sold a manuscript entitled *Clavicule Salomonis* for the considerable sum of £20. In the same letter he also referred to another manuscript entitled 'The Complete Book of Magic Science', which he described as 'one of my babes for at Denley's suggestion I made up the MS from other sources and made him several copies one after another'.[47] As a surviving sale catalogue from 1820 demonstrates, Denley's shop represented the greatest repository of magical knowledge in early nineteenth-century England apart from the British Library, the Bodleian and Cambridge University Library.[48] Amongst many other works on astrology, alchemy and witchcraft, we find a manuscript entitled 'Paracelsus's Occult Philosophy' for a very reasonable 10s. 6d., a copy of the 'Lemegeton', supposedly transcribed from a 1512 manuscript selling for £3 13s. 6d., Casaubon's *True and Faithful Relation* for £2 2*s.*, and, amongst the many unique manuscripts he was selling from Ebenezer Sibly's private collection, 'The Clavis: or Key to Unlock the Mysteries of Magick of Rabby Soloman'. It is no surprise to find that Denley also offered a 1665 edition of Scot's *Discoverie*, which he pointedly observed, contained 'wood cuts of magical seals'. The price was £1 11*s.* 6*d.* Denley's catalogue also demonstrates the demand for English versions of Agrippa's *Third* and *Fourth Books* at the time. While a 1533 first edition of *De occulta philosophia* could be had for a mere £2 2*s.*, a copy of Freake's translation bundled with a rare eighteenth-century reprint of the *Fourth Book* cost £2 12*s.* 6*d.* An original of Turner's translation of the *Fourth Book* was on sale for the princely sum of £4 14*s.* 6*d.* The reason people would have paid such prices was because they were not sufficiently educated to make use of the cheaper Latin originals. Maybe it was the demand from cunning-folk, therefore, that made such mark-ups commercially viable.

The availability of these literary riches led some well-known men of letters to resort to Denley's occult emporium. The popular Victorian novelist Sir Edward Bulwer-Lytton was a favourite client, while Samuel Taylor Coleridge borrowed books from Denley in preparation for a lecture he delivered at the London Philosophical Society 'On Tales of Witches, Apparitions etc'.[49] There is little evidence, unfortunately, of Denley's more humble customers. He certainly had a good mail order trade, however, and provincial cunning-folk can surely be counted as being amongst his clientele. As well as transcribing abstruse alchemical, mystical, masonic and geomantic texts, Denley and Hockley produced straightforward practical spell books in manuscript, some presumably made to order. One surviving example, drawn up by Hockley in 1829, and entitled 'Occult Spells', consists of a medley of charms extracted from sixteenth- and seventeenth-century texts on magic and astrology, including those by Reginald Scot, William Lilly, and Joseph Blagrave.[50] Hockley also copied items from the *Petit Albert*, a manuscript in the British Museum, and another manuscript dated 1583, presumably from Denley's collection. In terms of content 'Occult Spells' is similar to *Witchcraft Detected and Prevented.* With its own section on the discovery and prevention of witchcraft, it would have likewise appealed to the more practical needs of cunning-folk rather than learned, ceremonial magicians.

Denley was not the only one producing magical manuscripts on a commercial basis. The entrepreneurial cunning-man John Parkins also sold hand-copied grimoires. At the back of his *Book of Miracles* he advertised that ladies and gentlemen could be favoured with a 'curious and interesting work, which is prepared and constantly sold here at our office, in MS'. It cost the considerable sum of twenty to thirty guineas, however, and consisted of 'The Grand Oracle of Heaven: or The Art of Divine Magic. From the Urim, Thummim and *Sanctum Sanctorum*', together with 'The Grand Treasury of Divine Wisdom and Magic'. Parkins warned interested customers that each order would take six weeks to complete.[51] It was presumably a version of a manuscript he advertised five years earlier as the 'Grand Portable Celestial Oracle', which among other things contained 'the art of healing the sick and diseased; discerning, mitigating, and preventing all accidents and dangers in their nativities, by spiritual astrology'.[52] Although there is no record of Parkins's library, the Pseudo-Paracelsian works translated by Robert Turner seem to have been one of his main influences. The reference to Urim and Thummim was probably lifted from *Paracelsus of the Chymical Transmutation*,[53] and the use of the term 'lamen' to describe the charms he sold, and the content of those charms, was most likely based on the various 'lamens' described in detail in *Paracelsus of the Supreme Mysteries of Nature.*[54]

Cunning-folk's desire for manuscripts was not just the consequence of the scarcity of printed works, however, but also an aspect of the magical tradition. Hand-written versions of occult texts were considered more potent, particularly when the materials were consecrated, and instructions were written using red and black ink on special parchment. Such manuscripts survive in greater numbers for the seventeenth century than any other period, presumably a consequence of the growing circulation of relevant printed material at this time. A particularly fine example is the 'The Secret of Secrets' of Moses Long, a Gloucestershire 'conjuror'.[55] Inscribed with the date 1683, this 190-page bound volume contains numerous instructions on conjuring spirits and angels, as well as describing the construction of magical rings for various uses ranging from the utterly pointless, such as making an 'elephant apye bearing a castle on his back', to the more practical purpose that 'catell or beasts may multiply and increase', and also to enable one 'to have a swift horse to beare thee suddenly'. It also contains useful charms to 'quench fire burning A house' and so that 'a thiefe enter not into thy house'. Judging from these instructions, the reproduction of various spirit characters, and a couple of magical circles one of which is a variation on a classic pentacle of Solomon, Long's 'Secret of Secrets' had been copied from another manuscript based in part on Agrippa's *Three Books*, the *Fourth Book*, the *Heptameron* and some version of the Key of Solomon. While Long's grimoire was a straightforward manual, other manuscripts owned by cunning-folk were basically notebooks. That belonging to the eighteenth-century Yorkshire cunning-man Timothy Crowther was discovered in an old bookstall over a hundred years after his death. Its contents illustrate the variety of interests such people had. Apart from various family memoranda, it contained aphorisms 'relating to decumbiture, diseases, and practice of physick', 'Choise aphorismes of Cardan' (the sixteenth-century Italian astrologer Girolamo Cardano), other aphorisms relating to comets, eclipses, agriculture, and the 'wether and metiors'. It also contained his own astrological calculations, several incantations against witchcraft and for 'recovering things stolen', as well as various medical remedies.[56] One of John Parkins's personal manuscript books has survived. It contains notes on urine-scrying taken from the works of William Salmon, horary astrological calculations regarding some of his clients, notes on astromantic divination, draft sections of his publications, and much else besides which cannot easily be understood, as Parkins used an abstruse form of shorthand.[57] Our inability to decipher it can be explained by a passage in one of his publications advertising that he taught stenography using 'a method peculiar to himself, which was never published'.[58]

London was undoubtedly the centre of the occult book trade. When, in 1856, the Staffordshire cunning-man James Tunnicliff told his tormented client Thomas Charlesworth that he needed to buy a 'spell-book' to remove the witchcraft that plagued Charlesworth's farm, it was to London that a letter was sent.[59] But there were other provincial booksellers who dabbled in the occult market. Around the same time as Denley, a Leeds bookseller, a man 'who had been by turns weaver, astrologer, Militiaman, Chartist, philosopher, and poet', was described as possessing a choice library on the 'Black Art'.[60] That these booksellers did not trade in magical works without criticism from some quarters is evident from the experience of an occult bookseller named George Bumstead. He commented in his memoirs that he had 'been censured by a few ignorant persons for dealing in old books relating to the "Occult Sciences"'.[61] In 1852, he published a sale catalogue of works on magic and astrology from which we gain some idea of the relative availability and cost of such books in Victorian England.[62] Heydon's *Theomagia* (1664), for example, was described as being 'very rare' and worth £1 8s. The 1651 edition of the *Three Books of Occult Philosophy* was being sold along with the 1665 edition of *The Fourth Book* for a reasonable £2 10s. The 'rare', uncut 1783 edition of *The Fourth Book* cost 15s.[63] Raphael's *Manual of Astrology* (London, 1828) was somewhat surprisingly described as 'scarce' and cost 7s. 6d. Along with such esoteric works, Bumstead also sold a range of old fortune-telling books. *The Conjuror's Vade Mecum; or Every Lady her own Fortune Teller* (1795) cost a rather surprising 4s. 6d., while *The Royal Book of Fate: Queen Elizabeth's Oracle of Future Events* (1834) was priced at 3s. 6d.

A book of magic absent from the above list of library contents, but which generated an inordinate notoriety decades after its publication, was Francis Barrett's *The Magus: or Celestial Intelligencer* (London, 1801).[64] Barrett, who was better known during his lifetime for his ballooning exploits, claimed to be very learned in matters pertaining to magic, astrology, and chemistry, and advertised that he gave private lessons on the occult sciences. Although Barrett certainly possessed a considerable knowledge of such matters, his own work, like that of Sibly, was far from original. *The Magus* largely consists of plagiarised chunks from several seventeenth-century occult texts, particularly Turner's edition of the *Fourth Book of Occult Philosophy*, and some manuscript or continental print of the *Clavicule Salomonis*. Barrett did not possess any of these works, and instead relied on the goodwill of John Denley, who made his own library available to him. The kindness was not returned. Barrett failed to acknowledge his benefactor, and did not even recompense the benevolent Denley with a free copy. Published by the entrepreneurial bookseller and publisher James Lackington, with various eye-catching plates, *The Magus* must have been an expensive book to produce. By the 1820s it was already worth £1 1s. on the second-hand market.[65] In 1818 Denley had the satisfaction of buying the printing blocks, copperplates and copyright of *The Magus* when Lackington put his stock up for sale. Several decades later the copperplates and woodcuts ended up in George Bumstead's sale catalogue priced £6 6s: a bargain for a book that was to become so influential.

In 1884 W. Sparrow Simpson, Sub-Dean of St Paul's Cathedral, thought it 'a marvel to any thoughtful person that such a book as Barrett's *Magus* should ever have been compiled', and wondered who were 'the patrons of such a work as this? Are there still practitioners of the black art?'[66] There certainly were, and many cunning-folk would undoubtedly have loved to own a copy of *The Magus*, as it provided a compilation of several rare and important occult texts in one volume. However, although in 1875 the London publishers Knight and Compton produced a rare facsimile of *The Magus*, it remained a scarce and highly prized book. In 1852 Bumstead was asking £1 11s. 6d. for a copy, which, to put it in context, was 3s. 6d. more than the price of an original of Heydon's *Theomagia*. Those copies that did become available were probably snapped up by urban, middle-class occultists before provincial cunning-folk could get their hands on them. By the 1950s it was said that, 'you cannot buy a copy of the *Magus* without months of searching, and then only at a very high price indeed. Few examples have even changed hands during the past quarter of a century'.[67]

Confirmation that early modern and modern cunning-folk possessed books and manuscripts of ritual magic leads us on to the question of how they were utilised. Some were obviously used in a purely cosmetic sense to impress clients. After numerous perusals of 'Wise Man' Wilkinson's books, J. S. Fletcher remarked, 'from the fact that they were all very clean at the margins I have always considered that the Wise Man kept them for show rather than for his own mental edification'.[68] Maria Giles used her magic book purely as a prop. She told her clients to place their hands upon it, and then, as one witness put it, 'she whispered something to the book'. Giles only bothered to open it to put her payment inside.[69] Did cunning-folk ever employ the arcane talismans, spells and conjurations contained in the *Fourth Book*, Scot's *Discoverie*, and the like? There is, indeed, good evidence that some of the more erudite practitioners dabbled with high magic as well as their usual folk magic practices. John Walsh admitted to drawing magic circles on the ground, setting within them two candles of virgin wax, and calling up spirits to help him detect stolen property.[70] Moses Long certainly practised the conjuration of angels and spirits, but was obviously conscientious about the dangers of slipping into the dark side of magic. On several occasions he added marginal notes in his grimoire expressing doubts about some of the conjurations contained therein. Concerning the invocation of Duros, Artus and Æbedel, he wrote, 'because I know not whether they be good evill I advise not to medle with them', and later on he warned, 'beware of all evill spts [spirits] and medle not with them for being enemies to all man kind, if they appear eyther willingly, or unwillingly they ever intend ye distruction of man kind'.[71] John Parkins's surviving manuscript suggests that he too experimented with the invocation of spirits and angels. A number of stories relate how either John Harries, or more likely Henry Harries, attempted to call up spirits by drawing a circle round himself and muttering invocations. Such tales are not without foundation. In a letter written to the London astrologer and occultist, 'Raphael', Henry inquired: 'would you deliver lectures unto me on the occult science that will without any ambiguity make Spirits appear; as what I had seen and read on that science I doubt their reality'.[72] Another Welsh cunning-man, of Llanrhaiadr-yn-Mochnant, put on a wonderful show of spirit conjuration for his clients. He wore:

> a cap of sheepskin with a high crown, bearing a plume of pigeons' feathers, and a coat of unusual pattern, with broad hems, and covered with talismanic characters. In his hand he held a whip, the thong of which was made of the skin of an eel, and the handle of bone. With this he drew a circle around him, outside of which, at a proper distance, he kept those persons who came to him, whilst he went through his mystic sentences and performances.[73]

This appears to be his imaginative version of the ritual for calling up spirits as described in the *Fourth Book*, where it is instructed that a circle be made on the floor, within which divine names, occult characters and pentacles were to be drawn. The magician was to furnish himself with 'holy papers, lamens, pictures, pentacles, swords, sceptres, garments of convenient matter and colour, and things of the like sort'. Once in the circle it was necessary to consecrate it with 'convenient gesture and countenance'; and after saying various prayers and orations he was ready to begin invoking 'the Spirit which he desireth, with a gentle and loving Inchantment'.[74]

Some cunning-folk obviously made serious attempts to conjure up angels, demons and spirits, but one suspects that others put on a theatrical semblance of conjuration without any serious intent to invoke such beings. A Yorkshire cunning-woman, even when merely telling fortunes, would make a show of drawing a circle on her cottage floor and taking her stand within it.[75] Although Anne Bodenham was accused of raising diabolic spirits using magical circles, and certainly had some knowledge of how to invoke them properly, the evidence suggests her use of circles was very simplistic. When identifying thieves she made a circle in the earth with a stick, then looked into her crystal, which was placed over a picture in a book, and spoke 'some words softly to herself'.[76] Anyone could draw a circle on the ground, of course, but not every cunning-person possessed a copy of the *Fourth Book, Key of Solomon*, or Scot's *Discoverie* from which they could learn the careful preparations and consecrations that had to take place beforehand, and the content of the invocations that had to be said within the circle. As Bodenham remarked under legal examination, 'those that have a desire to [do] it, doe read in books'.[77] Those books made it quite clear that spirits could not be raised on the spur of the moment or in a few minutes. In the *Heptameron*, for instance, it was stated that anyone planning to conjure up spirits or angels 'ought to be clean and purified by the space of nine daies before the beginning of the work, and to be confessed, and receive the holy Communion'.[78] Even for those cunning-folk who had the necessary texts, there were obviously far easier ways of detecting thieves than employing such a costly and time-consuming method. Anyway, the main use of grimoires, other than for show, was not to invoke spirits but rather to help in the construction of written charms. It is to this important aspect of cunning-folk's trade that we now turn.

# 6

## *Written Charms*

The popular demand for written charms was considerable, and their production an evidently lucrative trade. The surviving examples that can be firmly attributed to cunning-folk date mostly from the eighteenth and nineteenth centuries. They vary markedly in terms of their quality and sophistication. Although some are corrupted and difficult to decipher, it is important to stress that in general they were not meaningless gibberish made up on the spur of the moment, as some ignorant contemporaries suggested. Many contain mystical words and symbols that were deliberately used in specific contexts, and derived principally from printed books and manuscripts of magic, the Bible and chapbooks. An examination of the content of these charms serves to highlight both the intrinsic Christian content of magic, and the important role of cunning-folk and literacy in its transmission and dissemination.

Charms could be produced for a variety of purposes, such as the detection of thieves and the procurement of love, but the majority were concerned with the protection of humans and livestock from witchcraft and the curing of those already bewitched. Magical texts usually specified that such charms had to be written on either virgin or unborn parchment. The former was made from the skin of an animal that had not yet reached sexual maturity, while the latter was made from unborn animals that were either cut out of the uterus or aborted. Indeed, Robert Turner advertised in the *Fourth Book* that his publisher, Thomas Rooks, of the Lamb and Ink-Bottle near St Paul's, sold not only virgin parchment but also 'the best abortives' for producing one's own unborn parchment.[1] Eighteenth- and nineteenth-century cunning-folk sometimes adhered to the tradition of using parchment, though they were hardly likely to be fussy about its origin. Parchment, however, was considerably more expensive than paper and less easily obtained, so it is no surprise to find that it was usually only employed for smaller charms.

Most written charms contained a strong religious content. This is not unexpected, considering the sources from which they derived. They included passages from the Bible, appeals to the Holy Trinity, Catholic exorcisms, and lists of divine names in different languages. By way of initial example we can turn to the confession of the cunning-man Richard Walton. He described the charm he wrote down for his bewitched clients as follows: 'I usually gave them a piece of writing upon a piece of parchment, wherein was wrote the beginning of the first chapter of St John's Gospel, and several other parts of the Holy Scriptures'; as well as 'many of the divine names belonging to God and his Holy Angels'. According to Reginald Scot the Gospel of St John was known to be particularly effective as a charm against thieves.[2] It is ironic, therefore, that Walton actually employed it to protect from witchcraft the heifer of a horse-thief named Humphry Moussall. Part of the case against Walton rested on a statement by Moussall that the charm had actually been intended to preserve him from arrest. As Walton bitterly observed, if 'the unthinking gentlemen of the jury' had read it properly they would have realised it only concerned witchcraft, since the charm concluded by asking that 'the angel of god would preserve from witchcraft or evil tongues'. Nevertheless, he still penitently admitted that he 'did not do well in making a penny of the Holy Scriptures and the many divine names therein used'.[3] Scriptural passages were often reproduced in Latin, with the occasional smattering of Greek or Hebrew. Such passages were often badly spelt and grammatically poor, presumably from repeated copying. Not surprisingly, there was also considerable use of overtly magical words and phrases, spirit names, occult symbols, planetary signs, and astrological terms.

If a charm was intended to protect a human, the cunning-person would often conceal it in a little bag with the injunction that it be kept close to the body and should never be allowed to touch the ground. To avoid this fate, charms were sewn into clothing, worn around the neck or tucked into corsets. The wearers of John Parkins's lamens also had to read an imprecatory prayer every hour, and he further warned all his clients that their power would be effective only as long as they believed fervently in them. Swearing, lying and every other sin, even in thought, was to be avoided.[4] If not secreted on the person, charms were usually meant to be hidden somewhere around the house or outbuildings, most commonly above doors and windows, although the bedridden sometimes placed them in their pillows. Some were placed in tins or bottles, which is one of the reasons why they have survived today. If livestock were bewitched then the charm might also be buried in the ground where the affected animals grazed. Richard Walton instructed Humphry Moussall to bury his charm 'in the corner of the garden, to wards sun-rising, about a foot deep in the ground, laying a green turf upon it, and then fill up the hole again'.[5] The ingestion of charms was very rare, though in one instance a cunning-man ordered that a charm be fed to a bewitched cow in a pint of hot gruel.[6]

Even if they were comprehensible to the client, which was rarely the case, charms were not usually meant to be openly displayed or even read by their possessors. The owner of one charm told the Rev. Thomas Hawkins that 'he did *not* read it, and that he believed no one *could* read it'.[7] To this end, cunning-folk usually folded and sealed them with wax or stitched them up. There was the odd exception though. Around 1890 an old couple, living near Okehampton, Devon, bought a charm from a cunning-man to cure a bewitched horse. It contained a drawing of a magical seal surrounded by various cabalistic signs, and the following words, which the old man was told to read on three consecutive Sundays after its purchase:

> I do this to torture and torment that man or woman who has injured us, James C[____] and Ann C[____], and we do confine them in the lower regions for ever, never to trust us or our horse more for ever in the name of those three Holy Angels known and unknown, Tetragrammaton, Aurona-dall, Draconium, in the name of God the father, God the Son and God the Holy Ghost. Amen, Amen, Amen.[8]

This is not the place to undertake the difficult and laborious task of tracing the origin and meaning of all the signs, symbols, and language that make up these charms. Nevertheless, it is instructive to examine their content in more detail, and to consider from what sources cunning-folk may have constructed these charms in the first place.

The most simple and ancient of charm formulae was the word 'Abracadabra' written on a piece of parchment. A nineteenth-century Exeter cunning man sold just such a charm sewn up in a one-inch square black silk bag. It was for protection against witches and evil spirits, and cost the considerable sum of one guinea. The owner was instructed that should it ever fall to the ground it would lose its magical power.[9] Although the word abracadabra is now used light-heartedly, and is associated with stage magic, it was once considered one of the most powerful of words and not to be used in jest. Its origin is obscure, though we do know the Romans used it as an amulet against disease, and it therefore presumably had a long history of use in England.[10] More pertinent, perhaps, is that its potency was expounded in early modern printed works. In chapter eleven of Agrippa's *Third Book* there is an example of how to arrange the word in diminishing form, and Reginald Scot stated that 'Abracadabra written on a paper, with a certeine figure joined therewith, and hanged about ones necke, helpeth the ague'. The seventeenth-century antiquarian John Aubrey also suggested its use as a cure for diseases in general and the ague in particular, as did the astrologer-physician John Durant.[11] The formula also found its way into a couple of nineteenth-century popular publications on magical matters. It appeared in Smith's compendious *Astrologer of the Nineteenth Century*, and later in *The Private Companion*, where it was instructed that 'This mysterious triangle must be written upon a piece of square paper, which is then folded in such a manner as to conceal the triangle. A white thread in the form of a cross, closes this amulet, which is suspended from the neck by a linen ribbon.'[12] Knowledge of its power was obviously widespread during the early modern and modern periods, and there were a variety of sources from which cunning-folk could obtain examples of the formula.

A step up in terms of sophistication was provided by Reginald Scot's versions of a Latin talisman called the 'Paracelsian Charme', which were used for keeping witches and bad spirits away from buildings. Scot's adaptation ran as follows: 'Omnis spiritus laudet Dominum: Mosen habent et Prophetas: Exurgat Deus et dissipentur inimici ejus.'[13] It translates as 'Let every spirit praise the Lord: they have Moses and the prophets: Let God arise and his enemies be scattered.' The second segment of this sentence is from St Luke 16:29, and the third from Psalm 68. Around 1900 a version of this charm was obtained from an old farmer who lived in the district of Pendle, Lancashire. It was written on a small piece of paper in an 'illiterate hand', and was intended to be placed over the door of the house. On it was written, 'Omnes spiritu laudet domnum moson habent dusot propheates exurgrat disipentur inimicus'. The farmer also had another version of the same charm, labelled 'For the field', which had the added command, 'Let all the cattle in this field prosper'. When an old cow-house in neighbouring Yorkshire was pulled down several pieces of paper were found in holes above the stalls, on which was written:

> Omni Spiritones laudent Dominum
> habentu Mosa et Prophetores
> Excugat Deus et dissipentur
> Manu segas amori.
> Fiat. Fiat. Fiat.

A similar charm was also given to a client by a Nottinghamshire cunning-man in 1866 for protection against witchcraft:

> Omnes Spiritus laudent Dominum.
> Misericordiam habe Deus
> Desinetur Inimicus D. V.[14]

This was obviously a widely employed form of protective charm amongst cunning-folk.

It is likely that some of these nineteenth-century versions derived directly from Scot's *Discoverie*, but a more influential conduit for disseminating the formula – almost certainly taken from Scot originally – was a popular chapbook entitled *A Groatsworth of Wit for a Penny*. First published in the late seventeenth century, it was reprinted several times in London during the second half of the eighteenth century. More significantly, considering the geographical spread of the above examples, printers in several northern and midland towns also published it. One edition printed in Newcastle around 1770 claimed it was in its eleventh edition by that time, and early nineteenth-century versions were also printed in Warrington and Coventry. It was a run-of-the-mill fortune-teller with the usual sections on the signification of moles, physiognomy, and a list of good and bad days. Like many such chapbooks, it claimed to have a distinguished author, in this case the famed seventeenth-century astrologer William Lilly. What marks it out, though, is what it gave as a 'night-spell to catch thieves', which turns out to be a version of the Paracelsian Charm. The exact spelling varies in different editions, and this probably contributed to the discrepancies that occur in the handwritten versions. That which appears in the Newcastle edition is as follows:

> Omnes spiritus laudent Dominum,
> Mosem habent et prophetas,
> Exurgat Deus, dissipienter inimici.

It may be significant that the chapbook makes no mention of its effectiveness against witchcraft, only that it 'will drive away any Spirit that useth to haunt any House or Place; having it about one, no Thief can do you any Harm'. This would seem to confirm an earlier observation concerning chapbook publishers' self-censorship when it came to demonic magic and anti-witchcraft matters.[15] The author of the above edition did at least appear to allude to its original use against witches when he concluded, 'Authors say it will do so many more pretty tricks, besides'. *A Groatsworth of Wit* directed that the spell be written on virgin parchment and placed in the four corners of the house, garden or orchard. Judging from the corrupted spelling and the varied wording of all the handwritten examples, one suspects that numerous versions of the charm must have circulated in manuscript as well as printed form.

Another category of short charm comprises of those made up of brief lists of biblical, demonic and secret names, sometimes garbled, and occasionally reduced to gibberish, which usually end with an adjuration. The following example was found in an old hall in the neighbourhood of Bradford:

> Aon + hora + Cammall + + +
> Naadgrass + Dryadgrass + + +
> Arassund + yo + Sigrged + + +
> dayniss + Tetragrammaton E
> Inurmed E Soleysicke + + +
> domend + Ame + dias + hora + + M.
> Fiat.

An authority on handwriting judged it to have been written in a hand not earlier than George III. The great etymologist Walter Skeat also analysed it and concluded nothing could be made of it, though it has to be said that he was no expert in occult matters.[16] Apart from 'hora' and 'Fiat' which are Latin for 'hour' and 'let it be done', the only obviously recognisable word in the charm is 'Tetragrammaton' which was a secret name of God, and one of the most powerful words of magic. Otherwise 'Aon' is surely aeon, 'Ame' is presumably Amen, 'Cammall' is probably a misspelling of 'Camael' the angel of Mars, and 'Sigrged' could be a corruption of the spirit 'Sagrigrit'. Greek mythological derivations could be found for 'dayniss' and dryadgrass, the former coming from Adonis and the latter the Greek for woodland nymphs. The charm was presumably written for a person named E. Soleysicke.

A rather more coherent example of this category of charm comes from Somerset, and was written down on a scrap of paper probably during the late nineteenth century:

> Sator, arepo, Tenet, opera, Rotas,
> Jah, Jah, Jah,
> Enom Jah, Jah, Jah, Rethur [?]
> Gehuvah Siphereth, negach, Had
> Yesod, malkush, amaluim,
> Jouae Juest, Shadrach,
> Mishach abednago, be ye
> all present in my aid
> and for whatsoever I shall
> desire to obtain.[17]

The most interesting feature of this is the first line, which is a linear version of a well-known Latin magic word square, or acrostic, which reads the same horizontally and vertically, backwards and forwards. William Bottrell found that Cornish cunning-folk also wrote it on a piece of parchment in the form of a word square for protection against witchcraft.[18] A couple of examples of the word square have been found dating to the period of Roman occupation; one scratched on wall-plaster at Cirencester, the other on a sherd of pottery found during excavations in Manchester. Nearer in date to our period is an unusual Rotas-Sator square, carved on an oak board and dated 1614, which was fixed to the south wall of Great Gidding parish church in Cambridgeshire.[19] As with 'Abracadabra', though, it is extremely unlikely that examples from the modern period represent an unbroken continuation from Roman times. The author of the Somerset charm had presumably cobbled it together from several literary sources. As told in the *Book of Daniel*, Shadrach, Meshach and Abednago are the three defiant men who refused to worship King Nebuchadnezzar's golden image and were cast into a furnace. 'Gehuvah Siphereth, negach, Had Yesod, malkush' are variant spellings of the powerful divine names, Jehovah, Sephiroth, Netzach, Hod, Yesod, Malkuth.

A less esoteric charm, although similar in structure, was found over the door of a house in the neighbourhood of Burnley:

> Sun, Moon, Mars, Mercury, Jupiter, Venus, Saturn, Trine, Sextile, Dragon's Head, Dragon's Tail, I charge you all to gard this hause from all evils spirits whatever, and gard it from all Desorders, and from aney thing being taken wrangasly, and give this famaly good Ealth and Welth.[20]

The cunning-person who produced this was evidently not particularly conscientious in his or her work. Trine and sextile are not demons or words of power, but technical astrological terms for the aspects of the planets when separated by 120 and 60 degrees respectively. The author presumably found the words in some of his or her books and obviously thought them impressive names to 'conjure' with. Dragon's Head and Dragon's Tail are likewise astrological terms, which, as outlined by Agrippa in his *Three Books*, refer to two specific points in the passage of the moon. This example would suggest that its author was either ignorant of what he wrote down, or deliberately fobbed off his or her clients with a charm that contained little magical potency; not that clients would be aware of this fact of course.

While the above charm indicates a limited knowledge of magic, the following example betrays a certain sly cynicism. It was confiscated from a Lincolnshire cunning-man, William Martin of Bratoft, who was prosecuted in 1850 after selling it for ten shillings to Tobias Davison, whose wife was sick. The charm, wrapped in a little parcel, was opened in court. Inside were found some sticks, and a paper on which was written the word 'Abracadabra', the twelve signs of the zodiac, some fractional numbers and the following rhyme:

> By Saint Peter and Saint Paul,
> God is the maker of us all;
> What he gave to me I give to thee,
> And that is nought to nobody.[21]

This jocular verse is out of keeping with the solemn nature of its purpose, and one cannot help but think that Martin was having a private joke at the expense of his patients.

A medley charm from Cornwall, found in a small silk bag on the body of a deceased old woman, leads us back once again to Scot's *Discoverie*. The charm consisted of a piece of parchment three inches square on which was written the word 'NALGAH'.[22] Underneath this was a drawing described as a birdlike figure, with two pairs of wings, hovering over an egg. Written under the figure was the word 'TETRA-GRAMMATON'. On the reverse side was a diminishing 'Abracadabra', and the divine names 'Jehovah. Jah. Eloim. Shadday. Adonay', ending with the plea 'Have mercy on a poor woman'. Nalgah is a demonic name that does not appear in any of the printed magical texts mentioned in the previous chapter, except the anonymous 'Discourse on Devils and Spirits' appended to the 1665 edition of Scot's *Discoverie*. Nalgah is described therein as one of the 'seven good Angels, or Daemons', the others being Iubanladace, Yah-li-Yah, Maynom, Gaonim, Halanu and Kam a-Umi. The character or symbol of Nalgah as depicted in the 'Discourse' also corresponds well to the birdlike figure in the Cornish charm. The citing of Nalgah by cunning-folk makes perfect sense, considering that he was meant to appear 'to those that are devoted to the knowledge of Magick; teaching them how to exercise Infernal Witchcraft without danger ... he must be sought by hours, minutes, constellations, privacy and blood, etc'.[23] The name also appears in an early nineteenth-century charm from Yorkshire.[24] So the use of Nalgah in these charms must have derived either directly from the 1665 edition of *Discoverie*, or a manuscript grimoire that had borrowed from it. The latter proposition is likely, for in Hockley's 'Occult Spells' we find the same passage concerning Nalgah and a reproduction of his symbol.[25]

The importance of the second 'Discourse' in the 1665 edition of *Discoverie* is also evident from another charm, this time produced by William Harris, a Welsh quack who also offered to cure the bewitched. When Harris appeared before the Rhayader magistrates in 1867, the content of a charm he sold to one Edwin Jones was read out in court:

> The fourth is Maynom, one of the powers who hath the ability of superficient administration and protection, that is at one and the same time to be present

with many. His presence must be sought by humility and prayer; the fifth good genius is Gaomum, an angel of celestial brightness, who hath the peculiar ability of rendering his pupil invisible to any evil spirit whatsoever.

Compare this with the relevant passage in the 'Discourse' concerning the fourth and fifth good 'Angels and Daemons':

> Maynom one of the powers who hath the ability of subservient administration; that is, at one time to be present with many; he resembleth a ew with lamb, typifiying his nature in that appearance. Gaonim an angel, causing his pupil to go invisible, and transporting him at his pleasure in a moment, to the outmost parts of the earth.[26]

The discrepancies were perhaps the result of Harris writing the passage from memory. As Jones deposed in court, Harris 'sat down at a table and wrote something on a piece of paper, which he afterwards sewed up in a piece of cloth and gave to me'. However, Harris certainly possessed at least one occult literary source. When Samuel Philips, a carpenter, was diagnosed as bewitched, Harris instructed his accomplice daughter to 'write something out of a large book on a piece of paper; the paper was then given to the prisoner's wife who sewed it up in a piece of calico'.[27] Was this book a manuscript grimoire containing information drawn from the 1665 *Discoverie*? Or perhaps Harris actually possessed an original copy of the book, but did not have it with him when consulted by Jones. The 1665 edition is certainly a large folio (nothing particularly unusual in that respect), but its size would certainly have impressed a carpenter whose experience of literature was probably restricted to the Bible and small popular publications.

While the above medley charms were miscellanies of occult words, phrases and symbols, invocation charms were longer and their content more formal and structured.[28] The following impressive example was bought for 2s. 6d. from a cunning-man near Halifax in 1807. It was written on both sides of a sheet of paper and folded into a triangular form. Several seals were affixed to it:

> In the name of Jesus Christ, I call upon thee through power will command such creatures, Drimoth, Bellmoth, Lymock, I conjure you up to fetch me back the watch of J\_\_\_\_ C\_\_\_\_r, that was stolen on the ninth day of August, 1807, in the house of man, to bring the matter to true light, and to confess the said watch and to the part the owner, to have his watch again in so short

time as may be pleasing and acceptable to the Almighty. God will have the whole matter made known in this order without any further trouble unto the parties. I. G. H. name of the angels Satan and Agemon, that you attend me in the hour acceptable to the Almighty God, and send unto me a spirit called Sagrigg, to torment the thief both day and night that he do fulfil my command, and desire to fetch back the watch in nomen de patri an filii. (Here follows some more unintelligible latin.) I by these creatures shall make them to yield through God's help, to their sorrow, by the authority of the Omnipotent, the Father, the Son, and the Holy Ghost, and by the holy virgin Mary mother of our Lord Jesus Christ, and the holy angels and archangels, and of St Michael and St John the Baptist, and in behalf of St Stephen and all the martyrs, St Sylvester and all the confessors, the holy virgins, and all the saints in heaven and earth. Unto whom there is given power to bind all those spirits to bring the thief to judgement, that have stolen the watch. And here, we do excommunicate, damn, curse, and bind with the knots and bonds of excommunication all the thieves, male or female, that have committed this theft or mischief to J____ C____, of Causeyfoot, or have accepted any part thereof to their own use. Let them have part with Judas who betrayed Christ, Amen. – – Let their children be made orphans. Cursed be the thief, be they in the field, in the grove, in the woods, in their houses, barns, chambers, and beds, that have stolen the watch. And cursed be they in church, the church yard – – in eating, in waking, in sleeping, in drinking, in sitting, kneeling, standing, lying, in all their works, in their body and soul, and in their five wits. And cursed be the heart, back, liver, bowels, and spleen. And cursed be their head, – – and their arms, – – and the hands which took the watch. And cursed be their flesh, and cursed be their bones, and the marrow that is within their bones. And cursed be they – – by the milk of the virgin Mary. I conjure thee Lucifer, with all they soldiers, by the Father, Son, and Holy Ghost – – that the thief rest not day or night, till though restore the watch again to J____ C____, acceptable to Almighty God – – Bring them to destruction. – – And let the torments of hell be strong upon them for ever. Amen.[29]

This was actually an abbreviated transcription of the charm, for it apparently contained considerable repetition of some passages. It was, in fact, a version of a long-established charm against thieves that Scot called 'Saint Adelberts cursse'.[30] The major difference between Scot's version and the above is that the latter starts with the conjuration of the spirits 'Drimoth, Bellmoth and Lymock'. But this is, in itself, further confirmation that the charm derived from the *Discoverie*, for these are variant spellings of the spirits Orimoth, Belimoth and Lymocke, who also appear in a conjuration later on in the *Discoverie* 'To speake with spirits'. The line 'send unto me a spirit called Sagrigg' also appears in the same conjuration, except that the spirit is called 'Sagrigrit'.[31] A briefer conjuration for the same purpose was found amongst the papers of Joseph Railey in 1857:

> I do conjure, constrain, adjure, and command you spirits. Analaya, Analla, Anacar, in the name of the Father, and of the Son, and of the Holy Ghost, by Alpha and Omega, the Beginning and the End, by the general ressurrection, and by Him who shall come to judge the quick and the dead, and the world by fire, and, by the general ressurrection at the last day, and by that name that is called Tetragrammaton, that you cause the person who stole the goods in question to bring back the same.

Below the writing was a triangle with a cross at each corner, with illegible inscriptions along each side and down the centre.

A number of lengthy charms dating from the late eighteenth to the early twentieth century can be found in the collections of the National Library of Wales and the Welsh Folk Museum, and yet more examples survive in private hands.[32] They consist mostly of elements found in the charms already discussed, and usually begin with an adjuration such as the following from an unpublished original:

> + Lignum sanctae crusis, defendat me a malis, presentibus, preateritus & futuris, interioribus & exterioribus ++ Margaret Richards +++ omnes spiritus laudet dominum: Mosen habent et prophetas: Exergat Deus et disipenture inimiciessus + O Lord Jesus Christ I beseech thee to preserve me, and all that I posses from the powers of all evil men, women, spirits, or wizards or hardness of heart, and this I will trust thou will do by the same power as thou didst cause the blind to see the lame to walk and they that were possessed with unclean spirits to be in their own minds Amen ++ [33]

There then follows a list of holy names including the three wise men, and divine names such as Elohim, Adonay and Tetragrammaton. After this there is a row of astrological symbols as well as the signs of the archangels Gabriel and Michael. To one side is a diminishing abracadabra (note also the inclusion of the Paracelsian charm within the body of the text). An almost identical version of this charm was found in the mid nineteenth century when an old cow-house was being pulled down.

It had been placed in a tin box and buried in the wall. Instead of the name 'Margaret Richards', the name of another purchaser, 'Daniel Evans', had been inserted. The son of Daniel Evans, who took over the tenancy of the farm, remembered his father obtaining the charm from a cunning-man and apothecary of Machynlleth, to protect his cattle from the witchcraft.[34]

A recurring feature of at least half of the surviving Welsh charms, all of which are very similar in structure and content, though they are written in several different hands, is the drawing in the right-hand bottom corner of a circular magical seal containing various occult symbols. Earlier this century one such charm was sent to the British Museum for examination. It was suggested that it was akin to some medieval papal seals, but that 'possibly the author himself had no very set plan in mind when he arranged them'.[35] In fact, the original author of this Welsh charm-type knew exactly what he was doing. The seal had nothing to do with papal insignia. Although similar types of 'seal' can be found in the *Key of Solomon*, the only example which corresponds exactly with that on the Welsh charms is one of two printed side by side in Scot's *Discoverie*, bearing the instruction 'Who so beareth this sign about him, let him fear no fo, but fear GOD'.[36] It is obvious, therefore, why it was added to the arsenal of protective words and symbols contained in these charms. Let us give credit to some cunning-folk for knowing the meaning of what they wrote down. That other cunning-folk also used the same seals is evident from a charm produced by the nineteenth-century Plymouth cunning-woman Mary Catherine Murray. It was written on parchment, or 'skin' as she called it, and as described in court, contained several 'signs', against two of which were the words, 'Whosoever beareth this sign all spirits will do him homage' and 'Whosoever beareth this sign need fear no foe'. These are close paraphrases of the sentences beneath Scot's two seals.[37] It is further worth noting that in an occult manuscript written largely by Thomas Parker between 1693 and 1695, but augmented by another hand in the early eighteenth century, there are roughly drawn copies of both protective seals.[38] All this is further proof, if it were needed, that the *Discoverie* was the most influential source of practical magic for cunning-folk until the twentieth century.

To return to the Welsh charms, one of their striking aspects is that, apart from those passages written in Latin, the text was nearly always in English. It is possible that this was a deliberate attempt to make them even more mystifying to a Welsh-speaking public. Yet many of these charms were found in areas of the country where the Welsh language was hardly dominant by the nineteenth century. More to the point, the content of most of the charms ultimately derived from English sources. There was no real reason to bother translating them since they were not meant to be read. The fact that almost identical versions of the same charm exist in different handwritings suggests that either knowledge of the charm was passed on through several generations of cunning-folk in the same family – like the Harries – or that an unrelated opportunist purchased one of the charms as a template to help set him or herself up in the trade.

Most cunning-folk seem to have had just one or two stock charms that they reproduced over and over again, personalising them by adding the client's name or the nature of the area or animal to be protected. The quality and sophistication of the charms provide at least some indication of the relative educational level of the cunning-folk who produced them, though unfortunately they tell us little about their own perceptions of what they were doing. A well-written charm only confirms that the cunning-person was proficient at the act of writing, not that he or she believed in the efficacy of their charms, or even knew anything about the symbols, signs and names contained therein. In other words, the charm might merely show that a cunning-person was good at copying. We can assume with some confidence that those cunning-folk who possessed impressive collections of occult books, or those like John Parkins and Timothy Crowther who made their own manuscript compilations of astrology and magic, had a lively interest in ritual magic and an earnest belief in the charms they produced.[39] It is also likely, however, that many cunning-folk possessed very little knowledge of ritual magic and occult philosophy, but by one means or another obtained some simple written formulae that they copied out with little thought. Nevertheless, for the clients of cunning-folk the ability to write and copy out charms was in itself an exhibition of power, in addition to the magical strength of what was written. The illiterate depended on an intermediary who possessed the requisite skills to reproduce the potent charms and amulets they required, while the literate needed someone who had access to the rare written and printed sources of magic from which charms originated.

# 7

# *European Comparisons*

Although this book is principally concerned with British cunning-folk, much can be learnt by comparisons with their counterparts elsewhere in Europe. The term 'cunning-folk', which has been defined and employed throughout this book, obviously has little meaning in other languages, so can we really use the term in a European context? Several eminent historians of European witchcraft have decided to use it in their discussions of magical practitioners, rather than refer to them by their various names in the main European languages.[1] For me the term is valid if the same criteria apply as have already been outlined in this book. So, if elsewhere in Europe we find magical practitioners offering the same breadth of services – love magic, thief detection, fortune-telling, herbal medicine, unbewitching, blessing – then I think 'cunning-folk' provides a useful, all-embracing comparative term. In France many, though by no means all of those known variously as *devins-guérisseurs*, *désenvoûteurs*, *désensorceleurs* and *leveurs de sorts*, carried on a similar breadth of trade, as did *toverdokters* and *duivelbanners* in the Netherlands, *kloge folk* in Denmark, *Hexenmeisters* in German lands, *curanderos* in Spain, and *saludadores* in Portugal. It has to be remembered of course that, as in England, each individual magical practitioner might have had his or her own specialities. But on a regional European level there are also some broader differences in the social make-up of cunning-folk, the way in which they went about their business, and the magical practices they employed. It is the identification and examination of these differences that casts new light upon the characteristics of the English tradition. To begin with, however, it is important to be aware of the nature and extent of our sources. As in England, the activities of cunning-folk throughout Europe were considered illegal for the long duration of the period with which this book is concerned, and much of our knowledge consequently derives from trial documents. However, for the early modern period in particular, the social, religious and legal policies that determined patterns of prosecution, were quite diverse amongst the various kingdoms, princedoms, republics and city states of Europe, resulting in an uneven coverage of cunning-folk and their activities.

Throughout much of early modern Europe cunning-folk could, in theory, be tried under the same secular statutes as suspected witches. The predominant intellectual view, particularly amongst Protestants, was that beneficial and harmful magical practitioners were very much the same: people in either explicit or implicit league with the devil. In theory, there was potential for thousands of cunning-folk to perish at the stake along with those condemned as witches. In practice, no such thing happened. As in England, and for the same reasons, relatively few cunning-folk were prosecuted under secular statutes for witchcraft. Those that were, were also usually dealt with more leniently by the courts than those convicted as witches, often facing banishment rather than burning. In some areas this differential punishment was actually stipulated in the relevant statutes. The Carolina Code (1532) of the Holy Roman Empire recommended more merciful treatment towards those who presumed to tell fortunes or practised magic. The Danish witchcraft ordinance of 1617 also specified that cunning-folk were to be fined and exiled, while witches were to be burned.[2]

Another set of secular laws under which cunning-folk were prosecuted in some regions related to medical practice. Whereas in England until the mid nineteenth century there was a largely unrestricted medical market, elsewhere in Europe the secular authorities made more concerted attempts to protect the interests of the orthodox medical profession in the face of competition from cunning-folk and other unofficial healers. It has been suggested that in Hungary the cessation of the witch trials in the mid eighteenth century, which involved a number cunning-folk, was partly brought about by the introduction of a wave of medical statutes, aimed at defining and restricting the role of different healers in public practice. As a result, authoritarian concern shifted from the role of cunning-folk as witches to cunning-folk as healers. In Denmark the Kvaksalver law of 1794, which was directed against those who took 'it upon themselves to cure illnesses among the peasantry in spite of the fact that they are completely unknowing in the art of medicine', specifically referred not only to 'quacks' but 'cunning men or women'. Prosecutions under the law were not infrequent. Nowhere, perhaps, did the medical profession lobby the legislature harder than in eighteenth-century France, both before and after the Revolution. The principal targets of French legislation were secret remedies and their vendors, but the related issue of magical healers also received considerably more formal attention from the medical fraternity than in England.[3] While the English medical profession was not lost for words when it came to quacks, or 'pretenders' to medical legitimacy and respectability, they were remarkably quiet about the profusion of cunning-folk and other magical healers. In contrast to France, here there were no concerted attacks on such people by the medical profession at this period. Yet no matter whether there were legal restrictions or a policy of *laissez-faire*, in practice cunning-folk were no less active in France, Denmark and Hungary than they were in England. It was one thing to pass a law and another to enforce it. The Hungarian public hygiene reforms largely failed. In Denmark the Kvaksalver law still required that a physician or apothecary lodge a personal complaint before the state would take action, and evidently insufficient numbers were motivated enough to enter legal proceedings to threaten the position of cunning-folk in Danish society in any way.

It was generally the religious judicial institutions rather than the secular that expressed the most concern about cunning-folk and were the most active in suppressing them. Some of the best sources we have on the subject resulted from the interest and bureaucratic scrupulousness of the permanent Papal Inquisitions in Spain (1478–1834), Portugal (1536–1821) and Italy (from 1542 on). Primarily set up to root out heretics, particularly among converted Jews and Muslims, and, after the Reformation, Protestants and their Catholic sympathisers, they became increasingly preoccupied with those who practised magic. While cases concerning 'superstition' made up only a small percentage of the business of the Portuguese and Spanish Inquisitions, the Roman Inquisition took a keen interest in all aspects of popular magical practice from the late sixteenth century onwards.[4] However, historians' understandable preoccupation with the Inquisition has, perhaps, overshadowed the importance of the regular episcopal courts in Catholic countries, which also dealt with moral and spiritual offences by both clerics and lay people. These courts dealt with many cases of illicit magic as well.[5]

It was not just Catholic ecclesiastical courts that sought to suppress cunning-folk and punish people for consulting them. Until the pervasive influence of such institutions declined during the eighteenth centuries, Lutheran and Calvinist Protestant church councils also took particular exception to those who practised magic for supposedly beneficial purposes. In newly reformed Strasbourg, Lutheran pastors and magistrates joined forces in a concerted effort to rid the city of cunning-folk and diviners.[6] Such people also appear in some of the very first cases brought before the consistory of the Genevan Reformed Church set up by Calvin. In 1542, for instance, Aymon Peronet was summoned for using 'certain medicines and cures for the sick, and for using certain spells'. Out of 530 people excommunicated in the rural districts around Geneva between 1567 and 1569, seventy-eight (15 per cent) were guilty of 'superstition', which in most cases concerned the consultation of magical practitioners.[7] In the Calvinist Hungarian city of Debrecen, pastors urged magistrates to purge the town of cunning-folk. The Scottish Presbyterians also dealt with such people, along with the usual range of moral offenders, in their lower courts known as kirk sessions. These continued to deal with magical practitioners and their clients decades after the Church of England had lost interest. In April 1700, for instance, a man appeared before the congregation at Balfron to confess his sin in consulting a cunning-man or charmer named Donald Ferguson, 'where by he cast off much of the fear of God and yielded to Satan'.[8] In the Protestant Netherlands church synods and councils also took a strong stance against magical practices. During the first half of the seventeenth century the provincial synod of Overijssel repeatedly asked the secular authorities to take action against, 'magical healing, divination, conjuration and other such abominations'. In 1615 ministers requested that visits to blessers, exorcists, and witch doctors also be expressly forbidden. The courts of the Dutch Reformed Church continued to admonish and exclude from Holy Communion both cunning-folk and their clients until the early eighteenth century. One of the last recorded cases heard before the church council of the Dutch province of Zeeland concerned a woman who, in 1729, had gone to consult some cunning-folk in Flanders to detect the whereabouts of stolen property.[9] In the multitude of states, cities and princedoms that were to become modern Germany all three major churches, Lutheran, Catholic and Calvinist, were active in condemning the consultation of cunning-folk. Yet, in Reformation Rothenburg, a large imperial town which effectively became Lutheran in 1544, there was a significant gap between condemning and suppressing popular magic. Although the ecclesiastical visitations repeatedly brought the 'problem' of cunning-folk to the attention of the town authorities, no concerted effort was ever made to deal with them.[10] Despite the obvious lack of success and secular incentive to suppress popular magic, the ecclesiastical courts in some German-speaking territories apparently persisted in confronting such offenders right up until the early nineteenth century.[11]

It was suggested early on in this book that only a tiny minority of those prosecuted for witchcraft in English secular courts were cunning-folk; but what about the situation in other parts of Europe – particularly in areas where the legal persecution of witches was far more intense? It has been suggested by Richard Horsley that in parts of Switzerland, Austria and France cunning-folk, or more precisely cunning-women, made up a significant proportion, nearly a half in some areas, of those tried as witches.[12] If this was the case why have historians of continental witch-trials had so little to say about cunning-folk? Well, first, the interpretation of the evidence is unconvincing.[13] When one looks at the secondary sources he relied on, particularly the work of William Monter and Etienne Delcambre, it becomes apparent that Horsley based his assumption on a limited amount of cases, misreading of the texts, and the conflation of accusations of witchcraft with prosecutions for witchcraft.[14] Furthermore, the most recent authoritative survey of European witchcraft concludes that cunning-folk made up only 'a minuscule fraction' of those prosecuted. A detailed assessment of the trial records of the duchy of Lorraine, one of the areas Horsley cited, suggests that out of 2000 people executed no more than twenty were magical healers of some description.[15] This tallies well with the situation in England. In the Netherlands too, hardly any examples have been found. That in these regions under 2 per cent of those accused or executed were cunning-folk is a long, long way from the impression created by Horsley. Nevertheless, despite the failings of Horsley's analysis, his attempt to focus on the important role of cunning-folk was still commendable.

Of course, the experience in other regions of Europe was bound to be different, and it is quite likely that elsewhere cunning-folk were more prone to prosecution as witches, but as yet either the sources are insufficient or few historians have conducted the relevant analyses. In Norway not a few cunning-women were accused of *maleficium*, but there are no figures to give a more exact picture. In Hungary it seems a significantly higher percentage of practitioners were tried for harmful magic, a number of whom were actually identified as witches by other cunning-folk. This was certainly the case in the city of Debrecen, where there was particularly bitter rivalry. In one extraordinary instance, four practitioners who lived in two nearby streets were burned for witchcraft. A client had consulted them, and each had accused the other of bewitchment. Not knowing which was the real witch, he reported all four of them to the authorities.[16] The evidence for Finland varies. Although in one region studied accusations of *maleficium* against 'soothsayers and healers' were uncommon, a countrywide survey seems to suggest they were fairly frequently prosecuted for the crime.[17] Overall, this is an area of witchcraft studies that has not received enough attention, so any European generalisations are highly speculative.[18] Nevertheless, I will brazenly venture to suggest that the low level of cunning-folk *prosecutions* for *maleficium* in England was mirrored in most of Western Europe. That is not to say, though, that *accusations* of *maleficium* against cunning-folk were as infrequent – that is a quite different and even more indeterminate matter. As the ethnographic and court records for nineteenth-century England reveal, it was not uncommon for cunning-folk to be suspected of harmful magic, and the situation was surely no different in previous centuries. This just goes to show the interpretational gap between a suspicion, an accusation and a prosecution when it comes to analysing witchcraft.

Considering that much of Western Europe tried suspected witches under a quite different legal system to that in England, it might be expected that significantly different patterns of cunning-folk prosecutions for *maleficium* occurred. Under English common law, the onus was on the victim of crime to present information against their supposed bewitchers. Apart from the atypical and unofficial activities of the witch-finder Matthew Hopkins (between 1645 and 1647), there was no authoritarian hunt for suspected witches. Under continental Roman law, however, inquisitorial procedure allowed judges and court officials to instigate legal proceedings and to investigate personally alleged crimes, using formal and informal interrogation and torture. Under such a legal system there was more potential for cunning-folk to get dragged into a spiral of witchcraft accusations. On the Continent, as in England, both beneficial and harmful magic were sometimes interpreted as one and the same crime, witchcraft. But whereas under common law, those making accusations were usually of a social level that made a distinction between practitioners of good and bad magic, an investigating judge under Roman law might act according to the intellectual or theological orthodoxy rather than popular discrimination. If during an investigation into alleged witchcraft a witness mentioned certain cunning-folk as being involved in a beneficial curative role, the judge might interpret this in a quite different light, suspecting that they were part of the same infernal sisterhood or brotherhood as the witches they had been employed to combat. The cunning-folk mentioned would consequently also be taken in for interrogation. No doubt a number of cunning-folk were unfortunate enough to get caught up in such a series of events. The application of torture, furthermore, would understandably lead cunning-folk to admit to diabolic relations, as the case of Katherina Hoser, a cunning-woman from Kulmbach in Germany illustrates. In 1569 Hoser was brought before the local Lutheran authorities to answer for her 'superstitious' activities. She promised to renounce her trade, but apparently went back on her word. It was not long before she was arrested and slung in prison by the secular authorities. It was now that her interrogation began. At first, Hoser denied any dealings in harmful magic, but before long successive bouts of torture led her to admit to having formed a pact with the devil. In the minds of her interrogators she proved the suspected link between benign magic and satanic worship.[19] Despite the terrible evidence of this and other cases, the experience and implementation of justice varied widely across Europe, on a localised basis, and many prosecutions for witchcraft and magic involved only minimal investigation, which helps explain why, despite the potential for significant cunning-folk prosecutions, levels seem to have remained low on the whole.

Prior to the Protestant Reformation in the first half of the sixteenth century, most people throughout western Europe had roughly the same experience of organised religion. The Catholic Church offered a well-defined range of spiritual services to guide and comfort people throughout their lives. The seven sacraments punctuated their experience, from baptism to the last rites, and many people imbued these rituals with profound magical significance. The priesthood, through the sacrament of ordination, were deemed to have a special relationship with God, and priests were the mediators via whom God delivered His blessings upon the people. No wonder, then, that the priest was popularly believed to possess supernatural powers, which were further enhanced by the various religious services and rites he had at his disposal. The mass was thought to have an actively benign influence upon the sick as well as facilitating spiritual communion. The recitation of Latin prayers, notably Paternosters and Aves was encouraged, and was seen to have a magical effect. The special rite of exorcism vividly demonstrated the church's commitment to intervene directly in the protection of its flock from supernatural attack. For many there was no real distinction between charms, prayers and exorcisms. In a sense, magic was basically religious devotion put to specific practical ends. The veneration of saints and holy wells, pilgrimages, processions and the miraculous powers of relics were all accepted and integrated into religious worship. The church also sold consecrated candles, crosses, holy water and rosaries, which had their own benign potency, and were incorporated into various forbidden magic rituals as well.

Protestants condemned all these aspects of religious practice as idolatrous 'superstition', and a programme of both inculcation and suppression was set in motion in Protestant states to reform both the nature of popular devotion and the relationship between laity and clergy. In attempting to redefine the boundaries between religion and magic, organised religion in Protestant areas withdrew from its long-held role as a resourceful ally in the day-to-day struggle against misfortune and malign forces. But it was not only the Protestants who tried to reform the popular perception of piety. Following several meetings of the Council of Trent in the mid sixteenth century, the Catholic Church embarked on a programme of reform as well. Partly in response to the spread of Protestantism in its various forms, and partly arising from an increased awareness of the gap between official devotion and popular religion, the Catholic hierarchy attempted to demarcate clearly, at the parish level, the often blurred line between the sacred and the profane. They also employed the term 'superstition' to describe all rites, charms and rituals that were believed to effect what only the church and its representatives could legitimately achieve, or which went beyond the prescribed boundaries of clerical service. For the laity to employ Latin prayers for curative purposes was superstitious profanity, but if the clergy employed the same it was an act of piety. In 1597 the episcopal tribunal of Novara punished an elderly healer, Francesco Poletto, for curing the bewitched by merely instructing them to say one Our Father and forty-one Hail Marys every morning for a week.[20] Innocuous enough advice it would seem, but Poletto had no ordained right to suggest such things. It was hammered home that only the clergy, through God, could truly ascertain whether someone was bewitched, and only clerical prayers and remedies were effective. All those, such as cunning-folk, who professed to have the same abilities and powers, were guilty of sacrilege at least, and of diabolism at worst.

The theological reasoning behind the classification of pious and profane religious practices may have been straightforward for the educated, but it was lost on many of the laity, who believed prayers and sacramentals were imbued with their own holy power independent of the clergy. Unsurprisingly the reform programme initiated at Trent proved difficult to enforce on the ground, even with the help of the Inquisitions and the episcopal courts. In the spirit of local competition many priests continued to transgress the prescribed boundaries of supernatural service. Nearly 20 per cent of charges of 'superstition' investigated by the Inquisition of Modena between 1580–1600 concerned clerics.[21] The most obvious proof of failure was that cunning-folk and other magical healers remained widespread and popular long after ecclesiastical tribunals went into decline.

The above very brief sketch of attitudes towards popular religion during the sixteenth century provides the necessary background in assessing the extent to which the Reformation affected the role of magic in society. In theory the English Reformation should have removed the clergy from the world of popular magic, and to a considerable extent it did so – by reducing the sacraments, destroying relics, scrapping pilgrimages, denouncing holy wells, banning the trade in sacramentals and condemning their popular usage in healing and the prevention of misfortune, debunking the mystique of Latin prayers by translating them into the vernacular, and refusing to exorcise the possessed. As the example of Richard Napier and others indicates, however, at parish level many Anglican clergymen continued to involve themselves with the magical concerns of their laity, even if their sacred arsenal was badly depleted.

Considering the paucity of pre-Reformation information on English cunning-folk, one way of assessing the impact of religious change upon them is by making comparisons with the situation in those countries that remained Catholic. A central issue in this respect was the relationship between cunning-folk and the priesthood in a communal context. In Catholic countries cunning-folk were in direct competition with the clergy, particularly in the field of diagnosing and healing witchcraft. Officially the Catholic clergy should not have been offering services such as fortune-telling, thief detection and love magic, but in practice some were, and therefore the competition with cunning-folk was all the stronger. One result of this competition may have been to keep fees for some magic services low, as clerical involvement in healing the bewitched usually incurred little direct expense. It is possible, therefore, that the Reformation in England heralded an era of greater prosperity and social importance for cunning-folk. They were as affected by the laws of supply and demand as any other trade or profession, and reduced competition in the unbewitching business may have led to price inflation, as higher prices could be asked for this aspect of their trade. The void left by the clergy's partial withdrawal from popular magic may also have led to the proliferation of cunning-folk. One could certainly seek confirmation for this scenario in the various statements made during the 1540s and 1550s concerning the pernicious growth of such people in the kingdom, a view which was affirmed in the Elizabethan Act of 1563.

Moving from the general to the specific, one of the most conspicuous contrasts between magical practitioners in Anglican England and Catholic Europe concerns the predominantly female trade in love magic. The Inquisition and ecclesiastical court records from Spain and Italy are full of women interrogated for plying love charms and potions. It would also seem, from the Italian evidence at least, that it was quite a specialist female business.²² In England at the same period and beyond, by contrast, there is no evidence of significant gender differentiation in the field of love magic. It was an integral part of trade for both cunning-men and -women. Furthermore, female clients seem to have had no particular preference for female practitioners above men when it came to consultations on matters of the heart. The wealth of information provided by the Mediterranean Inquisitions and ecclesiastical courts has led to suggestions that love magic was more important as a female preoccupation in Italy, Spain and Portugal due to the nature of social relations there. The argument is that women were more culturally restricted in terms of financial independence than in Protestant communities and consequently more materially reliant on men. Love magic, therefore, assumed a greater importance and was a primarily female concern. However, it is necessary to qualify this assumption. First, it is probable that the records disproportionately magnify the gender bias. Female practitioners were more likely to be picked up by the Inquisition and the episcopal courts: partly because the unusual financial independence magic brought them made them more conspicuous; partly because of the association between prostitution and love magic; and partly because of the general perception that women were more drawn to 'superstition'. For these reasons male love magicians are probably under-represented in the archives. Secondly, while the early modern English court records, both secular and ecclesiastical, are not as rich as those of the Mediterranean concerning this aspect of magic, the trade was nevertheless the focus of serious concern in newly Protestant England as well, particularly in aristocratic circles. The Conjuration Act of 1542 specifically mentioned the crime of provoking 'any person to unlawful love'. Furthermore, nineteenth-century prosecutions and ethnographic sources show that love magic was widely practised in England both by professionals and privately.

Even taking male under-representation into account, there is no doubt that women still predominated in the trade in Mediterranean countries. As well as looking for broad cultural explanations, such as the importance of marriage as a survival strategy, perhaps the female dominance of the trade also had something to do with the presence of the male priest-figure in the magical equation. The Catholic clergy had a large stake in certain aspects of magical practice, particularly in unbewitching and healing.

The male domination of other areas, such as treasure-seeking and astrology, was ensured by their greater access to literary knowledge. The two areas where women could successfully vie with men and assert themselves in the occult market were fortune-telling and love magic. With the clergy out of the equation and the male presence reduced, the field of magical practice opened up significantly, giving more opportunity for females to compete and to diversify their business: in other words they could become cunning-women rather than remaining mere fortune-tellers or love specialists. Once this happened, as in post-Reformation England, the professional practice of love magic became less discernibly gendered. This explanation is largely conjecture, but it is a theory that needs considering. More research in other Protestant countries will hopefully throw some light on the matter.

Another area of 'cunning-trade' where there was a significant divergence between England and Western Europe was treasure-seeking. Although there is considerable evidence for treasure conjuration in early modern England, there are no extant cases of English cunning-folk professing to conjure up spirits to find treasure after the early eighteenth century. In contrast, it remained a very popular practice in much of Europe, though by the late eighteenth century the nobility and clergy had largely given it up, leaving the field to cunning-folk and itinerant conjurors. In Europe prosecutions for treasure-seeking continued well into the modern period. In 1750, for example, a cunning-man of Basque origin, Gratien Detcheverry, was tried at Bayonne. Amongst other charges he had claimed to find treasure with the aid of his grimoire. Jeanne-Marie Villefranque gave evidence that Detcheverry promised she would be able to conjure up a considerable horde of treasure if she bought a 'very rare book, full of secrets, called agripa noir'. This was presumably a copy of his own Spanish manuscript of the same name, which was confiscated and publicly burnt by the authorities. The following decade a Brabant cunning-man, Joseph Saucin, was prosecuted by Jean Hausselet after promising but failing to obtain for him a hidden treasure of a thousand florins by invoking the devil. Saucin was flogged, branded and banished. In 1802 a Danish treasure-seeker named Jens Clemmensen was arrested and his copy of *Cyprianus* confiscated. Clemmensen had managed to convince some villagers in Sæbygård that with the aid of his book he had discovered that 'in a mound on Bjel Hill was hidden gold, guarded by a dragon'. He declared he was going to dig it up but required the aid of six men who had to pay him thirty pieces of silver in order to obtain their share.²³ Right up until the mid nineteenth century cunning-folk were still being prosecuted in France for professing to conjure up treasure. In 1808, for instance, a couple were arrested in the department of Oise, one of whom claimed to have gained the necessary powers after signing a pact with the devil. Twenty years later a cunning-man in the Charente was employed by two men to reveal a treasure that was reputed to lie hidden in a field they had recently bought.²⁴

The reason for the early withdrawal of cunning-folk from the trade in England certainly does not relate to any declining belief in a landscape full of buried treasure. Prehistoric burial mounds, standing stones and underground passages continued to be associated with treasure folklore.²⁵ Nor is their any sign of the English displaying less cupidity or consequent stupidity, since gypsy fortune-makers continued to ply their trade successfully until the twentieth century. Although most such itinerants usually only offered to multiply real money by magic, a few also claimed to find hidden treasure.²⁶ But, compared to the situation on the Continent, particularly France, in eighteenth- and nineteenth-century England, there was little popular preoccupation with searching for buried treasure, and cunning-folk did not offer the service. It is debateable whether the latter fact was responsible for the former trend or vice-versa. Both, however, were symptoms of the same factor – the limited distribution of literary magical knowledge.

Treasure conjuration was very much tied up with the tradition of learned magic. If one looks at the evidence from both the early modern and modern periods, the possession of occult texts played a crucial role. In the numerous cases brought before the Mediterranean Inquisitions and episcopal courts, the *Clavicule of Solomon* emerges as an essential tool for any self-respecting treasure-seeker, as it contained the necessary rituals for conjuring spirits either to help find treasure or to control those guarding it. The trade in manuscripts was brisk. At the end of the sixteenth century a Neapolitan magician paid thirty-eight gold coins for a collection of occult manuscripts including the *Fourth Book* and the third book of the *Clavicule*. Another contemporary paid twelve ducats alone for a full copy of the latter.²⁷ Several decades later, the extent of the trade was causing serious concern among Inquisitors. They prosecuted the prime targets, booksellers, but copying went on in many backrooms. When the house of one Venetian love magician was searched in 1654, the authorities found numerous magical texts, including the *Clavicule*, in various stages of completion.[28] Despite the best efforts of the Inquisition, there were large numbers of the *Clavicule* and the *Fourth Book* in circulation throughout Italy well into the eighteenth century – far more than in England. When the treasure-seeking fever subsided amongst the clergy and higher social echelons, there remained a relatively large pool of texts for lower-class magical practitioners to drink from, presumably at a more reasonable price.

More significant, however, was the continental growth of cheap, popular printed versions of the *Clavicule* and the like. The contrast between England and France has already been highlighted in this respect, but one of the ramifications of this can be seen in the relative strength of the treasure-seeking tradition. There was not the same access to relevant knowledge. For a few pence eighteenth- and nineteenth-century French cunning-folk could easily obtain a comprehensive arsenal of early modern information on demonic conjuration. Chapbooks were hardly the most impressive of literary formats, so continental cunning-folk also made written compilations of their contents in more awe-inspiring manuscript books. The act of transcription, particularly onto parchment, imbued the spells and conjurations with a power absent from low-grade print. The existence of these manuscripts, in turn, demonstrates the influence and impact of popular literature on the tradition of folk magic. Thus Detcheverry's 'Agripa Noire' actually had little to do with either Agrippa's works, or the spurious *Fourth Book*, but was rather a compilation of conjurations from a variety of chapbook grimoires, with some definite copying from an edition of *Le Dragon noir*, and was probably translated into Spanish from French sources. The grimoire of an eighteenth-century Breton, François Merret, consists of a compilation of seventy-six useful charms, conjurations and talismans culled from chapbooks such as *Le Dragon rouge*. Jens Clemmensen's manuscript, entitled 'Julius Ciprianus den XII & D. J. Faustus Dreyfaices Höllen Schwang', was also likely to have been compiled from popular publications, as was another contemporary

Norwegian version entitled 'Cyprianus eller Swart-Bogen [Black-Book]', which was owned and added to by Christopher Hammer.[29]

Just as significant as cunning-folk's *access* to such knowledge was the widespread popular *awareness* of the ability to obtain treasure magically. Nineteenth-century French labourers may not have been able to read chapbook grimoires, but many were aware of what they contained and the possibilities they held out to those who could use them. Furthermore, those who could read, and adventurously decided to bypass cunning-folk, could attempt to conjure up treasure themselves. During the early nineteenth century several French men were arrested after persuading people to buy, for twenty francs, a booklet that contained instructions on how to find treasure with the aid of a spirit.[30] The story of treasure-seeking in eighteenth- and nineteenth-century Europe is inextricably tied up with the story of popular print. In England the restricted circulation of magic texts, particularly the *Clavicule*, and subsequently the intriguing absence of chapbook grimoires during the publication boom of the eighteenth century, sent a once thriving activity into decline.

There has been considerable discussion in recent decades concerning the survival of shamanism in the magical traditions of Europe, particularly in the Balkans and north-east Europe. Based on the evidence from early modern witchcraft trials and more recent ethnographic research, it has been mooted that the practices and beliefs of some European cunning-folk, particularly in the south and east, displayed shamanic qualities. This ties in with the wider notion that cunning-folk represented an archaic survival of pan-European, pre-Christian religion. Referring to witchcraft and magic in early modern France, for instance, one historian has stated that, 'cunning-folk are perhaps the most complete embodiment of the conglomeration of Roman Catholic doctrine, magical practices, animism, paganism, and common sense that were all to be found in the villagers' mental world'. Can we really talk of paganism and animism with regard to cunning-folk? More recently, a fine translation of a fascinating German study of a sixteenth-century Alpine healer, Chonrad Stoeckhlin, was published under the altered title of the *Shaman of Oberstdorf*.[31] Shamanism in early modern Germany? England is even further away geographically and culturally from the main focus of this debate, but some engagement with it is instructive.

What is shamanism? The term is a scholarly construct open to a variety of definitions.³² In its broadest usage the term describes any magical healer who achieves an altered state of consciousness by means of drugs, drums, dance or chant, and who once in this state mediates between his or her clients and the 'other world' of spirits and gods. For the purposes of this discussion, though, I shall stick to the policy of restricting the term to the characteristic practices and beliefs surrounding the trance mediums of several Siberian tribal cultures. This follows the distinction made by the influential Mircea Eliade and others, between classic shamanism as found in the specific cultural contexts of Siberia and central Asia, and shamanism in a generic sense, which relates to those healers around the world sharing similar concepts and practices.³³ The Siberian shaman was a magical healer and seer who gained his or her powers from communication with the spirit world by entering an ecstatic trance, usually achieved via the use of drum beats and chants. The wearing of symbolic costumes and headdresses, representing animal or tree forms, was a common feature in their rituals but was not essential. Shamans claimed to make contact with the other world by sending their own spirit there, or via the conduit of spirit helpers who could take on an animal form. Like cunning-folk, the Siberian shaman performed a range of services including healing, detecting lost or stolen goods, and divination. Shamanism, however, was not synonymous with paganism. It was a system of belief that operated within a variety of religious paradigms. Some shamans in the former Soviet Union were, for example, practising Muslims. In a European context, that meant that there was no practical incompatibility between Christianity and shamanistic practices. Indeed, if one accepts a broad definition of shamanism, it could even be argued that nineteenth-century spiritualists were shamans, though there is an obvious cultural gulf between a Siberian shaman and a Victorian medium.

Let us look briefly now at the evidence for shamanism in Europe. Culturally the closest Europeans to the indigenous Siberians were and are the Saami or Lapps, whose traditional arctic territories are now part of Russia, Sweden, Finland and Norway, though for much of the period covered by this book Denmark and Sweden controlled the Saami regions of the latter two countries. During the seventeenth and early eighteenth centuries the Protestant clergy of Scandinavia waged a campaign against what they saw as the 'heathenish' magical practices of the Saami, and their trance magicians in particular. A late example of this concern is evident in a court case in 1682 involving apparent idol worship in Swedish Lappmarken, following which a special witchcraft commission was sent to the region to investigate the continuation of paganism and magic amongst the Saami.[34] Lapland gained the reputation in England of being a stronghold of witchcraft in all its guises. James I mentioned it in his *Daemonologie*, and even during the late eighteenth century an English chapbook provided 'a short description of the famous Lapland Witches'.[35] There is, though, little evidence that either the church or the secular authorities were successful in eradicating the Saami shaman, for the basic reason that the shamanic tradition was apparently already decaying in the region by the early modern period. Trials for witchcraft and magic in the area of present day Finland, of which they were perhaps as many as 2000, reveal little evidence for the widespread practice of shamanism as evinced by the public performance of ecstatic trance, aided by the characteristic ritual drums and 'laula' chants of the Saami.[36] There are certainly references to the continued use of drums, but rarely in direct association with trance ritual. It seems, furthermore, that such drums were invested more generally with magic and divinatory powers beyond their use by shamans. In 1688, for instance, Olaf Sjulsson, a school-trained, Saami village constable, petitioned the authorities to allow Saami herders to use divining drums instead of compasses to find their way back to their huts.[37] It is also likely that non-Saami cunning-folk and diviners adopted drums as a showy accoutrement to impress customers and legitimate their powers, just as English cunning-folk displayed their books of conjuration without actually using them properly.

Despite the lack of explicit references to recognisable shamanism in the court records, there are, nevertheless, examples of associated beliefs concerning trance mediation. Trial records and later ethnographic sources reveal seers and cunning-folk who displayed similar traits. One example is the magical healer Juha Talonpoika, who was accused in 1733 of 'falling into a trance or going dead like the Lapps'. According to his own testimony, however, Juha stated that he experienced shaking, fainting fits, which one witness described as epileptic, during which he received divine inspiration to heal.[38] There is no evidence that Juha ritualistically entered into a soul-travelling trance state like that induced by shamans, and the district court cleared him of any such association. What he and others prosecuted for similar behaviour in the region were practising was in fact a generic form of faith healing apparent even today in the world of Christian evangelism.

Another strong focus of academic interest in shamanic survival in Europe has focused on the *táltosok* of Hungary.[39] As in Finland, some of these magical practitioners also found themselves caught up in the witchcraft trials of the seventeenth and early eighteenth centuries, and subsequently figured prominently in the work of folklorists and ethnographers. A *táltos* was usually marked out at birth by having an extra finger or being born with teeth. As recorded in later folk legends, during childhood they also underwent some profound psychic experience such as being tormented by spirits or having visions of dismemberment. As the *táltos* trial evidence shows – there are records of some twenty-six in all – the *táltos* performed a similar range of tasks as cunning-folk, but healing the bewitched and finding treasure were their particular specialities. A good example was Örzse Tóth, who was tried in 1728. Her abilities were confirmed by her having three double teeth at birth, and her soul frequently journeyed to the other world where she met the Virgin Mary and received medicine directly from Jesus. She also had a helping spirit in the form of a dragon. The powers she gained from these relations enabled her to cure the sick, detect thieves, unbewitch, bewitch, see hidden treasure, and predict deaths.[40]

Some scholars have felt comfortable with translating *táltosok* as 'shamans'.[41] One of the main reasons is that some *táltosok* claimed that on certain occasions their souls would join those of others, often in animal form, to do spirit battle against evil forces to protect their villages and towns. Similar communal soul-battlers have been identified elsewhere in Europe, most famously the *benandanti* investigated by the Venetian Inquisition, who claimed to leave their bodies at night to protect the crops of their community against witches.[42] Some *táltosok* also assumed solitary soul patrols. Örzse Tóth claimed that during a recent earthquake her town would have sunk had her spirit not gone around the place to protect it.[43] Despite these characteristics it is unwise to equate the figure of the *táltos* with the shaman – and for good reason. Crucially, there is little or no evidence that the *táltos* spirit journeys, like those of Siberian shamans, were induced by publicly performed, ritually induced trance states. Instead they usually occurred during sleep, were the result of supposedly innate clairvoyance, or, as with some Finnish seers, were brought on by fits, real or otherwise. In Siberia, shamans were only one group amongst other magical practitioners offering similar services, so their importance in their respective cultural groups should not be overemphasised. Likewise in Hungary, and in central and south-eastern Europe more generally, there was a wide diversity of magical practitioners, some sharing similar characteristics to the *táltos*, and by association elements of archetypal shamanism, others operating using books of conjuration.[44]

If shamanism is an inappropriate description for the source of the *táltosok*'s power, what about calling them cunning-folk? The leading Hungarian experts on the subject, Éva Pócs and Gábor Klaniczay, refrain from labelling the *táltosok* as cunning-folk, though another eminent scholar, Tekla Dömötör, apparently had no reservations about including them under such an umbrella term. Her basis for doing so was by comparing the *táltosok* with the role and practices of English cunning-folk as described in the work of Alan Macfarlane and Keith Thomas. As has already been mentioned, court records suggest that most *táltosok* carried on a range of practices and functions similar to those of cunning-folk. Furthermore, they also reveal that with regard to treasure-seeking, for example, *táltosok* did not rely solely on their spirit relations, but, like cunning-folk, also employed practical tools such as scrying-mirrors; and in other areas of divination they employed mechanistic methods such as the interpretation of fingernails.[45] Yet there remains one significant difference between the *táltosok* and English cunning-folk: the latter sought spirit aid through ritual conjurations derived from literary sources, whereas the former used their innate ability to tap the spirit world. The results were often the same, however. If a non-Hungarian term is to be applied then cunning-folk seems the most appropriate. The one important exception concerns the battling *táltos*. There is little evidence for English or other western European cunning-folk engaging in either soul-gatherings or communal protection programmes. In this respect, at least, some but by no means all those described as *táltos*, ought to be made distinct from both cunning-folk and shamans.

Moving further westwards, the link with shamanism becomes even more culturally tenuous, despite similar concepts and motifs being found. This is because the idea of soul travel or communication with the spirit world was not culturally specific, let alone definably shamanistic. While there was presumably a commercial motive in labelling Chonrad Stoeckhlin a 'shaman', there was also a credible interpretive reason in that he claimed that his magical abilities derived from his periodic travels with the *Nachtschar* or 'phantoms of the night'. These journeys would begin with the appearance of an angel guide, at which point he would, in his own words, be 'overcome by lethargy, an unconsciousness'.[46] One might call this state trance-like, but considering these visits mostly occurred at night, as with the *benandanti*, one might also describe it as sleep. Once in this state, whatever it was, his soul left his body and joined the travelling spirits for two to three hours at a time. But the concept of journeying with the denizens of the other world, whether fairies, trolls, angels, demons or spirits of the dead, was widespread across Europe, including early modern England. So too was the notion that some cunning-folk derived powers from such supernatural beings, though this tradition was stronger and lasted longer in Ireland and Sicily. In both these regions cunning-folk were thought to have gained the ability to heal fairy-inspired illnesses from special contact with such beings. The Inquisition accounts of the Sicilian *donas de fuera* reveal a rich tradition of magical practitioners claiming fairy powers, enabling them to offer a similar range of services as English cunning-folk. The *donas*, mostly women, said they had 'sweet blood' which obliged them to travel regularly in spirit with groups of fairies, with whom they indulged in singing, dancing, feasting and lovemaking.

In England there are numerous accounts from both the early modern and modern periods of people claiming they had taken part in nocturnal fairy revels, though such experiences were usually portrayed as chance encounters rather than the result of design. Unlike the experiences claimed by Stoeckhlin, furthermore, the *donas* and other continental fairy healers, English meetings with the fairies, like those confessed to by John Walsh, were usually conducted corporally and not spiritually. Yet, while the notion of fairy fraternising was certainly a vibrant aspect of English popular *belief*, it was not as integrated into the world of popular *magic* as elsewhere. Whereas in Ireland the problem of fairy-inspired illness and fairy changelings continued until the last century, in England it had largely disappeared by the mid sixteenth century. The associated need to acquire fairy knowledge was accordingly reduced.

Examining the varying emphasis magical practitioners placed on fairy relations and innate spirit mediation at a regional level leads us back to those two major cultural influences – religion and literacy. All the evidence points to the conclusion that in post-Reformation England cunning-folk could rarely build a reputation solely on birthright or fairy association, unlike the *táltosok*, *donas* and their ilk. For cunning-folk the possession of literacy and literature was crucial, the inference being that when it came to assessing their worth, people placed more emphasis on the acquisition of written knowledge than other sources of magical inspiration. Public criteria and expectation shaped the way cunning-folk constructed their reputation. Aspiring but illiterate English cunning-folk were handicapped, and the odds were stacked against them achieving real success because, unlike some of their continental counterparts, the fairy source strategy had limited client appeal. Stoeckhlin, on the other hand, lived in a culture where illiteracy was not necessarily a professional handicap. As a herdsman he had already acquired some reputation for healing skills, but to broaden his practice he could tap into the profound belief in the *Nachtschar* as a source of power. 'It was his participation in this myth', Behringer noted, 'that enabled him to take on a charismatic role in his community.'[47] Whether he made up the stories of his soul journeys, or whether he really experienced some form of altered state of consciousness, is not important because the purpose of his stories was primarily to legitimate his claim to special knowledge, and that is precisely what he achieved. It is also surely no coincidence that the Sicilian *donas* were lowly women, as, for that matter, were the remaining seventeenth century English fairy healers. To be female and poor was the greatest barrier to literacy.[48]

It is tempting to link the differential importance of literacy in popular magic to the impact of Protestantism. Maybe the Protestant emphasis on the solitary contemplation of the Bible, which obviously required both its translation into the vernacular and the encouragement of a degree of popular literacy, elevated the popular importance of written knowledge to a higher degree than in Catholic and Orthodox areas. There is certainly strong evidence to confirm that literacy was more widespread in Protestant regions during the early modern period.[49] In this sense, the cautious growth of literacy did not banish the fairy but rather reduced the potency of fairy power. This is particularly apparent in Protestant Celtic areas like Wales, where fairy lore remained an established strand of belief well into the nineteenth century, but where the reputation of cunning-folk or *dyn hysbys* did not rest on the possession of fairy magic. Perhaps we should see John Walsh as operating on the cusp of change brought about by the Reformation – the last period in England when the fairy was as mighty as the word.

While fairy encounters, whether in spirit or in body, were usually beyond the direct control of the individual, self-induced soul travel, as practised by shamans, was also an aspect of English witchcraft belief. In England, however, it was usually the witch and not the conjuror who was believed to send his or her spirit around and about the community at night, usually to torment people and horses in their sleep. We find such beliefs particularly in relation to the physical experience of sleep paralysis – or 'nightmare', 'hag-riding' and 'witch-riding' as it was variously known – which involved nocturnal hallucinations and a sense of suffocating immobility.[50] Sufferers claimed to see witches flying though their bedroom windows and straddling them. Even in mid nineteenth-century Surrey, there is a reliable report of a woman who believed a witch came through her window at night and took her away on nocturnal flights until four in the morning. Her husband, who explained to a local magistrate that she did not know who it was who whirled her out of bed, had employed a cunning-man to find out. Her flights were physically and mentally distressing, and as her husband reported, 'when she comes back, poor thing, she's all in a pucker, like'.[51] We therefore find the same fundamental belief in, and perhaps experience of, voluntary and involuntary soul flight in Victorian England as in sixteenth-century Italy and eighteenth-century Hungary, but it is less apparent, and differently focused and culturally interpreted. As has been observed, 'the traits which underpin Siberian shamanism occur naturally in individuals throughout humanity, although they are given different cultural expression at particular times and places.'[52] Once such widely shared core beliefs and experiences as soul travel, spirit communication and fairy gatherings are recognised, referring to the shamanistic characteristics of magical practitioners loses its relevance in a European context. That said, neither should the acceptance of this reductionist point blind us to the significant variations between magic practitioners in different European cultures at different times, and also the diversity of popular beliefs that surrounded them, and which they helped to shape.

This leads us back, in a roundabout way, to the applicability of the term 'pagan' to cunning-folk. The origins and exact meaning of the word are problematic, and this is not the place to debate them. But in reference to Europe it can be uncontroversially used it to describe the pre-Christian worship of multiple gods and spirits. By the medieval period the church may not have obliterated all signs of pre-Christian beliefs and practices in England, but it had effectively suppressed all vestiges of paganism as a religion and as a mode of worship. Even in areas of Scandinavia and the Baltic, where paganism was widespread several centuries after its demise in western and southern Europe, there is little evidence for explicitly pagan activities beyond the fifteenth century.[53] Those pre-Christian beliefs and practices that remained only did so because they were assimilated into the Christian corpus of belief either at a popular or official level – the two were not necessarily the same. Some simple healing charms used in England into the twentieth century, for instance, have direct origins in known pagan charms. The names of Germanic pagan gods were merely replaced by biblical figures.[54] Yet this process of assimilation was so complete that, although some such pre-Christian magic continued, to label it pagan is to misrepresent the people who used it and the context in which it was used.

As lay magical healers, cunning-folk certainly filled a pre-Christian role in society, just as the priest occupied a pre-Christian role as official mediator between the living and the spirit world, between the mortal and the immortal. But few historical insights are to be gained from seeking an archaic or shamanic lineage for cunning-folk. Such people were products of the religious cultures of their time and place, and they operated within the social boundaries and belief systems of their present, not their distant past. In pagan Europe there were people like cunning-folk, just as there were blacksmiths, weavers and potters, but to emphasise their pagan roots is about as meaningful or meaningless as pointing out the pagan origins of early modern potting.

# 8

## Cunning-Folk in the Twentieth Century

When people first hear about cunning-folk two questions often crop up: 'Why did they disappear?' and 'Are there still any cunning-folk today?' This final chapter will address these interrelated questions, but to do so properly it is necessary to consider the existence of cunning-folk on a conceptual as well as a physical level. I have reiterated throughout this book that cunning-folk should be defined by the range of services they provided, and most crucially by their role as unbewitchers. Should we also categorise them as being bound by the past? In other words, is it appropriate to use the term to describe people offering similar services in contemporary English society? One might dismiss this as a rather pedantic point, but if someone today labels themselves as a cunning-man, wise-woman or white witch they are self-consciously claiming to be part of a long-held tradition, and assuming a role which flourished and had meaning in a type of society substantially divorced from our own. Before considering further the applicability of the concept in today's society we need go back and trace the decline of cunning-folk during the early years of the twentieth century.

There is no doubt that by the time of the First World War there were far fewer cunning-folk operating in England than there had been fifty years before, and by the 1940s they seem to have disappeared altogether. The evidence for this comes from two main observations. First, that court cases involving cunning-folk dried up in the first decade of the century, and secondly, ethnographic and folklore sources from the period reveal less and less information concerning cunning-folk, or at least relating to those still active. In contrast, there is plenty of evidence for the continued popularity of astrologers and fortune-tellers of all sorts. They and gypsy magicians were frequently prosecuted up until the legal changes brought about by the 1951 Fraudulent Mediums Act. The reason the prognosticators thrived while cunning-folk disappeared can be firmly attributed to the declining relevance of witchcraft in English society.[1] Quite simply, without witches there were no cunning-folk. The economic and social structure of English society underwent profound changes during the late nineteenth and early twentieth century. Close-knit communities whose existence had been based on local economies in which barter was as strong a currency as cash, where oral traditions and local beliefs had been maintained through anchor families who had stayed put for generations, and where everyone had a stake in agriculture or livestock rearing, disintegrated under the impact of urbanisation and mechanisation, and of expanding national and international markets. As a result of these broad changes, and many other related developments, the scope for witchcraft accusations was reduced. At the same time, the growth of agricultural insurance, personal banking and an embryonic welfare state lessened the financial impact of ill-health and livestock deaths. When there was no longer a need to explain misfortunes in terms of witchcraft, people no longer gained reputations as witches, and cunning-folk effectively went out of business. It was not only the basis of their trade that was undermined, though, but also the source of their power. As the literate section of society shifted from being the minority to the majority, witchcraft lost its mystique, and the power popularly invested in cunning-folk diminished accordingly.

One of the last cunning-folk prosecuted in England was the widow Ellen Hayward (b. 1836) of Cinderford. Her trial at the Littledean petty sessions in 1906 was reported both locally and nationally, and the information provided by the newspapers gives us a useful insight into the role of a wise-woman in Edwardian rural society. First, though, we must step back in time a little because Hayward's first brush with the press had occurred a year earlier.[2] In May 1905 around fifty pounds was stolen from the house of John Markey, a resident of May Hill. Markey suspected a neighbour and a warrant was procured to search his house, but no trace of the stolen money was found. Frustrated by such official means, Markey went to consult Ellen Hayward. According to villagers, Hayward instructed Markey to look into a crystal and he would see a vision of the thief. What he saw was the face of one of his own family: the consequences of this revelation were to be terrible for the Markeys. Mental illness plagued the family and the introduction of Ellen Hayward in their affairs acted as a trigger. To begin with, one of John's daughters, Mrs Barnes, and his granddaughter, started smashing up their house and had to be removed to Gloucester Asylum. Then John's wife broke down under the strain and ran off. A search party was sent to look for her but no trace could be found. She emerged from Newent Wood several days later complaining that she was being troubled by witches. During her disappearance the state of mind of John's second son, George, deteriorated rapidly, and he soon began to rage uncontrollably, talking of 'witchery' and breaking whatever came to hand. He ran off bootless down the road, and was later picked up as a wandering lunatic. He had only recently married for the second time, his first wife having died in an asylum.

Hayward was hardly to blame for these tragic events, but the focus of attention soon fixed upon her. Although the sensational events in May Hill had been widely reported in the national press, not even Ellen could have foreseen that the affair would become a parliamentary matter. On the 31 May, Mr McVeagh, Member of Parliament for Down South, stood up in the House of Commons and asked the Home Secretary, Mr Akers Douglas, if he was aware of the 'practice of witchcraft' at May Hill and other parts of Gloucestershire. 'In view of the alarm in the locality,' he went on, 'what action would be taken by the authorities to suppress witchcraft?' Akers Douglas replied that he had made enquiries about the Markeys and the 'supposed witch', and confirmed that 'if sufficient evidence is forthcoming to justify a prosecution, proceedings will be taken by the local police against the woman who was consulted'. In the event, no further proceedings were taken regarding the May Hill affair. Nevertheless, all the bad press led Hayward to agree to an interview with a journalist in the hope of clearing her reputation. Her hopes were to be dashed because the journalist did not portray her in a flattering light, reporting that 'her hair is tangled and tousled and ragged, grey wisps hanging about her unquestionably dirty, old face'. Not surprisingly, Hayward steered the conversation away from the subject of witchcraft and magic, and basically enlarged upon her role as an herbalist. 'I have cured hundreds of tumours and thousands of sores', she said, and further observed, 'I have cured eight cases of cancer, but you can't cure a cancer when it has spread in more than thirteen different directions'.

The newspapers soon lost interest in Hayward, as did the politicians, and her normal business resumed, though her spell in the limelight made her more cautious in what she said and did for her clients. She made sure never to demand payment, for example, it being taken for granted that customers would offer her money anyway, and she also stopped keeping casebooks. Yet, despite this policy of discretion, in May 1906 she found herself in court charged 'for that between 24 November, 1905, and 1 March 1906, at Cinderford, [she] unlawfully did use certain craft or means or device, to wit, by pretended witchcraft, deceive and impose on one of His Majesty's subjects'. That subject was James Davis an illiterate, sixty-six-year-old hurdle-maker of Pauntley, Worcestershire. Davis deposed that the previous year two cows and three of his pigs had fallen ill, and a 'travelling woman' had confirmed his suspicions that a woman named Amos had bewitched them out of spite. Having gathered from the newspapers 'what the wise woman at Cinderford had done in the Markey case', he decided to call upon her help in the matter and sent her 2s. 6d. in a letter written by his sister Hannah Elton. Shortly after he went to see Hayward, travelling a distance of over thirty miles, and told her he wanted the witchcraft removed from his surviving pig. After he had paid her another five shillings, she gave him some unspecified advice, and the pig got better. Weeks later the pig had a relapse, however, and Davis himself was taken seriously ill. Despite his poor condition, in December he undertook another long journey down to Cinderford and asked Hayward to 'put him right'. She said he was suffering from influenza, and he gave her a sovereign, which she said was too much. Hayward continued in bad health, and began to suspect that Hayward had been paid to put a spell upon him. At the end of February he went to see Hayward for a third and last time, rebuking her saying, 'I should think he gave you a good sum of money to serve me like this'. He told her that, if she did not take the spell off soon, 'he would put it in Government's hands', to which she replied in consternation, that 'she was afraid it was another Markey's case'. Davis believed his enemies, Mr and Mrs Amos, were behind his misery, and asked Hayward to 'put it heavily' on them to stop, offering her another 2s. 6d., but she refused. She gave him some medicine, and in a subsequent letter wrote that 'God would take the spell off'. God did not, so Davis reported her to the police. On the 7 May Police Constable Packer was sent down to the Newent district to make enquiries, and the following day he received the following letter from Hayward explaining her business:

> I have been ill twelve weeks, and cannot remember any man coming to me from Pauntley or Redmarley. Numbers of people have been to see me for different complaints, and have brought me money. I have given people advice for treatment of pigs, cows, and horses, but I cannot give dates. I tell them what to do, and they put it down on paper. I have received postal orders from people, but cannot say who. I have been very cautious with my advice since Markey's affair. My profession is a herbalist. I have not taken the names and addresses of people visiting me for over twelve months, I am not able to, I am seventy years of age. I have studied physiology, but have not done any for four years. I do no harm to nobody.

When called before the magistrates, Hayward said that she placed her faith in God, who 'had always promised that his children should not want', and claimed the medicine she gave Davis was merely a cup of tea. Hayward evidently had many satisfied customers, since the court received numerous letters testifying to her successes as a herbal healer. Much to her relief, the magistrates dismissed the case, and she was able to return to relative anonymity.[3]

A couple of weeks after the trial an anonymous well-wisher was moved to write an indignant and rather rambling letter to the local newspaper. It was signed 'ANTI-OPPRESSION' and read as follows:

> Sir, is there no way, in the interests of the community and our boasted civilization and good name, of putting a stop to the persecution of Mrs Hayward? Everybody locally knows the preposterous suggestion of witchcraft has no grounds in fact. Certainly the local magistrates do, and so does the police, I think. Who is at the bottom of it? Is it envious doctors, or is the police anxious for a job? ... I think it is time the public, scores of whom have benefited by the old lady's advice and service, should take some form of publicly protesting against the spying and prosecuting, which may easily come to persecuting of this particular woman. I suggest, in the meantime, that the local magistrates, who know, or can easily know, that the woman makes no sort of claims to witchcraft, as has been proved twice, and has done an enormous lot of good in relieving suffering – these magistrates should give the tip to the chief constable, or superintendent of police, or who ever is responsible, to stop it ... I think the public ought to show their indignation in some way, for they talk, or a good many of them do, indignantly enough.[4]

The author of this letter was obviously educated, and apparently unaware of Hayward's magical dealings. Judging from the fact that similar letters had been sent to the local magistrates, she had a pool of clients who saw her only as a herbalist – and a good one. While some people in the region still looked upon Hayward as a mistress of magic, a wise-woman, the focus of her reputation was shifting to her role as a natural healer. Over the centuries numerous examples can be found of cunning-folk who maintained a separate trade as 'respectable' herbalists, so Hayward's dual reputation was not unusual in itself, but one gets the impression that for the last of the cunning-folk orthodox herbalism, as distinct from the use of herbs in conjunction with charms, became increasingly important as unbewitching and the detection business tailed off. The writing was on the wall as far as cunning-trade was concerned, and to protect those aspects of business that were still viable, cunning-folk such as Hayward perhaps resisted getting involved with the residual demand for witch-doctoring. By doing so, they effectively contributed to the demise of their old selves. This may have left people like James Davis unsatisfied with their treatment, but Davis represented a dwindling customer base. Another aspect of this trend was the move away from diagnosing to merely supplying remedies. By and large the only reason sick people went to cunning-folk was to have their suspicions of witchcraft confirmed. As people stopped seeking such explanations they were more ready to accept doctors' diagnoses, and to take their medicine, only resorting to alternative medicine when orthodox treatment failed. It is highly unlikely that Hayward's cancer patients were diagnosed by her. She merely provided an alternative avenue of cure rather than an alternative explanation of cause.

There is some evidence that a few cunning-folk carried on business into the 1930s in areas like the west country, but a close examination of such reports usual reveal that most of those referred to as 'white witches' and 'wise-men' were actually charmers. Thus, in a flurry of articles and letters on the topic of 'white witches' in Devon newspapers in October 1934, the main details actually concerned charmers, particularly those who continued to cure ringworm.[5] Similarly, Ruth Tongue in her book of Somerset folklore, much of it collected during the first half of the century, referred frequently to the presence of conjurors and white witches, but once again the activities described are usually those of charmers. In the 1930s the Cornish folklorist and antiquarian William Paynter also presented some evidence for the continued resort to cunning-folk but confused the issue by talking of palmists and astrologers in the same context.[6] It is true that in parts of western England charmers of ringworm, warts and internal bleeding in livestock continued to operate in significant numbers until the 1970s, and a few still do, but there is a big difference both conceptually and in practice between them and cunning-folk.[7] Over the border into Wales, an article by a Montgomeryshire doctor, W. LL. Davies, provides a useful glimpse into the last years of cunning-trade during the late 1930s. According to Davies, at the time of writing Montgomeryshire conjurors were mainly dealing with failed butter-making, animal diseases 'such as lameness, growths of all kinds, warts, etc', and 'minor ailments in the farmer's family, such as warts, dog-bites, boils, wounds of all kinds, bleeding, and even indigestion'.[8] The activities of cunning-folk, it would seem, had largely been reduced to the farmyard. No thief detection, no love magic, and the only witch-doctoring was centred on the stable and dairy. Davies gave no recent accounts of human unbewitching, stating only that the belief in witches and witchcraft had been widespread 'until very lately'.[9] One of the last places the nefarious work of witches was to be found was in the churn, but farm butter-making was on its last legs at this time, and when the churns fell into disuse so to did the role of cunning-folk. Once again, charmers continued to be called on, while cow-doctors and herbalists dealt with the other residual elements of rural cunning-trade.

Claims have been made that the last of the cunning-folk passed on their magical knowledge to Wiccans and other modern 'witches', thereby maintaining a continuous link with the magical as well as the herbal traditions of the past. The most influential of these claims concerns an Essex wise-man named George Pickingill of Canewdon, Essex. Pickingill died in 1909 and was certainly one of the last practising cunning-folk in the county, but he was never a major regional figure like William Brewer, James Tuckett, James Murrell or John Wrightson. The only reason he attracted so much interest is because in 1962 the author Eric Maple included an account of his activities, stitched together from interviews with elderly residents from Canewdon and surrounding villages, in a populist history of witchcraft.[10] During the following decade a story began to gain serious currency in pagan witchcraft circles that

Pickingill had been a hereditary high priest of the 'Old Religion', and was responsible for nine secret covens of pagan witches. It was even put forward as fact that the infamous Aleister Crowley had been a member of one of these covens and that masons and occultists from all over Britain, America and Europe had sought instruction from the great master Pickingill.[11] The leading historian of pagan witchcraft, has carefully investigated these fanciful claims, and found no factual basis to support any of them.[12] My own understanding of the evidence leads me to the same conclusion. 'Old George' was a simple rural cunning-man whose small world of village affairs never crossed with that of middle-class occultists. He received a Christian burial and the idea that he was a pagan priest would probably make him turn in his grave. The desire to find an ancient inheritance has led some modern witches to accept seductive but entirely unsubstantiated claims, which have only served to undermine less sensational but more reasonable connections between the popular wizards of the past and the witches of the present.

A few modern healers have directly inherited simple healing charms, herbal knowledge and divinatory skills from a continuous line stretching back at least to the oral traditions of the nineteenth century, and so can legitimately claim to have a true link with the past. Most, however, have rediscovered and recreated the popular magical practices of that past from the work of historians, folklorists and neo-pagan writers on the subject. Yet this does not necessarily invalidate claims to be the heirs to cunning-folk. After all, the success of many such people was also built upon their access to literary sources rather than on a continuous oral tradition of folk magic. Fundamentally, there is little intrinsic difference between an aspiring conjuror today learning practical invocations from grimoires, obtained from the esoteric section of an Internet bookshop, and a nineteenth-century cunning-man who gained his knowledge from second-hand books ordered from John Denley or George Bumstead. The material in both instances may even be the same. The significant difference lies in the wider relationship between society and literature. Because literacy is no longer seen as a special ability, and no longer attracts the same level of popular respect, today's self-styled wise-women and -men will never achieve the same level of power, influence and social relevance in their respective communities as did their historic namesakes. Yet access to literary knowledge enables them to offer the same range of services, and can teach them how to employ the same sorts of magical practices, such as urine-scrying, witch-bottles, the construction of talismans and even the long defunct sieve and shears, all of which have long disappeared from the oral pool of knowledge. To function, however, aspiring contemporary cunning-folk have to have a client base that *demands* these services, otherwise they are not cunning-folk as characterised by what they did and how they were perceived by society over the previous five centuries and beyond.

Modernity and cunning-folk are not incompatible concepts. There is nothing essentially anachronistic about a cunning-woman who drives a car and who contacts clients on a mobile phone. As anthropologists have shown, the fear of bewitchment is real enough in some areas of Europe today, and consequently people identifiable as cunning-folk continue to exist, albeit with a substantially reduced clientele.[13] For sure, there is a big gap between the nineteenth century and the present in terms of the sophistication of personal communications, but so there was between the world of an Elizabethan cunning-woman and a Victorian practitioner who used the penny post and visited her clients by train. The continuity lies in the nature of their business, which changed relatively little and it was not until the early twentieth century that the continuity was broken. How many contemporary British white-witches regularly practise both thief magic and unbewitching on a commercial basis? A self-styled wise-woman today who does not deal with bewitched clients is not a wise-woman as defined historically. Witchcraft was the glue that held the concept of cunning-folk together. When the unbewitching business dried up during the early twentieth century, cunning-folk soon ceased to exist both in practice and in popular discourse.

This is not to belittle the role of modern magical healers. They continue to provide relief and comfort to people, just as cunning-folk did. Rather, it is an attempt to clarify where they *really* stand in relation to those formerly described as cunning-folk. People who refer to themselves as such ought to be fully aware of their relationship to their historical namesakes, and be aware of the conceptual and social differences that separate them. Many contemporary magical healers do show such awareness. Some feel a kinship with the practitioners of what they call the 'Old Craft', but refrain from explicitly labelling themselves.

Some feel no need to claim to be part of a continuous, indigenous tradition at all. Others cling to the ideas and practices of popular magic but seek to define themselves in new ways. Perhaps the most interesting of these new definitions is that of 'hedge witch', which effectively entered the language following the publication of Rae Beth's book of the same name. The term has now caught on both in this country and in the USA. Like cunning-folk, hedge witches are solitary practitioners and similarly practise herbalism, divination, and simple spells and rituals using everyday objects rather than the grand accoutrements of ceremonial magic – closer to the activities of rural James Baker and his magic spoon than the urban Wycherley and his consecrated sword. Despite these similarities, there is still a considerable gulf between hedge witches and cunning-folk, not only in relation to the unbewitching trade, but also from a religious point of view. Cunning-folk were essentially Christian. Whether conscientious churchgoers or not, they employed the Bible and Christian rites and rituals. Hedge witches, on the other hand, are mostly pagans in some form or another. They worship nature and have an animistic conception of the physical environment. This, in turn, is mirrored in the content of the spells and charms they use.

While many modern magical healers may feel an affinity with cunning-folk, few are on the same spiritual and moral wavelength. On a social and emotional level it is doubtful that many contemporary healers would get on well with the cunning-folk of the past. Honest, conscientious and effective cunning-folk certainly existed, but in general they were commercially hard-nosed, possessed a cynical streak, and were rather too prone to unscrupulous activities. I am not sure this is the sort of inheritance to which modern practitioners really want to lay claim. Whenever money mixes with the practice of magic, there will always be those who seek to exploit and defraud. Maybe the days of 'traditional' cunning-folk have not gone for good, though at present there is no market to sustain them in this country. Situations vacant. Only the following need apply: men and women with prior working experience outside the business, and entrepreneurial acumen. Must have competent literacy skills, possess own books of the trade, herbal experience, good divinatory skills, practical knowledge of conjuration, and intimate understanding of witchcraft. Working knowledge of astrology desirable. Own transport advisable. Formal dress optional.

The candidate will work from home, but must expect to be on call at all times, and be prepared to work with animals. Lack of scruples no barrier. Start of employment: when sufficient numbers of people complain of bewitchment once again.

# Notes

*Notes to Introduction*

1. Hutton, *Triumph*, p. 98. See also Davies, *Witchcraft, Magic and Culture*, p. 215.
2. Crawford, 'Evidences for Witchcraft in Anglo-Saxon England'; Jolly, *Popular Religion*; Griffiths, *Aspects of Anglo-Saxon Magic*; Flint, *Rise of Magic*.
3. See Cockayne (ed.), *Leechdoms*; Grattan and Singer, *Anglo-Saxon Magic*; Grendon, 'Anglo-Saxon Charms'; Pollington, *Leechcraft*; Cameron, 'Anglo-Saxon Medicine and Magic'.
4. Heywood, *Wise Woman*, sig. D4r.
5. Macfarlane, *Witchcraft*.
6. Davies, *Witchcraft, Magic and Culture*, pp. 214–29; Davies, *People Bewitched*, pp. 27–92; Davies, 'Cunning-Folk in the Medical Market-Place'; Davies, 'Cunning-Folk in England and Wales'; Hutton, *Triumph*, ch. 6; de Blécourt, 'Witch Doctors, Soothsayers'. See also Smith, 'The Wise Man'; Maple, *Dark World*, ch. 8.
7. Sharpe, *Instruments*, pp. 66–70, provides a brief but useful account.
8. One exception is the work of Roy Porter. See, for example, Porter, 'The People's Health'.

*Notes to Chapter 1: Cunning-Folk and the Law*

1. Crawford, 'Evidence for Witchcraft in Anglo-Saxon England', pp. 107–8.
2. Peters, *The Magician, the Witch and the Law*, pp. 112–20; Jones, 'Political Uses of Sorcery', 670–87; Kieckhefer, *Magic in the Middle Ages*, pp. 96–100.
3. Raine (ed.), *Depositions ... Durham*, p. 29.
4. Hale, *Precedents*, pp. 32, 102.
5. Kittredge, *Witchcraft*, p. 187.
6. Thomas, *Calendar of Plea and Memoranda*, 20 January 1375.
7. Riley, *Memorials*, pp. 472, 462.
8. Riley, *Memorials*, p. 518.

9. Martin, 'Clerical Life in the Fifteenth Century', p. 377.
10. Kittredge, *Witchcraft*, p. 197.
11. Nichols, *Narratives*, pp. 334–35.
12. Nichols, *Diary of Henry Machyn*, p. 251.
13. *Articles ... of Our Moste Dread Soveraigne Lady Elizabeth*, sig. B1r; Thomas, *Religion*, p. 541.
14. Coxe, *Short Treatise*, p. 10.
15. See, Thomas, *Religion*; Sharpe, *Instruments*.
16. *Disclosing of a Late Counterfeyted Possession by the Devyl*, sig. A2r; *Rehearsall Both Straung and True, of Hainous and Horrible Actes Committed by Elizabeth Stile*, sig. A2v; *True and Just Recorde, of the Information ... Taken at S. Oses*, sig. A3r.
17. James, *Daemonologie*, p. 76.
18. Thomas, *Religion*, p. 309.
19. *Lawes against Witches, and Coniuration*, pp. 6–7.
20. Cunnington, *Records*, p. 278; Winstedt, 'The Squires Family', p. 147.
21. Raine, *Depositions ... York*, p. 101.
22. Cockburn (ed.), *Calendar of Assize Records: Hertfordshire Indictments*, p. 2; Cockburn (ed.), *Calendar of Assize Records: Surrey Indictments*, pp. 129–30; Macfarlane, *Witchcraft*, p. 256; *Calendar of State Papers Domestic*.
23. Bund, *Worcester County Records*, p. 492; Atkinson, *Quarter Sessions Records*, p. 20.
24. Somerset Record Office, QS 112/72 and 118/30–1.
25. Harley, 'Historians as Demonologists'; de Blécourt, 'Witch Doctors, Soothsayers'; de Blécourt, 'Cunning Women, from Healers to Fortune Tellers'.
26. *Witch of Wapping*, p. 5.
27. *True and Just Recorde, of the Information ... Taken at S. Oses*, sig. A2r-A2v.
28. Raine, *Depositions ... York*, pp. 64–65.
29. Macfarlane, *Witchcraft*, p. 128.
30. Stearne, *A Confirmation*, p. 11.
31. Thomas, *Religion*, p. 311.
32. Purvis, *Tudor Parish Documents*, p. 199; Tyler, 'The Church Courts at York', p. 95; visitation of the diocese of Coventry and Lichfield, 1623. (Thanks to Darren Oldridge for reporting the latter case.)
33. See, for example, Gowing, *Domestic Dangers*; Houlbrooke, *Church Courts*; Ingram, *Church Courts*; Emmison, *Elizabethan Life*; Sharpe, *Defamation*; Tyler, 'The Church Courts at York'; Rushton, 'Women, Witchcraft, and Slander'.
34. Ewen, *Witchcraft*, p. 448. (Thanks to Darren Oldridge for reporting the 1636 case.)

35. Perkins, *A Discourse*, p. 255.
36. Bernard, *Guide*, sig. A6r.
37. Thompson, *Diocese of Lincoln*, pp. 210–11; Peacock, 'Extracts from Lincoln Episcopal Visitations', p. 262; Hale, *Precedents*, p. 163; Hussey, 'Visitations', p. 21; Purvis, *Tudor Parish Documents*, p. 200; Hale, *Precedents*, p. 219.
38. Macfarlane, *Witchcraft*, p. 285.
39. Thomas, *Religion*, p. 312.
40. Gaskill, *Crime and Mentalities*, p. 90; Curry, *Prophecy*, p. 105; Macfarlane, *Witchcraft*, p. 67.
41. Macfarlane, *Witchcraft*, pp. 68, 72.
42. *Articles ... Glocester* (1635), sig. B2v; *Articles ... Buckingham* (1639), sig. B4r.
43. *Articles ... Norwich* (1606), sig. B2r.
44. Gowing, *Domestic Dangers*, pp. 32–34.
45. Brinkworth, 'The Laudian Church in Buckinghamshire', p. 50.
46. Ravenscroft, *Dame Dobson*, p. 70.
47. Trotman, 'Seventeenth Century Treasure-Seeking', pp. 220–1.
48. *Breslaw's Last Legacy*, p. 40.
49. *Life and Mysterious Transactions of Richard Morris*; Dawson, *History of Skipton*, pp. 390–94.
50. *Gentleman's Magazine*, 31 (1761), p. 187; Gaskill, *Crime and Mentalities*, p. 116 n. 155.
51. Fisher, *Notes and Recollections*, pp. 22–23.
52. Phillips, *History of the Vale of Neath*, pp. 582–83.
53. Howell, *Cobbett's Complete Collection of State Trial*, ii, p. 1052n.; cited in Gaskill, *Crime and Mentalities*, p. 116.
54. *Leeds Mercury*, 28 February 1801; *The Times*, 25 April, 27 November 1801.
55. *Staffordshire Advertiser*, 18 October 1823.
56. See Davies, *Witchcraft, Magic and Culture*, pp. 54–56; Perkins, *Reform of Time*, p. 42.
57. *Gloucester Journal*, 24 July 1830; *The Times*, 24 July 1830.
58. Davies, 'Cunning-Folk in England and Wales', p. 101; Davies, *People Bewitched*, pp. 84–92.
59. Davies, 'Cunning-Folk in the Medical Market-Place', p. 65; *County and North Devon Advertiser*, 6 March 1846; Christie, 'Folklore in North Devon', p. 140.
60. *Berkshire Chronicle*, 28 May, 11 June, 25 June, 24 September, 3 December 1853; 17 May 1856; *Justice of the Peace*, 26 November 1864; 18 March 1865; *The Times* 13 February, 29 February 1868; *Newbury Weekly News*, 9 November 1871.
61. *Newbury Weekly News*, 9 November 1871.

62. *Briefe Description of the Notorious Life of John Lambe*, p. 2.
63. Baring-Gould, *Devonshire Characters*, p. 83.
64. Udal, *Dorsetshire Folk-Lore*, p. 217.

## Notes to Chapter 2: For Good or Evil?

1. Clark, *Thinking with Demons*, p. 459.
2. Perkins, *Discourse*, p. 174.
3. Perkins, *Discourse*, p. 176
4. Bernard, *Guide*, sig. A5v.
5. Cooper, *Mystery of Witch-Craft*, p. 4.
6. Gaule, *Select Cases*, pp. 30–31.
7. Stearne, *Confirmation*, p. 7.
8. Ady, *Perfect Discovery*, p. 40.
9. Bovet, *Pandaemonium*, p. 52.
10. Holland, *Treatise*, sig. F1v.
11. Perkins, *Discourse*, p. 176.
12. *The Divel's Delusions*, p. 2.
13. Holland, *Treatise*, sig. F4r.
14. Perkins, *Discourse*, pp. 208–9.
15. Mason, *Anatomie*, pp. 69–70.
16. Homes, *Daemonologie*, p. 22. See Clark, *Thinking with Demons*, ch. 11, for further discussion on Satan's natural abilities.
17. Homes, *Daemonologie*, p. 47.
18. Holland, *Treatise*, sig. G1r. See also Daneau, *Dialogue of Witches*, ch. 6.
19. Macfarlane, 'A Tudor Anthropologist'.
20. Holland, *Treatise*, sig. G2v.
21. On catechisms see Green, *The Christian's ABC*; Marsh, *Popular Religion*, pp. 82–86.
22. Cited in Clark, *Thinking with Demons*, p. 496.
23. Scot, *Discoverie*, book 1, ch. 3.
24. *Brideling, Sadling and Ryding, of a Rich Churle*, sig. A3r; *Wonderful Discoverie of the Witchcrafts of Margaret and Phillip Flower*, sig B2r.
25. Ady, *Candle in the Dark*; Filmer, *Advertisement*; Wagstaffe, *The Question of Witchcraft*; Webster, *Displaying of Supposed Witchcraft*.
26. See, Thomas, *Religion*, pp. 27–179; Duffy, *The Stripping of the Altars*; Hutton, *Rise and Fall of Merry England*; Marsh, *Popular Religion*.
27. Melton, *Astrologaster*, p. 17.
28. Darrell, *True Narration of the Strange and Grevous Vexation*, p. 1; Bower, *Doctor Lamb Revived*, p. 1.

29. Collinson, *Godly People*, p. 407; Raine, *Depositions ... York*, p. 127.
30. Elmer, 'Saints or Sorcerers'; Reay, *The Quakers*, pp. 68–71.
31. [Farnworth], *Witchcraft Cast Out*, p. 2.
32. *Witchcraft Cast Out*, pp. 5, 2, 11.
33. Fox, *Declaration of the Ground of Error and Errors*, p. 24.
34. Clark, *Thinking with Demons*, p. 497.
35. Brinley, *Discovery*, pp. 5, 46.
36. *Athenian Oracle: Being an Entire Collection*, p. 282.
37. Berry, 'An Early Coffee House Periodical and its Readers'. (Thanks to Tim Hitchcock for drawing my attention to this article.)
38. Davies, *Witchcraft, Magic and Culture*, p. 13.
39. *The Black Art Detected*, sig. A2v.
40. Boulton, *Possibility and Reality of Magick*, p. 184.
41. Hutchinson, *Historical Essay*, p. 227.
42. *The Review*, 20 October 1711.
43. Defoe, *Compleat System*, pp. 378–89.
44. Defoe, *Compleat System*, preface.
45. Defoe, *Compleat System*, p. 359.
46. *Life and Character of Harvey*, pp. 12, 20.
47. *Life and Character of Harvey*, pp. 63, 57.
48. Curry, *Prophecy and Power*, pp. 89–91.
49. *Life and Character of Harvey*, p. 72.
50. Collier, *Miscellaneous Works of Tim Bobbin*, pp. 147–56.
51. Defoe, *Compleat System of Magick*, preface.
52. Robertson, *Rochdale*, pp. 392–94.
53. Collier *Miscellaneous Works of Tim Bobbin*, pp. 150–51.
54. See Owen, *Welsh Folk-Lore*, pp. 212, 255–57.
55. *Life and Mysterious Transactions of Richard Morris*, p. 5.
56. *Life and Mysterious Transactions*, p. 5.
57. *Life and Mysterious Transactions*, p. 48.
58. Durbin, *Narrative of Some Extraordinary Things*, p. 54.
59. Heaton, *The Demon Expelled*, p. 40. (Thanks to Jason Semmens, who is working on the case, for bringing it to my attention.)
60. *Breslaw's Last Legacy*, p. ix.
61. *Breslaw's Last Legacy*, pp. 40–41.
62. *Breslaw's Last Legacy*, p. 101.
63. Ady, *Candle in the Dark*.
64. Hall, *Old Conjuring Books*, p. 155.
65. See the *Gloucester Journal*, 4 July 1814, 19 December 1814
66. Quennell, *Mayhew's London*, p. 491.

67. Hawkins, *Iniquity*, p. v.
68. Hawkins, *Iniquity*, pp. 27, 30.
69. See Porter, 'Witchcraft and Magic in Enlightenment, Romantic and Liberal Thought'; Sharpe, *Instruments*, pp. 247–50.
70. Hawkins, *Iniquity*, p. 21.
71. Hawkins, *Iniquity*, p. 21.
72. *Western Flying Post*, 26 August 1856.
73. Hawkins, *Iniquity*, pp. 26–27.
74. See, for example, *Extraordinary Life and Character of Mary Bateman*; *Life and Trial of Mary Bateman*; *York Herald*, 25 March 1809.
75. *Extraordinary Life and Character of Mary Bateman*, p. 56.
76. *Ecce Homo*. Francis X. King should be credited with bringing the career of Parkins to general attention. See his study of Francis Barrett, *The Flying Sorcerer*.
77. *Ecce Homo*, p. 67. For similar statements see Davies, *Witchcraft, Magic and Culture*, p. 7.
78. *Ecce Homo*, p. 68.
79. *Ecce Homo*, pp. 13 n. 3, 34 n. 10.
80. *Ecce Homo*, p. 2.
81. See, for example, Davies, *Witchcraft, Magic and Culture*, p. 50.
82. See Smith, 'The Wise Man', pp. 28–31.
83. Atkinson, *Forty Years*, p. 113.
84. Owen, *Welsh Folk-Lore*, p. 217.
85. Watson, *Somerset Life*, p. 66; Davies, *People Bewitched*, p. 64.
86. Udal, *Dorsetshire Folk-Lore*, p. 215.
87. Baring-Gould, *Devonshire Characters*, p. 82.
88. See Davies, 'Newspapers'.
89. For a couple of examples see the *York Herald*, 7 October and 4 November 1809.
90. *Taunton Courier*, 18 March 1819; *Staffordshire Advertiser*, 18 October 1823; Hunt, *Popular Romances*, p. 317; *Berkshire Chronicle*, 17 May 1856; *Newbury Weekly News*, 9 November 1871.
91. Forfar, *Wizard of West Penwith*; Yonge, *Cunning Woman's Grandson*; Morrison, *Cunning Murrell*; Kershaw, *Wise Woman of the Mill*.
92. Yonge, *Cunning Woman's Grandson*, pp. 18–19.
93. See Maple, 'Cunning Murrell'; Maple, *Dark World*, pp. 174–82; Hutton, *Triumph of the Moon*, p. 93; Davies, *Witchcraft, Magic and Culture*, pp. 114–15.
94. Kipling, *Rewards and Fairies*, p. 96.
95. Hardy, 'The Withered Arm'; Hardy, *Mayor of Casterbridge*, ch. 26; Hardy, *Tess of the d'Urbervilles*, ch. 21; March, 'Dorset Folklore', p. 481.

96. See More's morality tale, *Tawney Rachel*; Davies, *Witchcraft, Magic and Culture*, p. 159.
97. Yonge, *Cunning Woman's Grandson*, pp. 64, 226.
98. Forfar, *Wizard of West Penwith*, p. 39.
99. Yonge, *Cunning Woman's Grandson*, p. vi; Forfar, *Wizard of West Penwith*, p. 39.
100. Harrison, *Wise Woman*, p. 64.
101. [Warren], *Jane Lowe*, pp. 23–24.
102. [Warren], *Jane Lowe*, pp. 13, 48.
103. Gaule, *Select Cases*, pp. 160–67.
104. Gifford, *Dialogue*, sig. D4v; Mason, *Anatomie*, p. 59.
105. Hawkins, *Iniquity*, p. x.
106. Gifford, *Dialogue*, sig. M3v.
107. Parkins, *Cabinet of Wealth*, p. 5.
108. Lyne, *Sinfulness and Idolatry of Charms*, p. 22.
109. *The Times*, 13 April 1857; March, 'Dorset Folklore', p. 481.
110. Raine, *Depositions ... York*, pp. 204–5.
111. *Manchester Courier*, 26 January 1848.
112. Atkinson, *Forty Years*, p. 108.
113. Bower, *Doctor Lamb Revived*, p. 10.
114. Fletcher, *Recollections*, pp. 104–5; Taylor, 'Witches and Witchcraft', p. 172.
115. Davies, *People Bewitched*, pp. 78–83.
116. *Plymouth Herald*, 14 December 1867.
117. Davies, 'Cunning-Folk in England and Wales', pp. 102–3.

*Notes to Chapter 3: Who and Why*

1. Scot, *Discoverie*, book 1, ch. 2; Cooper, *Mystery of Witch-Craft*, p. 315.
2. Macfarlane, *Witchcraft*, map 7.
3. Hardy (ed.), *Hertford County Records*, p. 3.
4. Davies, *People Bewitched*, p. 27.
5. Melton, *Astrologaster*, pp. 21, 47.
6. *Spectator*, 9 October 1712; Southey, *Letters from England*, p. 295.
7. Thomas, *Religion*, p. 295; Davies, 'Cunning-Folk in England and Wales', p. 92; Davies, *People Bewitched*, ch. 2.
8. Jackson (ed.), *Diary of Abraham de la Pryme*, p. 56.
9. *Somerset and Dorset Notes and Queries*, 12 (1911), p. 33; *Examination of John Walsh*, no pagination; *Wonderful Discoverie ... Margaret and Phillip Flower* (London, 1619), sig. E4v; Pitt, *An Account of one Ann Jefferies*. See also Thomas, *Religion*, p. 727.

10. Heywood, *Wise-Woman*, sig. B4r; *Lincolnshire Notes and Queries*, 1 (1889), p. 131.
11. Davies, *Witchcraft, Magic and Culture*, p. 247.
12. *Brideling, Sadling and Ryding, of a Rich Churle*, sig. A3r; Gregory, 'Witchcraft, Politics', p. 35; Bower, *Doctor Lamb Revived*, p. 1; *Extraordinary Life and Character of Mary Bateman*.
13. *The Times*, 29 February 1868; March, 'Dorset Folklore', p. 111.
14. Harley, 'Historians as Demonologists', p. 12.
15. *Genuine Life and Confession of Richard Walton*, p. 11.
16. Wheater, 'Yorkshire Superstitions', p. 271; *Life and Mysterious Transactions*, p. 5; Davies, *People Bewitched*, p. 30.
17. Parkins, *Book of Miracles*, p. 59; Davies, *People Bewitched*, p. 49.
18. Macfarlane, *Witchcraft*, appendix 1, p. 276; Trotman, 'Seventeenth Century Treasure-Seeking', pp. 220–21; Bower, *Doctor Lamb Revived*, p. 1; *Examination of John Walsh*, sig. A4v.
19. Parkins, *Book of Miracles*, p. 17.
20. *Ecco Homo*, p. 69.
21. *Ecce Homo*, p. 69.
22. *Briefe Description of the Notorious Life of John Lambe*, pp. 1, 2, 6.
23. Burne, *Shropshire*, p. 188.
24. Thomas, *Religion*, p. 295.
25. Hamer, 'A Parochial Account of Llangurig', p. 267; Robertson, *Rochdale*, p. 392; Davies, *People Bewitched*, p. 87.
26. Davies, 'Cunning-Folk in England and Wales', pp. 99–100.
27. Macfarlane, *Witchcraft*, pp. 290, 291.
28. Ady, *Candle in the Dark*, p. 115.
29. Sennertus et al, *Sixth Book of Practical Physick*, pp. 89, 95.
30. Drage, *Daimonomageia*, pp. 34, 20.
31. Sennertus et al, *Sixth Book*, p. 99.
32. *True and Impartial Relation of the Informations against Three Witches*, p. 2; *True and Just Recorde ... S. Oses* (London, 1582).
33. Raine, *Depositions ... Durham*, p. 39.
34. J. S., *The Starr-Prophet Anatomised*, p. 1.
35. Drage, *Physical Nosonomy*, p. 27.
36. See MacDonald, *Mystical Bedlam*; Sawyer, 'Strangely Handled in All Her Lyms', pp. 461–85.
37. Thomas, *Religion*, p. 757.
38. Glanvill, *Saducismus Triumphatus*, p. 281.
39. Blagrave, *Physick*, p. 153.
40. Blagrave, *Physick*, p. 156.
41. Chanter, 'Parson Joe and his Book', pp. 87–88.

42. Dawson, *History of Skipton*, pp. 390–94; Obelkevitch, *Religion and Rural Society*, p. 290; Polwhele, *Traditions and Recollections*, p. 605.
43. On charmers and their charms see Davies, 'Charmers and Charming', pp. 41–53; Davies, 'Healing Charms in England and Wales', pp. 19–33.
44. See Thomas, *Religion*, pp. 217–18.
45. Davies, *People Bewitched*, pp. 51–52.
46. Macfarlane, *Witchcraft*, p. 127.
47. Davies, 'Cunning-Folk in the Medical Market-Place', p. 66; Davies, *People Bewitched*, p. 68; Atkinson, *Forty Years*, p. 110; *Life and Mysterious Transactions of Richard Morris*, pp. 39, 48.
48. *County and North Devon Advertiser*, 6 March 1846; *County and North Devon Advertiser*, 29 May 1846.
49. Atkinson, *Forty Years*, p. 124.
50. Burney, *The Cunning-Man*, p. 13.
51. Bernard, *Guide*, p. 131; Macfarlane, *Witchcraft*, p. 126. See also, Sharpe, *Instruments*, p. 69.
52. *The Herts Mercury*, 5 September 1829.
53. Bernard, *Guide*, p. 137.
54. See Thomas, *Religion*, p. 297.
55. *Leeds Mercury*, 9 August 1806.
56. Wheater, 'Yorkshire Superstitions', p. 271; Gutch, *County Folklore ... Yorkshire*, p. 65; *Somerset County Herald*, 15 May 1858; Pearson, *Annals*, p. 85; *Somerset County Herald*, 27 June 1863.
57. Hardy (ed.), *Hertford County Records*, i, p. 268; *Manchester Courier*, 26 January 1848.
58. Macfarlane, *Witchcraft*, pp. 127, 276.
59. Somerset Record Office, QS 118/30–1; Bower, *Doctor Lamb Revived*, p. 2.
60. Davies, *People Bewitched*, p. 41.
61. *Hertford Reformer*, 23 June 1838; Mackay, *Extraordinary Popular Delusions*, pp. 560–61; *Torquay Directory*, 2 February 1875; *Somerset County Herald*, 1 February 1873; *Stafford Chronicle*, 29 July 1882; *The Times*, 24 April 1851; Davies, *People Bewitched*, p. 67.
62. *Somerset County Herald*, 15 May 1858; *The Times*, 24 March 1857. For further examples from the modern period see Hutton, *Triumph of the Moon*, pp. 105–6; Davies, *People Bewitched*, chs 2 and 3; Davies, 'Cunning-Folk in England and Wales', pp. 94–95.
63. *Berkshire Chronicle*, 17 May 1856; *Plymouth, Devonport, and Stonehouse Herald*, 14 December 1867; *Norfolk Chronicle*, 12 August 1876; Davies, 'Cunning-Folk in the Medical Market-Place', p. 68. Were they related to the Gunters who are the subject of Sharpe's *Bewitching of Anne Gunter*?

64. *Taunton Courier*, 31 December 1890; Davies, *People Bewitched*, p. 66.
65. Thomas, *Religion*, p. 298; Briggs, *Witches and Neighbours*, p. 171.
66. Raine, 'Proceedings Connected with a Remarkable Charge of Sorcery'; *Lancashire and Cheshire Antiquarian Society* 54 (1939), pp. 19–20.
67. *Genuine Life and Confession*, pp. 11, 13, 15, 26–27.

*Notes to Chapter 4: Services*

1. Peacock, 'Extracts from Lincoln Episcopal Visitations', pp. 254–56; Turner, 'Brief Remarks', p. 58.
2. Raine, 'Proceedings Connected with a Remarkable Charge of Sorcery'.
3. Nichols, *Narratives*, p. 333.
4. Turner (ed.), *Paracelsus of the Supreme Mysteries*, p. 66.
5. Rowse, *Case Books of Simon Forman*, p. 101.
6. Trotman, 'Seventeenth Century Treasure-Seeking', p. 220. They were called Mosaic Rods after those that Moses and Aaron used to bloody the waters of Egypt, summon a plague locusts, and bring about other acts of divine judgement. See Exodus 7–8.
7. *The Brideling, Sadling and Ryding, of a Rich Churle*, p. 13.
8. Gregory, 'Witchcraft, Politics', p. 36.
9. Macfarlane, *Witchcraft*, p. 121.
10. Blagrave, *Astrological Practice*, p. 162.
11. Farnworth, *Witchcraft Cast Out*, p. 13.
12. *The Herts Mercury*, 5 September 1829.
13. *Leeds Mercury*, 2 May 1807.
14. *Newbury Weekly News*, 9 November 1871; *Berkshire Chronicle*, 24 September 1853.
15. Hardy (ed.), *Middlesex Calendar*, p. 45; Somerset Record Office, QS 118/30–1.
16. Somerset Record Office, QS 112/72.
17. *Newbury Weekly News*, 9 November 1871.
18. Christie, 'Folklore in North Devon', p. 143.
19. *Notes and Queries*, 14 August 1852, p. 145.
20. Hardy (ed.), *Middlesex Calendar*, pp. 199, 372.
21. Nichols, *Narratives*, p. 332.
22. Parkins, *Cabinet of Wealth*, p. 7.
23. Raine, *Depositions*, p. 205; *Ashton-under-Lyne Reporter*, 17 January 1857; *FLS News* 16 (1992), pp. 12–13.
24. *Extraordinary Life and Character*, p. 11; *Justice of the Peace*, 18 March 1865, p. 165.
25. Parkins, *Cabinet of Wealth*, p. 7.

26. *Extraordinary Life and Character*, p. 12; Davies, 'Cunning-Folk in the Medical Market-Place', p. 69.
27. Raine, *Depositions*, p. 204; Parkins, *Cabinet of Wealth*, pp. 8–9.
28. See Davies, *Witchcraft, Magic and Culture*, p. 228; Davies, *People Bewitched*, p. 43.
29. Parkins, *Book of Miracles*, pp. 62–63.
30. *True and Impartial Relation of the Informations against Three Witches*, p. 27.
31. Bernard, *Guide*, p. 23.
32. *Tryall and Examination of Mrs Joan Peterson*, p. 4; Blagrave, *Physick*, p. 168; Hawkins, *Iniquity*, p. ix; *The Times*, 13 April 1857; *Norfolk Chronicle*, 12 August 1876.
33. Hawkins, *Iniquity*, p. ix; Davies, *People Bewitched*, p. 77; *Warwick Advertiser*, 18 December 1875; Durbin, *Narrative of Some Extraordinary Things*, p. 55.
34. Sennertus et al, *Sixth Book*, p. 96.
35. Cited in Sharpe, *Bewitching of Anne Gunter*, p. 57.
36. Roberts, *Treatise of Witchcraft*, p. 53; *Plymouth, Devonport, and Stonehouse Herald*, 14 December 1867; *Tryall and Examination of Mrs Joan Peterson*, p. 4.
37. March, 'Dorset Folklore', p. 111.
38. *Berkshire Chronicle*, 17 May 1856; *Somerset County Herald*, 15 May 1858.
39. *True Examination and Confession of Elizabeth Stile*, sig. B2r.
40. *Most Wonderful and True Storie of a Certaine Witch*, pp. 24–25; Davies, *Witchcraft, Magic and Culture*, p. 219.
41. *The Times*, 7 April 1857.
42. *A Full and True Account of the Proceedings ... Holden in the Old Bayley*, p. 4. For further information on witch-bottles see Merrifield, *Archaeology*, pp. 163–75
43. *An Account of the Tryal and Examination of Joan Buts*, pp. 1–2.
44. Hawkins, *Iniquity*, p. x.
45. Blagrave, *Physick*, p. 153.
46. Roberts, *Treatise*, p. 53.
47. Bernard, *Guide*, p. 138.
48. Parkins, *Cabinet of Wealth*, p. 6.
49. Sennertus et al, *Sixth Book*, pp. 99, 100; Blagrave, *Physick*, p. 171.
50. Parkins, *The English Physician*, p. 32.
51. *A True and Just Recorde*, sig. A8v.
52. *The True Examination ... Elizabeth Stile*, sig. B1r.
53. Cited in Howse, *Radnorshire*, p. 197; Peach, *A Circumstantial Account*, p. 9; Davies, *Witchcraft, Magic and Culture*, p. 23.

54. *Stafford Chronicle*, 29 July 1882; *Wolverhampton Chronicle*, 26 July 1882.
55. Durbin, *A Narrative*, p. 54.
56. *Staffordshire Advertiser*, 7 March 1857.
57. Hawkins, *Iniquity*, p. 34.
58. *Notes and Queries*, 14 August 1852, 145; Davies, *People Bewitched*, fig. 1.
59. Hawkins, *Iniquity*, pp. viii, vi.
60. Train, *An Historical and Statistical Account*, p. 162.
61. Fletcher, *Recollections*, p. 109.
62. *Transactions of the Historic Society of Lancashire and Cheshire* 74 (1922), p. 178; *The Brideling, Sadling and Ryding*, sig. B3ʳ; Scot, *Discoverie*, Bk. 13, Ch. 30. See also Rosen, *Witchcraft*, p. 220.
63. Davies, 'Cunning-folk in the Medical Market-Place', pp. 65–66; *Western Morning News*, 26 November 1922; Robertson, *Rochdale*, pp. 392–94. See also Davies, 'Cunning-Folk in England and Wales', p. 99; Davies, *People Bewitched*, p. 39.
64. Heywood, *Wise-woman*, sig. D2ᵛ.
65. Harry Price Library. A reproduction can be found in Maple, *Magic, Medicine*, p. 144; Smith, 'The Wise Man', p. 29.
66. See Curry, *Prophecy and Power*, pp. 132–34.
67. *Drakard's Stamford and General Advertiser*, 5 October 1810; Parkins, *The English physician, enlarged*.
68. Parkins, *Cabinet of Wealth*, p. 14.
69. Parkins, *Book of Miracles*, pp. 63–64.
70. Parkins, *Cabinet of Wealth*, p. 17.

## Notes to Chapter 5: Books

1. See Thorndike, *History of Magic and Experimental Science*; Kieckhefer, *Magic*; Flint, *Rise of Magic*; Fanger (ed.), *Conjuring Spirits*.
2. Cited in Mathiesen, 'A Thirteenth-Century Ritual', p. 144.
3. Raine, 'Proceedings Connected with a Remarkable Charge of Sorcery' p. 76; Kittredge, *Witchcraft*, ch. 12; Nichols, *Narratives*, p. 334.
4. Sloane 3826. Useful extracts from manuscripts of this period can be found in Thompson, *Mysteries and Secrets of Magic*; Waite, *Ceremonial Magic*; Shah, *Secret Lore*.
5. See *Ende of the Secretes of Nature*; *Boke of Secretes*.
6. Gaule, *Mag-Astro-Mancer*, p. 180.
7. Agrippa, *Three Books*.
8. Porta, *Natural Magick*.
9. Hart, 'Observations on Some Documents Relating to Magic', p. 392.

10. I concur with Fanger, 'Plundering the Egyptian Treasure', p. 237 n. 8.
11. James I, *Daemonologie*, preface.
12. The *Dictionary of National Biography* speculates that Turner may have died in 1665, perhaps a victim of the plague.
13. Roberts and Watson, *John Dee's Library Catalogue*, pp. 57, 169.
14. Other publications illustrating the great interest in magic at this period include Philalethes, *Magia Adamica*; Warren, *Magick and Astrology Vindicated*; Ramsey, *Judicial Astrologie Vindicated and Demonologie Confuted*.
15. Scot, *Discoverie*, p. 251.
16. Scot, *Discoverie*, pp. 226, 251.
17. Scot, *Discoverie*, p. 262.
18. See Kraye, Ryan and Schmitt (eds), *Pseudo-Aristotle in the Middle Ages*.
19. Turner, 'Brief Remarks', p. 58.
20. Robert Lenkiewicz Library.
21. Sharpe, *Instruments*, p. 281.
22. Obituary recorded in the *Westmorland Gazette*, 8 June 1839.
23. *The Athenian Oracle*, p. 282; *Account of the Infancy, Religious and Literary Life of Adam Clarke*, pp. 43–50.
24. 'Memoirs of the Birth, Education, Life and Death of Mr John Cannon', Somerset Record Office, DD/SAS C/1193/4. Many thanks to Tim Hitchcock for making me aware of this manuscript and lending me his own transcripts.
25. Dupont-Bouchat, 'Le diable apprivoisé', p. 239.
26. See Sebald, 'The Sixth and Seventh Books of Moses', pp. 53–58.
27. Aag and Christensen (eds), *Fra Cyprianus til New Age*. For Mother Shipton see Davies, *Witchcraft, Magic and Culture*, pp. 142–47.
28. See Devlin, *The Superstitious Mind*. For accounts of the mystique still surrounding these works in parts of rural France see, Gaboriau, *La pensée ensorcelée*; Boncoeur, *Le village aux sortilèges*; Camus, *Pouvoirs sorciers*.
29. See Davies, *Witchcraft, Magic and Culture*, ch. 3.
30. For a thief charm see *High-German Fortune-Teller*, p. 22.
31. *Witchcraft Detected*, preface.
32. *Witchcraft Detected*, p. iii.
33. *Witchcraft Detected*, p. iv.
34. Digby, *A Late Discourse*.
35. Maple, 'Cunning Murrell', p. 40; Hamer, 'Parochial Account of Llangurig', p. 268; Fletcher, *Recollections*, p. 107.
36. *Bye-Gones*, February 5, 1913, pp. 11–12; Mee, *Magic in Carmarthenshire*.
37. See More, *Explanation of the Grand Mystery*.
38. When Sibly died in 1799 he left his occult manuscripts to his nephew,

who, with rather unseemly haste, sold them all to John Denley within a month; Hamill (ed.), *Rosicrucian Seer*, p. 60.
39. Bottrell, *Folk-Lore of West Cornwall*, p. 189.
40. Heydon, *Defence of Iudiciall Astrologie*; Heydon, *Astrological Discourse*.
41. *Life and Mysterious Transactions of Richard Morris*, p. 40.
42. Harland and Wilkinson, *Lancashire Folklore*, pp. 123–24.
43. *Character of a Quack-Astrologer*.
44. Thanks to Elizabeth Lawrence for tracking down this information.
45. Gutch, *County Folk-Lore ... Yorkshire*, p. 68; Davies (ed.), *Life and Opinions of Robert Roberts*, p. 40; Hole, *Witchcraft in England*, p. 152; Hardwick, *Traditions, Superstitions*, p. 120; *Liverpool Courier*, 28 October 1857; *Ashton-under-Lyne Reporter*, 17 January 1857; also in *Folklore Society News*, 16 (1992), pp. 12–13.
46. National Library of Wales, MS Peniarth 171B. See Jenkins, 'Popular Beliefs in Wales', p. 454.
47. Hamill (ed.), *Rosicrucian Seer*, p. 60.
48. Denley, *Catalogue*, pp. 81, 84, 89, 95, 118.
49. The Coleridge Collection of the Victoria University Library in Toronto recently acquired a letter from Coleridge to Denley concerning this transaction.
50. Robert Lenkiewicz Library.
51. Parkins, *Book of Miracles*, p. 72.
52. Parkins, *Cabinet of Wealth*, p. 12.
53. The Urim and Thummim are supposed to have been integral parts of the breast-plate worn by the Jewish high-priest, via which the will of God was transmitted. Mentioned several times in the Old Testament, the exact meaning of the terms are unknown, and despite early attempts to translate their meaning into English, from the mid sixteenth century onwards the words were left untranslated in English Bibles.
54. *Fourth Book*, pp. 61–62, also contains some advice on constructing 'lamens'.
55. 'The Secret of Secrets', Bodleian Library, MS Rawlinson D253.
56. Dawson, *History of Skipton*, pp. 391–94; *The Reliquary*, 23 (1882–83), pp. 197–202.
57. Wellcome Institute Library, MS 3770; King, *Flying Sorcerer*, pp. 41–44.
58. Parkins, *Cabinet of Wealth*, p. 15.
59. *The Times*, 24 March 1857.
60. Wheater, 'Yorkshire Superstitions', p. 271.
61. Bumstead, *Apology for an Old Bookseller*, p. 12. By 1870 a man named Millard seems to have become the principal dealer in occult texts.
62. Bumstead, *Occult Works*.

63. Gutch, *East Riding of Yorkshire*, p. 68; Davies, *Life and Opinions of Robert Roberts*, p. 40.
64. Much of Barrett's life is obscure, but what there is to know about him can be found in King, *The Flying Sorcerer*.
65. Denley, *Catalogue*, p. 84.
66. Simpson, 'On a Seventeenth-Century Roll', pp. 302–3.
67. Shah, *Secret Law of Magic*, p. 12.
68. Fletcher, *Recollections*, p. 108.
69. *Newbury Weekly News*, 9 November 1871.
70. *Examination of John Walsh*, no pagination.
71. 'Secret of Secrets', pp. 51, 61.
72. Davies, 'Cunning-Folk', p. 96. For stories see Davies, *Folk-Lore*, pp. 246, 253–55.
73. Hancock, 'The History of Llanrhaiadr-yn-Mochnant', pp. 329–30.
74. *Fourth Book*, p. 66.
75. Fletcher, *Recollections*, p. 109.
76. Bower, *Doctor Lamb Revived*, p. 6.
77. Bower, *Doctor Lamb Revived*, p. 32.
78. *Fourth Book*, p. 81.

*Notes to Chapter 6: Written Charms*

1. *Fourth Book*, p. 54.
2. Scot, *Discoverie*, p. 131.
3. *Genuine Life and Confession of Richard Walton*, pp. 14, 19.
4. *Ecce Homo*, p. 70.
5. *Genuine Life and Confession*, p. 20.
6. Evans, 'Exorcism in Wales', p. 276.
7. Hawkins, *Iniquity*, p. x.
8. *Transactions of the Devonshire Association*, 61 (1929), p. 128.
9. Hewett, *Nummits and Crummits*, p. 73.
10. Simpson, 'On a Seventeenth-Century Roll', pp. 307–11; Budge, *Amulets and Superstitions*, ch. 8; Cavendish, *Black Arts*, pp. 153–55.
11. Scot, *Discoverie*, p. 155; Aubrey, *Miscellanies*, p. 106; Durant, *Art and Nature*, p. 11.
12. Raphael, *Astrologer of the Nineteenth Century*, p. 505; Secundus, *Private Companion*, pp. 9–10.
13. Scot, *Discoverie*, p. 140.
14. Weeks, 'Charm against Witches and Evil Spirits', pp. 146–47; Henderson, *Folk-Lore of the Northern Counties*, p. 179; *The Times*, 27 October, 1866.

15. Davies, *Witchcraft, Magic and Culture*, p. 150.
16. Bell, 'A Written Charm', pp. 91–93.
17. A photo of the original can be seen in Merrifield, *Archaeology of Ritual and Magic*, pl. 46.
18. Bottrell, *Stories and Folk-Lore*, p. 190.
19. See Merrifield, *Archaeology of Ritual and Magic*, pp. 142–44; Sherlock, 'An Ancient Christian Word-Square at Great Gidding'.
20. Harland and Wilkinson, *Lancashire Folklore*, p. 62.
21. *The Times*, 30 March, 1850.
22. Bottrell, *Stories and Folk-Lore*, p. 190.
23. Scot, *Discoverie* (1665), 'A Discourse', p. 43.
24. Atkinson, *Forty Years*, p. 96.
25. Hockley, 'Occult Spells', p. 38.
26. Scot, *Discoverie* (1665), 'A Discourse', p. 43.
27. *Hereford Times*, 2 March 1867. See Davies, 'Cunning-Folk in the Medical Market-Place', for further details of the case.
28. More examples of charms not included here can be found in Dawson, *History of Skipton*, pp. 392–94; Gutch, *County Folk-Lore ... Yorkshire*, pp. 61–62; Harland, 'A Lancashire Charm, in Cypher, against Witchcraft and Evil Spirits', pp. 81–85.
29. Hawkins, *Iniquity*, pp. iv–v.
30. Scot, *Discoverie*, p. 150.
31. Scot, *Discoverie*, p. 251.
32. Charms in the National Library of Wales can be found under MSS 1248, 4937E, 6729, 9140, 11229B, 15557. For printed transcriptions of some Welsh charms see Isaac, *Coelion Cymru*, pp. 150–57; Jones, *Welsh Folklore and Folk-Custom*, pp. 127–28; D. R. T., 'Demonology and Witchcraft', pp. 143–50; Davies, 'The Conjuror in Montgomeryshire', pp. 158–70; *Byegones*, 17 October (1888); Merrifield, *Archaeology of Ritual and Magic*, pp. 151–54.
33. National Library of Wales, MS 9140.
34. Evans, 'Exorcism in Wales', pp. 274–77.
35. Davies, 'The Conjuror in Mongomeryshire', p. 170.
36. Scot, *Discoverie*, p. 232.
37. *The Times*, 13 and 17 December 1867.
38. Gaster, 'English Charms of the Seventeenth Century', pp. 78, 375–78.
39. Dawson, *History of Skipton*, pp. 390–94.

*Notes to Chapter 7: European Comparisons*

1. For example, de Blécourt, 'Witch Doctors, Soothsayers and Priests'; Briggs, *Witches and Neighbours*.
2. de Blécourt, 'Witch Doctors, Soothsayers', p. 293; Monter, *Witchcraft in France and Switzerland*, p. 171; Johansen, 'Witchcraft, Sin and Repentance', p. 420; Johansen, 'Denmark: The Sociology of Accusations', p. 341.
3. Várkonyi, 'Connection between the Cessation of Witch Trials', pp. 425–79; Rørbye, *Kloge folk*. For a good resumé of this work in English see Tangherlini, 'How Do you Know She's a Witch?'; Ramsey, *Professional and Popular Medicine in France*.
4. For a good, relevant overview of the historiography on magic and the Inquisition see Gijswijt-Hofstra, 'Witchcraft after the Witch-Trials', pp. 129–41. More particularly see Bethencourt, 'Portugal: A Scrupulous Inquisition'; O'Neil, 'Magical Healing, Love Magic and the Inquisition', pp. 88–115; O'Neil, 'Sacerdote ovvero strione'; Dedieu, 'The Inquisition and Popular Culture in New Castile', pp. 140–43; Martin, *Witchcraft and the Inquisition in Venice*; Sallmann, *Chercheurs de trésors*; Cassar, *Witchcraft, Sorcery and the Inquisition*.
5. See, for example, Gentilcore, *From Bishop to Witch*; Gentilcore, *Healers and Healing in Early Modern Italy*; Deutscher, 'The Role of the Episcopal Tribunal of Novara'; Tausiet, 'Witchcraft as Metaphor: Infanticide and its Translations in Aragón'.
6. Abray, 'The Laity's Religion: Lutheranism in Sixteenth-Century Strasbourg', p. 222.
7. Monter, *Ritual, Myth and Magic*, p. 45. See also Monter, 'Witchcraft in Geneva, 1537–1662'.
8. Kristóf, '"Wise Women", Sinners and the Poor'; Graham, *Social Life of Scotland*, p. 328 (Thanks to Mike Mullett for this reference). See also Christie, *Witchcraft in Kenmore, 1730–57*.
9. de Blécourt and Pereboom, 'Insult and Admonition: Witchcraft in the Land of Vollenhove', p. 120. Gijswijt-Hofstra, 'Witchcraft before Zeeland Magistrates and Church Councils', p. 115. See also, de Blécourt, 'Four Centuries of Frisian Witch Doctors', pp. 158–59.
10. Rowlands, 'Witchcraft and Popular Religion in Early Modern Rothenburg ob der Tauber'.
11. Schöck, 'Das Ende der Hexenprozesse – das Ende des Hexenglaubens?'; Gestrich, 'Pietismus und Aberglaube'. The relevant finding of both authors are summarised in Gijswijt-Hofstra, 'Witchcraft after the Witch-Trials', pp. 164–67.

12. Horsley, 'Who Were the Witches?', p. 712. See also Horsley, 'Further Reflections on Witchcraft and European Folk Religion'.
13. de Blécourt, 'Witch Doctors, Soothsayers and Priests', pp. 289–92.
14. Monter, *Witchcraft in France and Switzerland*; Delcambre, *Les devins-guérisseurs dans la Lorraine ducale*.
15. Briggs, *Witches and Neighbours*, p. 122; Briggs, 'Circling the Devil: Witch-Doctors and Magical Healers', p. 162.
16. Kristóf, '"Wise women", Sinners and the Poor', p. 107.
17. Naess, 'Norway: The Criminological Context', pp. 372–73; Klaniczay, 'Hungary: The Accusations and the Universe of Popular Magic', pp. 254–55; Pócs, *Between the Living and the Dead*; Dömötör, 'The Cunning Folk in English and Hungarian Witch Trials', pp. 183–87; Nenonen, *Noituus, taikuus ja noitavainot*, p. 439; Heikkinen and Kervinen, 'Finland: The Male Domination', p. 323.
18. Gijswijt-Hofstra, 'Witchcraft after the Witch-Trials', p. 176.
19. Dixon, 'Popular Beliefs and the Reformation in Brandenburg-Ansbach', pp. 129–34.
20. Deutscher, 'Role of the Episcopal Tribunal of Novara', p. 416 n. 57.
21. O'Neil, 'Sacerdote ovvero strione', p. 56.
22. For a concise summary of the evidence see, Gijswijt-Hofstra, 'Witchcraft after the Witch-Trials', pp. 131–39. More particularly see, O'Neil, 'Sacerdote ovvero strione', p. 56; O'Neil, 'Magical Healing, Love Magic and the Inquisition', pp. 314–20; Ortega, 'Sorcery and Eroticism in Love Magic', pp. 58–92; Martin, *Witchcraft and the Inquisition*, passim; Gentilore, *Bishop to Witch*, pp. 211–15; Ruggiero, *Binding Passions*, ch. 3; Scully, 'Marriage or a career?: Witchcraft as an Alternative in Seventeenth-Century Venice', pp. 857–76.
23. Traimond, *Le pouvoir de la maladie*, ch. 3; Dupont-Bouchat, 'Le Diable apprivoisé', p. 238; Henningsen, 'Witch Persecution after the Era of the Witch Trials', p. 134.
24. Mozzani, *Magie et superstitions*, p. 135; Devlin, *Superstitious Mind*, pp. 176–77.
25. See, for examples, Bord and Bord, *The Secret Country*, pp. 18–26, 191–96; Grinsell, *Ancient Burial Mounds of England*, pp. 70–85.
26. See Davies, *Witchcraft, Magic and Culture*, pp. 260–64.
27. Sallmann, *Chercheur de trésors*, p. 161.
28. Scully, 'Marriage or a Career?', p. 861.
29. Traimond, *Le pouvoir de la maladie*, pp. 109–11; Muyard, 'Un manuel de sorcellerie en Basse Bretagne au XVIIIe siècle'; Henningsen, 'Witch Persecution after the Era of the Witch Trials', pp. 134–5; National Library of Norway catalogue.

30. Mozzani, *Magie et superstitions*, p. 135.
31. Garrett, 'Witches and Cunning Folk in the Old Régime', p. 57; Behringer, *Shaman of Oberstdorf*.
32. Hutton, *Shamans*. My thanks to Ronald Hutton for generously providing me with a pre-publication version.
33. See, for example, Eliade, *Le chamanisme*; Eliade, 'Some Observations on European Witchcraft', pp. 149–72; Eliade, 'Shamanism: An Overview', pp. 202–8.
34. Edsman, 'A Manuscript Concerning Inquiries into Witchcraft in Swedish Lapland', p. 125. See also Edsman, 'A Swedish Female Folk Healer'.
35. James, *Daemonologie*, p. 68; *The History of the Lancashire Witches*.
36. Nenonen, *Noituus, taikuus*, pp. 444–45; Nenonen, 'Envious Are All the People'.
37. Edsman, 'A Manuscript Concerning Inquiries', p. 128.
38. Nenonen, '"Envious Are All the People"', pp. 78–79.
39. For discussion on Hungarian magicians in English see, Pócs, *Between the Living and the Dead*; Pócs, 'Hungarian Táltos and his European Parallels'; Hoppál, 'Traces of Shamanism in Hungarian Folk Beliefs'; Klaniczay, 'Hungary: The Accusations and the Universe of Popular Magic'; Klaniczay, 'Shamanistic Elements in Central European Witchcraft'; Dömötör, 'Cunning Folk in English and Hungarian Witch Trials'; Dömötör, *Hungarian Folk Beliefs*.
40. Pócs, *Between the Living*, pp. 135–38.
41. For example, Várkonyi, 'Connection between the Cessation of Witch Trials'.
42. Ginzburg, *The Night Battles*. See also Ginzburg, *Ecstasies*.
43. Pócs, *Between the Living*, p. 136.
44. Laura Stark-Arola's recent work on popular magic in nineteenth-century Finland also shows a diverse world of magical practitioners and practices without any concrete relationship to shamanism. See Stark-Arola, *Magic, Body and Social Order*.
45. See Pócs, *Between the Living*, pp. 144–45.
46. Behringer, *Shaman of Oberstdorf*, p. 23.
47. Behringer, *Shaman of Oberstdorf*, p. 86.
48. Henningsen, 'The Ladies from Outside', p. 199.
49. See, for example, Houston, *Literacy in Early Modern Europe*, pp. 147–50.
50. Davies, 'Hag-Riding'; Davies, *People Bewitched*, pp. 132–33.
51. *The Times*, 13 April 1857.
52. Hutton, *Shamans*, ch. 12.
53. See Hutton, *Pagan Religions*; Dowden, *European Paganism*; Jones and Pennick, *History of Pagan Europe*; Milis (ed.), *Pagan Middle Ages*.
54. See Davies, 'Healing Charms'.

*Notes to Chapter 8: Cunning-Folk in the Twentieth Century*

1. Davies, *Witchcraft, Magic and Culture*, ch. 6; Davies, *People Bewitched*, ch. 6.
2. *Dean Forest Mercury*, 26 May, 2 June 1905; *The Citizen*, 23 May, 29 May 1905.
3. *Dean Forest Mercury*, 18 May 1906.
4. *Dean Forest Mercury*, 1 June 1906.
5. *Western Morning News*, 8 October, 9 October, 11 October 1934; *Express and Echo*, 9 October 1934.
6. Tongue, *Somerset Folklore*, pp. 76–77; *Western Morning News*, 3 March 1932.
7. See Davies, 'Charmers and Charming'.
8. Davies, 'The Conjuror in Montgomeryshire', p. 158.
9. Davies, 'Conjuring in Montgomeryshire', 168.
10. Maple, *Dark World*, pp. 173–74.
11. Valiente, *Witchcraft for Tomorrow*, pp. 15–20; Lugh, *Old George Pickingill*; Liddell and Howard, *Pickingill Papers*.
12. Hutton, *Triumph*, pp. 290–98.
13. See de Blécourt, 'The Witch, her Victim, the Unwitcher'.

# Bibliography

### PRIMARY PRINTED SOURCES, 1500–1700

*A Briefe Description of the Notorious Life of John Lambe* (Amsterdam, 1628).

Ady, Thomas, *A Candle in the Dark* (London, 1656); 2nd edn published as *A Perfect Discovery of Witches* (London, 1661).

*A Full and True Account of the Proceedings at the Sessions ... in the Old Bayley, June 1 and 2, 1682* (London, 1682).

Agrippa, Cornelius, *Three Books of Occult Philosophy*, trans. James Freake (London, 1651).

*An Account of the Tryal and Examination of Joan Buts, for being a Common Witch* (London, 1682).

*An Ende of the Secretes of Nature, Set Forth by Albertus Magnus in Latine* (London, 1549).

*An Account of the Tryal and Examination of Joan Buts, for being a Common Witch* (London, 1682).

*A Rehearsall Both Straung and True, of Heinous and Horrible Actes Committed by Elizabeth Stile* (London, 1579).

*Ars Notoria: The Notory Art of Solomon*, trans. Robert Turner (London, 1657).

*Articles to be Enquired in the Visitation, in the Firste Yere of the Raigne of our Moste Dread Soveraigne* (London, 1564).

*Articles to be Enquired of in the Generall Visitation of the Archdeacon of the Diocesse of Glocester* (London, 1635).

*Articles to be Enquired of in the Visitation of the Archdeacon of Buckingham* (London, 1639).

*Articles to be Enquired within the Archdeaconrie of Norwich* (London, 1606).

*A True and Impartial Relation of the Informations against Three Witches* (London, 1682).

*A True and Just Recorde, of the Information, Examination and Confession of All the Witches Taken at S. Oses in the Countie of Essex* (London, 1582).

Aubrey, John, *Miscellanies* (London, 1696).
Bernard, Richard, *A Guide to Grand Jury Men* (London, 1627).
Blagrave, Joseph, *Blagrave's Astrological Practice of Physick* (London, 1671).
Bovet, Richard, *Pandaemonium: or The Devil's Cloyster* (London, 1684).
Bower, Edmund, *Doctor Lamb Revived: or Witchcraft condemn'd in Anne Bodenham* (London, 1653).
Brinley, John, *A Discovery of the Impostures of Witches and Astrologers* (London, 1680).
Casaubon, Meric, *A True and Faithful Relation of What Passed for Many Years Between Dr John Dee ... and Some Spirits* (London, 1659).
Cooper, Thomas, *The Mystery of Witch-Craft* (London, 1617).
Daneau, Lambert, *A Dialogue of Witches* (English translation, London, 1575).
Darrell, John, *A True Narration of the Strange and Grevous Vexation by the Devil, of Seven Persons in Lancashire* (London, 1600).
Digby, K., *A Late Discourse ... Touching the Cure of Wounds by the Powder of Sympathy* (London, 1658).
Drage, William, *A Physical Nosonomy* (London, 1665).
Drage, William, *Daimonomageia: A Small Treatise of Sicknesses and Diseases from Witchcraft and Supernatural Causes* (London, 1665).
Durant, John, *Art and Nature Joyn Hand in Hand* (London, 1697).
F[arnworth], R., *Witchcraft Cast Out from the Religious Seed and Israel of God* (London, 1655).
Filmer, Robert, *An Advertisement to the Jury Men of England, Touching Witches* (London, 1653).
Fox, George, *A Declaration of the Ground of Error and Errors, Blasphemy, Blasphemers and Blasphemies* (London, 1657).
Gaule, John, *The Mag-Astro-Mancer: or The Magicall-Astrologicall-Diviner Posed, and Puzzled* (London, 1652).
Gaule, John, *Select Cases of Conscience Touching Witches and Witchcrafts* (London, 1646).
Glanvill, Joseph, *Saducismus Triumphatus* (London, [1681] 1726).
Heydon, Christopher, *A Defence of Iudiciall Astrologie* (Cambridge, 1603).
Heydon, Christopher, *An Astrological Discourse* (London, 1650).
Heydon, John, *Theomagia: or The Temple of Wisdome* (London, 1664).
Heywood, Thomas, *The Wise-Woman of Hogsdon: A Comedie* (London, 1638).
Holland, Henry, *A Treatise against Witchcraft* (Cambridge, 1590).

Homes, Nathaniel, *Daemonologie and Theology* (London, 1650).
James VI and I, *Daemonologie* (London, 1603).
Lilly, William, *Christian Astrology* (London, 1647).
Mason, James, *The Anatomie of Sorcerie* (London, 1612).
Melton, John, *Astrologaster: or The Figure-Caster* (London, 1620).
More, Henry, *An Explanation of the Grand Mystery of Godliness* (Cambridge, 1661).
*Paracelsus of the Chymical Transmutation, Geneology and Generation of Metals and Minerals*, trans. Robert Turner (London, 1657).
*Paracelsus of the Supreme Mysteries of Nature*, trans. Robert Turner (London, 1656).
Perkins, William, *A Discourse of the Damned Art of Witchcraft* (Cambridge, 1608).
Philalethes, Eugenius, *Magia Adamica: or The Antiquitie of Magic* (London, 1650).
Pitt, Moses, *An Account of One Ann Jefferies* (London, 1696).
Porta, Giambattista della, *Natural Magic, by John Baptista Porta, a Neopolitane: in Twenty Books* (London, 1658).
Ramsey, W., *Judicial Astrologie Vindicated and Demonologie Confuted* (London, 1650).
Ravenscroft, Edward, *Dame Dobson: or The Cunning Woman. A Comedy* (London, 1684).
Roberts, Alexander, *A Treatise of Witchcraft* (London, 1616).
S. J., *The Starr-Prophet Anatomised and Dissected: or Judicial Astrologie and the Astro-mancers* (London, 1675).
Scot, Reginald, *The Discoverie of Witchcraft* (London, 1584; repr. New York, 1972).
Scot, Reginald, *The Discoverie of Witchcraft* (London, 1665).
Sennertus, Daniel, N. Culpeper and Abdiah Cole, *The Sixth Book of Practical Physick. Of Occult or Hidden Diseases* (London, 1662).
Stearne, John, *A Confirmation and Discovery of Witch Craft* (London, 1648).
*The Athenian Oracle: Being an Entire Collection of All the Valuable Questions and Answers in the Old Athenian Mercury* (3rd edn, London, 1728).
*The Boke of Secretes of Albartus Magnus* (London, c. 1565).
*The Brideling, Sadling and Ryding, of a Rich Churle in Hampshire, by the Subtill Practise of one Iudeth Philips, a Professed Cunning Woman* (London, 1595).

*The Character of a Quack-Astrologer: or The Spurious Prognosticator Anatomiz'd* (1673).

*The Disclosing of a Late Counterfeited Possession by the Devyl in Two Maydens within the Citie of London* (London, 1574).

*The Divel's Delusions: or A Faithfull Relation of John Palmer and Elizabeth Knott* (London, 1649).

*The Examination of John Walsh, before Maister Thomas Williams* (London, 1566).

*The Fourth Book of Occult Philosophy*, trans. Robert Turner (London, 1655).

*The Lawes against Witches, and Coniuration: And Some Brief Notes and Observations for the Discovery of Witches* (London, 1645).

*The Most Wonderful and True Storie of a Certaine Witch Named Alse Gooderige of Stapenhill* (London, 1597).

*The Tryall and Examination of Mrs Joan Peterson* (London, 1652).

*The Witch of Wapping: or An Exact and Perfect Relation of the Life and Devilish Practices of Joan Peterson* (London, 1652).

*The Wonderful Discoverie of the Witchcrafts of Margaret and Phillip Flower* (London, 1619).

Wagstaffe, John, *The Question of Witchcraft Debated* (London, 1669).

Warren, Hardick, *Magick and Astrology Vindicated* (London, 1651).

Webster, John, *The Displaying of Supposed Witchcraft* (London, 1677).

Wecker, John, *Eighteen Books of the Secrets of Art and Nature*, trans. and enlarged by R. Read (London, 1660).

## PRIMARY PRINTED SOURCES, 1700–1910

*A Groatsworth of Wit for a Penny: or The Interpretation of Dreams* (numerous editions consulted).

*An Account of the Infancy, Religious and Literary Life of Adam Clarke* (London, 1833).

Astley, Philip, *Natural Magic: or Physical Amusements* (London, 1785).

Boulton, Richard, *A Compleat History of Magick, Sorcery and Witchcraft* (London, 1715).

Boulton, Richard, *The Possibility and Reality of Magick, Sorcery and Witchcraft, Demonstrated* (London, 1722).

Breslaw, Philip, *Breslaw's Last Legacy: or The Magical Companion* (London, 1784).

Brewster, David, *Letters on Natural Magic* (London, 1834).

Bumstead, George, *Apology for an Old Bookseller* (Diss, 1882).

Bumstead, George, *Occult Works: A Catalogue of an Extraordinary and Singularly Curious Collection of 600 Works* (London, 1852).

Burney, Charles, *The Cunning-Man: a Musical Entertainment in Two Acts ... Originally Written and Composed by J. J. Rousseau* (London, 1766).

[Collier, John], *The Miscellaneous Works of Tim Bobbin, Esq* (Salford, 1812).

Defoe, Daniel, *A Compleat System of Magick: or The History of the Black-Art* (London, 1727).

Denley, John, *A Catalogue of Books and Manuscripts* (London, 1820).

Durbin, Henry, *A Narrative of Some Extraordinary Things That Happened to Mr Richard Giles's Children* (Bristol, 1800).

*Ecce Homo! Critical Remarks on the Infamous Publications of John Parkins, of Little Gonerby, near Grantham; better known as Doctor Parkins* (Grantham, 1819).

*Extraordinary Life and Character of Mary Bateman, the Yorkshire Witch* (2nd edn, Leeds, 1809).

Forfar, William Bentinck, *The Wizard of West Penwith* (Penzance, 1871).

Hardy, Thomas, *Tess of the d'Urbervilles* (London, [1891], 1981).

Hardy, Thomas, *The Mayor of Casterbridge* (London, [1886], 1988).

Hardy, Thomas, *The Short Stories of Thomas Hardy* (London, 1928).

Harrison, F. Bayford, *A Wise Woman* (London, 1883).

Hawkins, Thomas, *The Iniquity of Witchcraft, Censured and Exposed: Being the Substance of Two Sermons, Delivered at Warley, Near Halifax, Yorkshire* (Halifax, 1808).

Heaton, James, *The Demon Expelled: or The Influence of Satan and the Power of Christ, Displayed in the Extraordinary Affliction and Gracious Relief, of a Boy* (Plymouth, 1820).

Hutchinson, Francis, *A Historical Essay Concerning Witchcraft* (London, 1718).

Kershaw, Miriam, *The Wise Woman of the Mill* (London, 1902).

Kipling, Rudyard, *Rewards and Fairies* (London, 1910).

Lyne, Richard, *The Sinfulness and Idolatry of Charms* (Bodmin, 1817).

[More, Hannah], *Tawney Rachel: or The Fortune Teller; with Some Account of Dreams, Omens and Conjurors* (London, c. 1810).

Morrison, Arthur, *Cunning Murrell* (London, 1900).

Parkins, John, *The Book of Miracles: or Celestial Museum* (London, 1817).

Parkins, John, *The Cabinet of Wealth: or The Temple of Wisdom Including our Celestial Touchstone* (Grantham, 1812).

Parkins, John, *The English Physician Enlarged. To Which is Added The Family Physician* (London, 1814).

Parkins, John, *The Universal Fortune-Teller* (London, 1810).

Peach, Edward, *A Circumstantial Account of a Successful Exorcism* (London, 1836).

Raphael [Robert Cross Smith], *The Astrologer of the Nineteenth Century* (London, 1825).

Secundus, Merlin, *The Private Companion: Being a Familiar and Historical Elucidation of the Theory and Practice of Alchemy, Necromancy, Astrology, Cartomancy, etc.* (London, c. 1875).

*The Black Art Detected and Expos'd: or A Demonstration of the Hellish Impiety of Being or Desiring to Be a Wizzard, Conjuror, or Witch* (London, 1707).

*The Genuine Life and Confession of Richard Walton, a Reputed Conjuror* (London, [1733] 1744).

*The High-German Fortune-Teller* (London, c. 1750).

*The History of the Lancashire Witches: Also a Treatise of Witches in General* (London, c. 1785).

*The Life and Character of Harvey, the Famous Conjurer of Dublin* (Dublin and London, 1728).

*The Life and Mysterious Transactions of Richard Morris, Esq. Better Known by the Name of Dick Spot, the Conjuror, Particularly in Derbyshire and Shropshire* (London, 1799).

*The Life and Trial of Mary Bateman, the Yorkshire Witch* (Leeds, c. 1870).

[Warren, Susanna], *Jane Lowe, the Wise Woman and the Seventh Son* (London, 1862).

*Witchcraft Detected and Prevented: or The School of Black Art Newly Opened . . . By a Member of the School of Black Art, Italy* (2nd edn, Peterhead, 1824).

Yonge, Charlotte, *The Cunning Woman's Grandson: A Tale of Cheddar a Hundred Years Ago* (London, 1890).

## SECONDARY PRINTED SOURCES

Aag, Frid J. and Elisabeth S. Christensen (eds), *Fra Cyprianus til New Age* (Oslo, 1991).

Abray, Lorna Jane, 'The Laity's Religion: Lutheranism in Sixteenth-Century Strasbourg', in Hsia (ed.), *German People and the Reformation*, pp. 216–34.

Anglo, Sydney (ed.), *The Damned Art: Essays in the Literature of Witchcraft* (London, 1977).

Ankarloo, Bengt and Gustav Henningsen (eds), *Early Modern European Witchcraft: Centres and Peripheries* (Oxford, 1990).

Ankarloo, Bengt and Stuart Clark (eds), *Witchcraft and Magic in Europe: The Eighteenth and Nineteenth Centuries* (London and Philadelphia, 1999).

Atkinson, J. C., *Forty Years in a Moorland Parish: Reminiscences and Researches in Danby* (London, [1892] 1923).

Atkinson, J. C. (ed.), *Quarter Sessions Records*, North Riding Record Society, 4 (London, 1886).

Baring-Gould, Sabine, *Devonshire Characters and Strange Events* (London, 1908).

Barry, Jonathan, Marianne Hester and Gareth Roberts (eds), *Witchcraft in Early Modern Europe* (Cambridge, 1996).

Bell, C. C., 'A Written Charm', *Folklore*, 13 (1902), pp. 91–93.

Behringer, Wolfgang, *Shaman of Oberstdorf: Chonrad Stoeckhlin and the Phantoms of the Night*, trans. H. C. Erik Midelfort (Charlottesville, 1998).

Behringer, Wolfgang, *Witchcraft Persecutions in Bavaria*, trans. J. C. Grayson and David Lederer (Cambridge, 1997).

Berry, Helen, 'An Early Coffee House Periodical and its Readers: The *Athenian Mercury*, 1691–1697', *London Journal*, 25 (2000), pp. 14–34.

Beth, Rae, *Hedge Witch: A Guide to Solitary Witchcraft* (London, 1990).

Bethencourt, Francisco, 'Portugal: A Scrupulous Inquisition', in Ankarloo and Henningsen (eds), *European Witchcraft*, pp. 403–25.

Blécourt, Willem de, 'Cunning Women, from Healers to Fortune Tellers', in Hans Binneveld and Rudolf Dekker (eds), *Curing and Insuring* (Hilversum, 1993), pp. 43–57.

Blécourt, Willem de, 'Four Centuries of Frisian Witch Doctors', in Gijswijt-Hofstra and Frijhoff (eds), *Witchcraft*, pp. 157–67.

Blécourt, Willem de, *Termen van toverij* (Nijmegen, 1990).

Blécourt, Willem de, 'The Witch, her Victim, the Unwitcher and the Researcher: The Continued Existence of Traditional Witchcraft', in Bengt Ankarloo and Stuart Clark (eds), *Witchcraft and Magic in Europe: The Twentieth Century* (London, 1999), pp. 141–219.

Blécourt, Willem de, 'Witch Doctors, Soothsayers and Priests: On Cunning Folk in European Historiography and Tradition', *Social History*, 19 (1994), pp. 285–303.

Blécourt, Willem de and Freek Pereboom, 'Insult and Admonition: Witchcraft in the Land of Vollenhove', in Gijswijt-Hofstra and Frijhoff (eds), *Witchcraft*, pp. 119–32.

Boncoeur, J. L., *Le village aux sortilèges* (Paris, 1979).

Bord, Janet and Colin, *The Secret Country* (London, 1976).

Bottrell, William, *Stories and Folk-Lore of West Cornwall* (Felinfach, [1880] 1996).

Briggs, Robin, 'Circling the Devil: Witch-Doctors and Magical Healers in Early Modern Lorraine', in Clark (ed.), *Languages of Witchcraft*, pp. 161–79.

Briggs, Robin, *Witches and Neighbours* (London, 1996).

Brinkworth, E. R. C., 'The Laudian Church in Buckinghamshire', *University of Birmingham Historical Journal*, 5 (1955–6), pp. 31–59.

Budge, Wallis, *Amulets and Superstitions* (London, 1930).

Bund, J. W. Willis (ed.), *Worcester County Records: Calendar of the Quarter Sessions Papers*, 1 (Worcester, 1900).

Camus, Dominique, *Pouvoirs sorciers* (Paris, 1988).

Cassar, Carmel, *Witchcraft, Sorcery, and the Inquisition: A Study of Cultural Values in Early Modern Malta* (Malta, 1996).

Cavendish, Richard, *The Black Arts* (London, [1967] 1977).

Chanter, J. F., 'Parson Joe and his Book', *Devon and Cornwall Notes and Queries*, 8 (1914–15), pp. 87–88.

Christie, J., *Witchcraft in Kenmore, 1730–57: Extracts from the Kirk Sessions Records of the Parish* (Aberfeldy, 1893).

Christie, Peter, 'Folklore in North Devon', *Transactions of the Devonshire Association*, 128 (1996), pp. 139–54.

Clark, Stuart (ed.), *Languages of Witchcraft* (London, 2001).

Clark, Stuart, *Thinking with Demons: The Idea of Witchcraft in Early Modern Europe* (Oxford, 1997).

Cockburn, J. S. (ed.), *Calendar of Assize Records. Home Circuit Indictments. Elizabeth I and James I*, 10 vols (London, 1975–85).

Collinson, Patrick, *Godly People: Essays on English Protestantism and Puritanism* (London, 1982).

Crawford, Jane, 'Evidence for Witchcraft in Anglo-Saxon England', *Medium Ævum*, 32 (1963), pp. 107–8.

Cunnington, B. H., *Records of the County of Wiltshire* (Devizes, 1932).

Curry, Patrick, *A Confusion of Prophets: Victorian and Edwardian Astrology* (London, 1992).

Curry, Patrick, *Prophecy and Power: Astrology in Early Modern England* (Oxford, 1989).

Davies, J. H. (ed.), *The Life and Opinions of Robert Roberts, a Wandering Scholar as Told by Himself* (Cardiff, 1923).

Davies, J. S. (ed.), *An English Chronicle* (Camden Society, 1856).

Davies, Owen, *A People Bewitched: Witchcraft and Magic in Nineteenth-Century Somerset* (Bruton, 1999).

Davies, Owen, 'Charmers and Charming in England and Wales from the Eighteenth to the Twentieth Century', *Folklore*, 109 (1998), pp. 41–53.

Davies, Owen, 'Cunning-Folk in England and Wales during the Eighteenth and Nineteenth Centuries', *Rural History*, 8 (1997), pp. 93–109.

Davies, Owen, 'Cunning-Folk in the Medical Market-Place during the Nineteenth Century', *Medical History*, 43 (1999), pp. 55–73.

Davies, Owen, 'Hag-Riding in Nineteenth-Century West Country England and Modern Newfoundland: An Examination of an Experience-Centred Witchcraft Tradition', *Folk Life*, 35 (1996–7), pp. 36–53.

Davies, Owen, 'Healing Charms in Use in England and Wales 1700–1960', *Folklore*, 107 (1996), pp. 19–33.

Davies, Owen, 'Methodism, the Clergy, and the Popular Belief in Witchcraft and Magic', *History*, 82 (1997), pp. 252–65.

Davies, Owen, 'Newspapers and the Popular Belief in Witchcraft and Magic in the Modern Period', *Journal of British Studies*, 37 (1998), pp. 139–66.

Davies, Owen, 'Urbanization and the Decline of Witchcraft: An Examination of London', *Journal of Social History*, 30 (1997), pp. 597–617.

Davies, Owen, *Witchcraft, Magic and Culture, 1736–1951* (Manchester, 1999).

Davies, W. LL., 'The Conjuror in Montgomeryshire', *Montgomeryshire Collections*, 45- 46 (1937–40), pp. 158–70.

Dawson, W. Harbutt, *History of Skipton* (London, 1882).

Dedieu, Jean Pierre, 'The Inquisition and Popular Culture in New Castile', in Haliczer, *Inquisition*, pp. 129–46.

Delcambre, Etienne, *Les devins-guérisseurs dans la Lorraine ducale: leur activité et leur méthode* (Nancy, 1951).

Deutscher, Thomas, 'The Role of the Episcopal Tribunal of Novara in the Suppression of Heresy and Witchcraft, 1563–1615', *Catholic Historical Review*, 77 (1991), pp. 403–21.

Devlin, Judith, *The Superstitious Mind: French Peasants and the Supernatural in the Nineteenth Century* (New Haven and London, 1987).

Dixon, C. Scott, 'Popular Beliefs and the Reformation in Brandenburg-Ansbach', in Scribner and Johnson (eds), *Popular Religion*, pp. 129–34.

Dömötör, Tekla, *Hungarian Folk Beliefs* (Bloomington, 1982).

Dömötör, Tekla, 'The Cunning Folk in English and Hungarian Witch Trials', in Venetia Newell (ed.), *Folklore Studies in the Twentieth Century* (Suffolk, 1980), pp. 183–87.

Dowden, Ken, *European Paganism* (London and New York, 2000).

Duffy, Eamon, *The Stripping of the Altars: Traditional Religion in England, 1400–1580* (New Haven and London, 1992).

Dupont-Bouchat, Marie-Sylvie, 'Le diable apprivoisé: la sorcellerie revisitée. Magie et sorcellerie au XIXe siècle', in Muchembled (ed.), *Magie et sorcellerie*, pp. 235–66.

Edsman, Carl-Martin, 'A Manuscript Concerning Inquiries into Witchcraft in Swedish Lapland ("Trolldomsrannsakningar i Lappmarken"), 1649–1739 by Erik Nordberg', *ARV: Scandinavian Yearbook of Folklore*, 39 (1983), pp. 121–37.

Edsman, Carl-Martin, 'A Swedish Female Folk Healer from the Beginning of the Eighteenth Century', in Edsman (ed.), *Studies in Shamanism* (Stockholm, 1967), pp. 120–65.

Eliade, Mircea, *Le chamanisme et les techniques archaiques de l'extase* (Paris, 1951).

Eliade, Mircea, 'Some Observations on European Witchcraft', *History of Religions*, 14 (1974), pp. 149–72.

Eliade, Mircea (ed.), *The Encyclopaedia of Religion*, xiii (London, 1987).

Elmer, Peter, '"Saints or Sorcerers": Quakerism, Demonology and the Decline of Witchcraft in Seventeenth-Century England', in Barry, Hester and Roberts (eds), *Witchcraft*, pp. 145–83.

Emmison, F. G., *Elizabethan Life: Morals and the Church Courts, Mainly from Essex Archidiaconal Records* (Chelmsford, 1973).

Evans, Griff., 'Exorcism in Wales', *Folklore* (1892), pp. 275–76.

Ewen, C. L'Estrange, *Witch Hunting and Witch Trials* (London, 1929).

Ewen, C. L'Estrange, *Witchcraft and Demonianism* (London, 1933).

Fanger, Claire (ed.), *Conjuring Spirits: Texts and Traditions of Medieval Ritual Magic* (Stroud, 1998).

Fanger, Claire, 'Plundering the Egyptian Treasure: John the Monk's *Book of Visions* and its Relation to the *Ars Notoria* of Solomon', in Fanger (ed.), *Conjuring Spirits*, pp. 216–50.

Fisher, Paul Hawkins, *Notes and Recollections of Stroud, Gloucestershire* (London, 1871).

Fletcher, J. S., *Recollections of a Yorkshire Village* (London, 1910).

Flint, Valerie, *The Rise of Magic in Early Medieval Europe* (Princeton and Oxford, 1991).

Gaboriau, Patrick, *La pensée ensorcelée* (Les Sables-d'Olonne, 1987).

Clarke Garrett, 'Witches and Cunning Folk in the Old Régime', in Jacques Beauroy et al (eds), *The Wolf and the Lamb: Popular Culture in France* (Stanford, 1976), pp. 53–64.

Gaskill, Malcolm, *Crime and Mentalities in Early Modern England* (Cambridge, 2000).

Gaster, M., 'English Charms of the Seventeenth Century', *Folklore*, 21 (1910), pp. 375–78.

Gentilcore, David, *From Bishop to Witch: The System of the Sacred in Early Modern Terra d'Otranto* (Manchester, 1992).

Gentilcore, David, *Healers and Healing in Early Modern Italy* (Manchester, 1998).

Gestrich, Andreas, 'Pietismus und Aberglaube: zum Zusammenhang von popularem Pietismus und dem Ende der Hexenverfolgung im 18. Jahrhundert', in Lorenz and Bauer (eds), *Das Ende der Hexenverfolgung*, pp. 269–86.

Gibson, Marion, *Early Modern Witches: Witchcraft Cases in Contemporary Writing* (London and New York, 2000).

Gibson, Marion, *Reading Witchcraft* (London and New York, 1999).

Gijswijt-Hofstra, Marijke, 'Witchcraft after the Witch-Trials', in Ankarloo and Clark (eds), *Witchcraft and Magic in Europe: The Eighteenth and Nineteenth Centuries*, pp. 95–189.

Gijswijt-Hofstra, 'Witchcraft before Zeeland Magistrates and Church Councils, Sixteenth to Twentieth Centuries', in Gijswijt-Hofstra and Frijhoff (eds), *Witchcraft*, pp. 103–19.

Gijswijt-Hofstra, Marijke and Willem Frijhoff (eds), *Witchcraft in the Netherlands* (Rotterdam, 1991).

Ginzburg, Carlo, *Ecstasies: Deciphering the Witches' Sabbath* (London, 1990).

Carlo Ginzburg, *The Night Battles: Witchcraft and Agrarian Cults in the Sixteenth and Seventeenth Centuries* (Baltimore and London, 1983; first published in Italian 1966).

Gowing, Laura, *Domestic Dangers: Women, Words and Sex in Early Modern England* (Oxford, 1996).

Graham, Henry Grey, *The Social Life of Scotland in the Eighteenth Century* (London, [1899] 1901).

Green, Ian, *The Christian's ABC: Catachisms and Catechising in England c. 1530–1740* (Oxford, 1996).

Gregory, Annabel, 'Witchcraft, Politics and "Good Neighbourhood" in Early Seventeenth-Century Rye', *Past and Present*, 133 (1991), pp. 31–66.

Grinsell, L. V., *The Ancient Burial Mounds of England* (2nd edn, London, 1953).

Gutch, Mrs, *County Folklore: Concerning East Riding of Yorkshire* (London, 1912).

Hale, William, *A Series of Precedents and Proceedings in Criminal Causes* (London, 1847).

Haliczer, Stephen, *Inquisition and Society in the Kingdom of Valencia, 1478–1834* (Oxford, 1990)

Haliczer, Stephen (ed.), *Inquisition and Society in Early Modern Europe* (Totowa, 1987).

Hall, Trevor H., *Old Conjuring Books: A Bibliographical and Historical Study* (London, 1972).

Hamer, Edward, 'A Parochial Account of Llangurig', *Montgomeryshire Collections*, 3 (1870), pp. 262–73.

Hammill, John, *The Rosicrucian Seer* (Wellingborough, 1986).

Hancock, T. W., 'The History of Llanrhaiadr-yn-Mochnant', *Montgomeryshire Collections*, 6 (1873), pp. 329–30.

Hardwick, Charles, *Traditions, Superstitions and Folk-Lore* (London, 1872).

Hardy, W. J. (ed.), *Hertford County Records: Notes and Extracts from the Sessions Rolls 1581–1698*, i (Hertford, 1905).

Hardy, William Le (ed.), *County of Middlesex Calendar to the Sessions Records*, i (London, 1935).

Harland, John, 'A Lancashire Charm, in Cypher, against Witchcraft and Evil Spirits', *Historic Society of Lancashire and Cheshire Proceedings*, 4 (1852), pp. 81–85.

Harland, J. and T. T. Wilkinson, *Lancashire Folklore* (London, 1882).

Harley, David, 'Historians as Demonologists: The Myth of the Midwife-Witch', *The Journal for the Social History of Medicine*, 3 (1990), pp. 1–26.

Hart, W. H., 'Observations on Some Documents Relating to Magic in the Reign of Queen Elizabeth', *Archaeologia*, 40 (1866), pp. 389–97.

Heikkinen, Antero and Timo Kervinen, 'Finland: The Male Domination', in Ankarloo and Henningsen (eds), *Early Modern European Witchcraft*, pp. 319–39.

Henderson, William, *Notes on the Folk-Lore of the Northern Counties of England* (London, [1866] 1879).

Henningsen, Gustav, '"The Ladies from Outside": An Archaic Pattern of the Witches' Sabbath', in Ankarloo and Henningsen (eds), *Early Modern European Witchcraft*, pp. 191–215.

Henningsen, Gustav, 'Witch Persecution after the Era of the Witch Trials: A Contribution to Danish Ethnohistory', *ARV : Scandinavian Yearbook of Folklore* 44 (1988), pp. 103–53.

Hewett, Sarah, *Nummits and Crummits* (London, 1900).

Hole, Christina, *Witchcraft in England* (London, 1977).

Hoppál, Milhály, 'Traces of Shamanism in Hungarian Folk Beliefs', in Milhály Hoppál (ed.), *Shamanism in Eurasia* (Göttingen, 1984), pp. 430–49.

Horsley, Richard A., 'Further Reflections on Witchcraft and European Folk Religion', *History of Religions*, 19 (1980), pp. 71–95.

Horsley, Richard A., 'Who were the Witches? The Social Role of the Accused in the European Witch Trials', *Journal of Interdisciplinary History*, 9 (1979), pp. 689–715.

Houlbrooke, Ralph, *Church Courts and the People during the English Reformation* (Oxford, 1979).

Houston, R. A., *Literacy in Early Modern Europe: Culture and Education, 1500–1800* (London and New York, 1988).

Howell, T. B. (ed.), *Cobbett's Complete Collection of State Trials and Proceedings*, 33 vols (London, 1809–26).

Howse, W. H., *Radnorshire* (Hereford, 1949).

Hsia, R. Po-chia (ed.), *The German People and the Reformation* (Ithaca and London, 1988).

Hunt, Robert, *Popular Romances of the West of England* (3rd edn, London, 1881).

Hussey, Arthur, 'Visitations of the Archdeacon of Canterbury', *Archaeologia Cantiana*, 26 (1904), pp. 17–51.

Hutton, Ronald, *The Pagan Religions of the Ancient British Isles* (Oxford, 1991).

Hutton, Ronald, *The Rise and Fall of Merry England* (Oxford, 1994).

Hutton, Ronald, *The Triumph of the Moon* (Oxford, 1999).

Hutton, Ronald, *Shamans: Siberian Spirituality and the Western Imagination* (London, 2001).

Ingram, Martin, *Church Courts, Sex and Marriage in England, 1570–1640* (Cambridge, 1987).

Isaac, Evan, *Coelion Cymru* (Aberystwyth, 1938).

Jackson, C. (ed.), *The Diary of Abraham de la Pryme, the Yorkshire Antiquary* (Durham, London and Edinburgh, 1870).

Jeaffreson, J. C., *Middlesex County Records*, 4 vols (London, 1886–92).

Jenkins, Gereint H., 'Popular Beliefs in Wales from the Restoration to Methodism', *Bwletin y Bwrdd Gwybodau Celtaidd*, 27 (1977), pp. 440–62.

Johansen, Jens Christian, 'Denmark: The Sociology of Accusations', in Ankarloo and Henningsen (eds), *European Witchcraft*, pp. 339–67.

Johansen, Jens Christian, 'Witchcraft, Sin and Repentance: The Decline of Danish Witchcraft Trials', *Acta Ethnographica Hungarica*, 37 (1991–2), pp. 413–23.

Jones, Prudence, and Nigel Pennick, *A History of Pagan Europe* (London, 1995).

Jones, T. Gwynn, *Welsh Folklore and Folk-Custom* (London, 1930).

Jones, William R., 'Political Uses of Sorcery in Medieval Europe', *Historian*, 34 (1972), pp. 670–87.

Kaplan, S. L. (ed.), *Understanding Popular Culture: Europe from the Middle Ages to the Nineteenth Century* (Berlin and New York, 1984).

Kieckhefer, Richard, *Magic in the Middle Ages* (Cambridge, 1989).

King, Francis X., *The Flying Sorcerer* (Oxford, 1992).

Kittredge, George L., *Witchcraft in Old and New England* (Cambridge, Massachusetts, 1929).

Klaniczay, Gábor, 'Hungary: The Accusations and the Universe of Popular Magic', in Ankarloo and Henningsen (eds), *Early Modern European Witchcraft*, pp. 219–57.

Klaniczay, Gábor, 'Shamanistic Elements in Central European Witchcraft', in Hoppál (ed.), *Shamanism in Eurasia*, pp. 404–22.

Kristóf, Ildikó, '"Wise women", Sinners and the Poor: The Social Background of Witch-Hunting in a Sixteenth- to Eighteenth-Century Calvinist City of Eastern Hungary', *Acta Ethnographica Hungarica*, 37 (1991–92), pp. 93–123.

Liddell, E. W. and Michael Howard, *The Pickingill Papers* (Chieveley, 1994).

Lorenz, Sönke and Dieter Bauer (eds), *Das Ende der Hexenverfolgung* (Stuttgart, 1995).

Lorenz, Sönke and Dieter Bauer (eds), *Hexenverfolgung. Beiträge zur Forschung* (Würzberg, 1995).

Lugh, *Old George Pickingill and the Roots of Modern Witchcraft* (Wiccan Publications, 1982).

MacDonald, Michael, *Mystical Bedlam: Madness, Anxiety, and Healing in Seventeenth-Century England* (Cambridge, 1981).

Macfarlane, Alan, 'A Tudor Anthropologist: George Gifford's *Discourse* and *Dialogue*', in Anglo (ed.), *The Damned Art*, pp. 140–56.

Macfarlane, Alan, *Witchcraft in Tudor and Stuart England* (London, 1970).

Mackay, Charles, *Extraordinary Popular Delusions and the Madness of Crowds* (2nd edn, London, 1852).

Maple, Eric, 'Cunning Murrell', *Folklore*, 71 (1960), pp. 36–43.

Maple, Eric, *Magic, Medicine and Quackery* (London, 1968).

Maple, Eric, *The Dark World of Witches* (London, 1962).

March, H. Colley, 'Dorset Folklore Collected in 1897', *Folklore* 10 (1899), pp. 107–12.

Marsh, Christopher, *Popular Religion in Sixteenth-Century England* (London, 1998).

Martin, C. Trice, 'Clerical Life in the Fifteenth Century, as Illustrated by Proceedings of the Court of Chancery', *Archaeologia*, 60/2 (1907), pp. 353–78.

Martin, Ruth, *Witchcraft and the Inquisition in Venice, 1550–1650* (Oxford, 1989).

Mathiesen, Robert, 'A Thirteenth-Century Ritual to Attain the Beatific Vision from the *Sworn Book* of Honorious of Thebes', in Fanger (ed.), *Conjuring Spirits*, pp. 143–63.

Mee, Arthur, *Magic in Carmarthenshire: The Harries of Cwrt-y-cadno* (Cardiff, 1912).

Merrifield, Ralph, *The Archaeology of Witchcraft and Magic* (London, 1987).

Milis, Ludo (ed.), *The Pagan Middle Ages* (Woodbridge, 1998).

Monter, William, *Ritual, Myth and Magic in Early Modern Europe* (Brighton, 1983).

Monter, William, *Witchcraft in France and Switzerland* (Ithaca and London, 1976).

Monter, William, 'Witchcraft in Geneva, 1537–1662', *Journal of Modern History*, 43 (1971), pp. 179–204.

Mozzani, Eloïse, *Magie et superstitions de la fin de l'Ancien Régime a la Restauration* (Paris, 1988).

Muchembled, Robert (ed.), *Magie et sorcellerie en Europe du moyen âge à nos jours* (Paris, 1994).

Muyard, F., 'Un manuel de sorcellerie en Basse Bretagne au XVIIIe siècle', *Annales de Bretagne et des Pays de l'Ouest*, 99 (1992), pp. 291–97

Naess, Hans Eyvind, 'Norway: The Criminological Context', in Ankarloo and Henningsen (eds), *Early Modern European Witchcraft*, pp. 367–83.

Nenonen, Marko, '"Envious Are All the People, Witches Watch at Every Gate": Finnish Witches and Witch Trials in the Seventeenth Century', *Scandinavian Journal of History*, 18 (1993), pp. 77-91.

Nenonen, Marko, *Noituus, taikuus ja noitavainot* (Helsinki, 1992).

Nichols, John Gough, *Narratives of the Days of the Reformation* (Camden Society, 1859).

Nichols, John Gough (ed.), *The Diary of Henry Machyn, Citizen and Merchant-Taylor of London* (Camden Society, 1848).

Nordland, Odd, 'The Street of "the Wise Women": A Contribution to the Sociology of Folk-Medicine', *ARV: Journal of Scandinavian Folklore*, 18-19 (1962-3), pp. 263-74.

Obelkevitch, James, *Religion and Rural Society: South Lindsey, 1825-75* (Oxford, 1976).

Oja, Linda, *Varken Gud Eller Natur: Synen på Magi i 1600-och 1700-talets Sverige* (Stockholm, 1999).

Oldridge, Darren, *The Devil in Early Modern England* (Stroud, 2000).

O'Neil, Mary, 'Magical Healing, Love Magic and the Inquisition in Late Sixteenth-Century Modena', in Haliczer (ed.), *Inquisition*, pp. 88-115.

O'Neil, Mary, 'Sacerdote ovvero Strione: Ecclesiastical and Superstitious Remedies in Sixteenth-Century Italy', in Kaplan (ed.), *Understanding Popular Culture*, pp. 53- 84.

Ortega, M. Sánchez, 'Sorcery and Eroticism in Love Magic', in M. E. Perry and A. J. Cruz (eds), *Cultural Encounters: The Impact of the Inquisition in Spain and the New World* (Berkeley and Oxford, 1991), pp. 58-92.

Owen, Elias, *Welsh Folk-Lore* (Aberystwyth, 1896).

Palgrave, Francis, 'The Confessions of Richard Bishop and Robert Seyman, before the Privy Council, Touching Certain Prophecies Connected with Popular Commotions in Norfolk', *Norfolk Archaeology*, 1 (1847), pp. 209-23.

Peacock, Edward, 'Extracts from Lincoln Episcopal Visitations', *Archaeologia*, 48/2 (1885), pp. 249-69.

Pearson, Alexander, *Annals of Kirby Lonsdale* (Kendal, 1930).

Perkins, Maureen, *The Reform of Time: Magic and Modernity* (London and Sterling, 2001).

Peters, Edward, *The Magician, the Witch and the Law* (Philadelphia, 1978).

Philips, D. Rhys, *The History of the Vale of Neath* (Swansea, 1925).

Pócs, Éva *Between the Living and the Dead* (Budapest, 1999).

Pócs, Éva, 'Hungarian Táltos and his European Parallels', in Milhály Hoppál and Juha Pentikäinen (eds), *Uralic Mythology and Folklore* (Budapest and Helsinki, 1989), pp. 251–76.

Polwhele, R., *Traditions and Recollections* (2 vols, London, 1826).

Porter, Roy, 'The People's Health in Georgian England', in Tim Harris (ed.), *Popular Culture in England, c. 1500–1850* (London, 1995), pp. 124–43.

Porter, Roy, 'Witchcraft and Magic in Enlightenment, Romantic and Liberal Thought', in Ankarloo and Clark (eds), *Witchcraft and Magic in Europe*, pp. 191–283.

Purvis, J. S., *Tudor Parish Documents* (Cambridge, 1948).

Quennell, Peter (ed.), *Mayhew's London* (London, 1969).

Raine, James (ed.), *Depositions and other Ecclesiastical Proceedings from the Courts of Durham* (Surtees Society, 1845).

Raine, James (ed.), *Depositions from the Castle of York* (Durham, 1861).

Raine, James, 'Proceedings Connected with a Remarkable Charge of Sorcery', *Archaeological Journal*, 16 (1859), pp. 71–81.

Ramsey, Matthew, *Professional and Popular Medicine in France, 1770–1830: The Social World of Medical Practice* (Cambridge, 1988).

Reay, Barry, *The Quakers and the English Revolution* (London, 1985).

Riley, Henry Thomas, *Memorials of London and London Life* (London, 1868).

Roberts, Julian and Andrew G. Watson, *John Dee's Library Catalogue* (London, 1990).

Robertson, William, *Rochdale and the Vale of Whitworth* (Rochdale, 1897).

Rosen, Barbara (ed.), *Witchcraft in England, 1558–1618* (Amherst, 1969).

Rowlands, Alison, 'Witchcraft and Popular Religion in Early Modern Rothenburg ob der Tauber', in Scribner and Johnson (eds), *Popular Religion*, pp. 101–19.

Rowse, A. L., *The Case Books of Simon Forman* (London, [1974] 1976).

Ruggiero, Guido, *Binding Passions* (Oxford, 1993).

Rushton, Peter, 'Women, Witchcraft and Slander in Early Modern England: Cases from the Church Courts of Durham, 1560–1675', *Northern History*, 18 (1982), pp. 116–32.

Ryan, W. F. and C. B. Schmitt (eds), *Pseudo-Aristotle in the Middle Ages: The Theology and other Texts* (London, 1986).

Rørbye, Birgitte, *Kloge folk og skidt folk. Kvaksalveriets epoke i Danmark* (Copenhagen, 1976).

Sallmann, Jean-Michel, *Chercheurs de trésors et jeteuses de sorts* (Paris, 1986).

Sawyer, Ronald C., '"Strangely Handled in All her Lyms": Witchcraft and Healing in Jacobean England', *Journal of Social History*, 22 (1988–9), pp. 461–86.

Schöck, Inge, 'Das Ende der Hexenprozesse – das Ende des Hexenglaubens?', in Lorenz and Bauer (eds), *Hexenverfolgung*, pp. 375–89.

Scribner, Bob and Trevor Johnson (eds), *Popular Religion in Germany and Central Europe, 1400–1800* (London, 1996).

Scully, Sally, 'Marriage or a Career?: Witchcraft as an Alternative in Seventeenth-Century Venice', *Journal of Social History*, 28 (1995), pp. 857–76.

Sebald, Hans, 'Shaman, Healer, Witch: Comparing Shamanism with Franconian Folk Magic', *Ethnologia Europaea*, 14 (1984), pp. 125–42.

Sebald, Hans, 'The 6th and 7th Books of Moses: The Historical and Sociological Vagaries of a Grimoire', *Ethnologia Europaea*, 28 (1988), pp. 53–58.

Shah, Idries, *The Secret Lore of Magic: Books of the Sorcerers* (London, 1957).

Sharpe, James, *Defamation and Sexual Slander in Early Modern England: The Church Courts of York*, Borthwick Papers, 58 (1980).

Sharpe, James, *Instruments of Darkness: Witchcraft in England 1550–1750* (London, 1996).

Sherlock, Davis, 'An Ancient Christian Word-Square at Great Gidding', *Proceedings of the Cambridgeshire Antiquarian Society*, 72 (1982–3), pp. 90–93.

Simpson, W. Sparrow, 'On a Seventeenth Century Roll containing Prayers and Magical Signs', *Journal of the British Archaeological Association*, 40 (1884), pp. 297- 332.

Smith, Kathryn C., 'The Wise Man and his Community', *Folk Life*, 15 (1977), pp. 24–35.

Stark-Arola, Laura, *Magic, Body and Social Order* (Tampere, 1998).

T., D. R., 'Demonology and Witchcraft', *Montgomeryshire Collections*, 37 (1915), pp. 143–50.

Tangherlini, Timothy, '"How Do You Know She's a Witch?": Witches, Cunning Folk and Competition in Denmark', *Western Folklore*, forthcoming.

Tausiet, Maria, 'Witchcraft as Metaphor: Infanticide and its Translations in Aragón in the Sixteenth and Seventeenth Centuries', in Clark (ed.), *Languages of Witchcraft*, pp. 179–97.

Taylor, M. R. T., 'Witches and Witchcraft', *Folklore*, 46 (1935), pp. 171–72.

Thomas, A. II., *Calendar of Plea and Memoranda. Rolls of the City of London, AD 1364–1381* (Cambridge, 1929).

Thomas, Keith, *Religion and the Decline of Magic* (London, 1971).

Thompson, A. Hamilton, *Diocese of Lincoln Visitations of Religious Houses, 1436–1449* (Oxford, 1927).

Thompson, C. J. S., *Mysteries and Secrets of Magic* (London, 1927).

Thorndike, Lynn, *The History of Magic and Experimental Science* (8 vols, New York, 1923–58).

Tongue, Ruth, *Somerset Folklore* (Llanerch, [1965] 1995).

Tourney, Garfield, 'The Physician and Witchcraft in Restoration England', *Medical History*, 16 (1972), pp. 143–55.

Traimond, Bernard, *Le pouvoir de la maladie: Magie et politique dans les Landes de Gascogne, 1750–1826* (Bordeaux, 1988).

Train, Joseph, *An Historical and Statistical Account of the Isle of Man* (Douglas, 1845).

Trotman, E. E., 'Seventeenth-Century Treasure-Seeking at Bridgwater', *Somerset and Dorset Notes and Queries*, 27 (1961), pp. 220–21.

Turner, Dawson, 'Brief Remarks, Accompanied with Documents, Illustrative of Trial by Jury, Treasure-Trove, and Invocation of Spirits', *Norfolk Archaeology*, 1 (1847), pp. 41–65.

Tyler, P., 'The Church Courts at York and Witchcraft Prosecutions, 1567–1640', *Northern History*, 4 (1970), pp. 84–109.

Udal, John Symonds, *Dorsetshire Folk-Lore* (Hertford, 1922).

Valiente, Doreen, *Witchcraft for Tomorrow* (London, 1978).

Várkonyi, Ágnes, 'Connection between the Cessation of Witch Trials and the Transformation of the Social Structure Related to Hygiene', *Acta Ethnographica Hungarica*, 37 (1991–92), pp. 425–79.

Waardt, Hans de, 'From Cunning Man to Natural Healer', in Hans Binneveld and Rudolf Dekker (eds), *Curing and Insuring* (Hilversum, 1993), pp. 33–43.

Waite, Arthur Edward, *The Book of Ceremonial Magic* (London, 1911).

Watson, W. Willis, *Somerset Life and Character* (London, 1924).

Weeks, William, 'Charms against Witches and Evil Spirits', *Folk-Lore*, 31 (1920), pp. 146–47.

Wheater, William, 'Yorkshire Superstitions', *Old Yorkshire*, 4 (1883), pp. 265–71.

Wilson, Stephen, *The Magical Universe: Everyday Ritual and Magic in Pre-Modern Europe* (London and New York, 2000).

Winstedt, E. O., 'The Squires Family', *Journal of the Gypsy Lore Society*, third series, 16 (1937), pp. 145–55.

# Index

Abano, Peter de, 123, 133
abortion, 102
abracadabra, 150, 154
Acts of Parliament,
  conjuration and witchcraft
    (1542) 4, 6–7, 8, 173; (1563)
    6–7, 8, 172; (1604) 8, 9, 10,
    11, 18, 20; (1736) 20–21, 37,
    41
  vagrancy, 10, 23–24, 25, 28
  Fraudulent Mediums Act, 187
Adelbert, Saint, 157
Ady, Thomas, 30, 35, 47, 76
Africa, 49, 50
Agrippa, Cornelius, 6, 121–22, 123,
  126, 127, 128, 129, 131, 133, 136,
  137, 138, 139, 141, 142, 144, 150,
  154, 174, 175, 176
Alfred, King, 1
Allen, William, 11, 99
Amos, Mr and Mrs, 190
Ardennes, 130
Articles of Visitation, 5
Ashmole, Elias, 124
Astley, Philip, 47
astrologers, astrology, 42, 43, 48,
  72, 73, 78–81, 90, 95, 100, 116,
  122, 123, 133, 134, 135, 136, 137,
  141, 148, 154, 158
*Athenian Mercury*, 38, 129
Atkinson, John, 53–54, 63, 84
Atkinson, Thomas, 86
Aubrey, John, 150
Austria, 167

Baker, James, 86, 88, 107, 196
Baker, Richard, 72
Baldock, Ralph, 2
Banastre, William, 14
Banks, Peter, 62, 101, 102
Baring-Gould, Sabine, 27, 54
Barrett, Francis, 73, 142–43
Bartlett, Mrs, 72, 107
Bate, William, 11
Bateman, Mary, 50, 72, 102
Battersby, Nicholas, 10, 11
Bean, Sarah, 55
Beare, Dr, 78
Bedfordshire, 31
Belgium, 174
Bellett, Ann, 11
Belton, Mariot de, 2
*benandanti*, 182
Bennett, Anne, 71, 72, 95
Berewold, Robert, 2
Berkshire, 25, 56, 80, 85, 88, 94, 106,
  108
Berkyng, John, 3
Bernard, Richard, 15, 18, 29, 30, 86,
  104, 110
Berry, William, 70
Bert, Dr, 78
Beth, Rae, 196
Beveridge, William, 135
Bible, 1, 100–1, 102, 134, 147, 148,
  150, 154, 183, 196
Bickerstaff, Isaac, 42
Blagrave, Joseph, 80–81, 96, 104, 109,
  110, 139

Bobbin, Tim, *see* Collier, John
Bodenham, Anne, 36, 63, 71, 73, 86, 87, 145
Bodin, Jean, 77
Bolingbrooke, Roger, 1
Bonner, Edmund, 6
Bottrell, William, 153
Boulton, Richard, 39–40
Bourn, Dr, 109
Bovet, Richard, 30
Breslaw, Phillip, 21, 46
Brewer, William, 84, 87, 89, 110
Brinley, John, 38
Bristol, 112
Brome, Isabella, 2
Brooks, James, 90
Broughton, Mother, 68
Buchan, P., 131
Buckinghamshire, 18, 19, 79
Buckley, John, 122
Bulwer-Lytton, Edward, 139
Bumstead, George, 142, 143, 194
Burgh, Hubert de, 1
Burney, Charles, 85
Burrell, Cuthbert, 103
Butler, John, 134
Butler, Joseph, 87, 112
Buts, Joan, 109

Calvin, Jean, 166
Cambridgeshire, 122, 153
Cannon, John, 129
Carolina Code, 164
Carre, Widow, 16
Casaubon, Meric, 124, 138
catechisms, 38
Catholicism, 35–36, 49, 111, 165, 170–72, 177
Chaffer, Clayton, 101, 137
Chambers, Mother, 16
Charlemagne, 131
Charlesworth, Thomas, 88, 89, 112, 141

charming, 19, 67, 83–84, 85–86, 192, 193, 194
Cheshire, 113
Chestre, John, 2
Clarke, Adam, 128–29
Clarke, Edith, 19
Clarke, Thomas, 126
Clegate, Henry, 36
Clegg, George, 43–45, 74, 114
Clemmensen, Jens, 174, 176
Cobham, Eleonor, 1
Cokars, John, 125
Coleman, Dorcas, 78
Coleridge, Samuel Taylor, 139
Collander, John, 84, 86
Collier, John, 43–45
Colmer, John, 72
Compton, Dr, 80
compurgation, 17
Cooke, Christopher, 137
Cooke, Rev., 24
Cooper, John, 136
Cooper, Thomas, 30, 67
Corneille, Thomas, 20
Cornwall, 56, 57, 62, 70, 153, 155
Cotton, William, 87
Cox, Francis, 6
Cranmer, Archbishop Thomas, 5
Crossby, Jane, 101
Crowley, Aleister, 194
Crowther, Timothy, 22, 82, 141, 160
Croxton, Mrs, 5
Culliford, Frederick, 64, 105
Culpeper, Nicholas, 79, 110, 116, 134
Cumbria, 18, 86
Curson, John, 93
Cyprianus, 130, 174, 176

Darrell, John, 36
Davies, W. LL., 193
Davis, James, 190–91, 192
Davis, Mary, 97
Davison, Tobias, 154

# INDEX

Davye, John, 5
Dawson, William, 85
Death, Thomas, 78
Dee, John, 124
Defoe, Daniel, 40–41, 42, 43, 135
Delcambre, Etienne, 167
Denley, John, 138–39, 142, 194
Denmark, 163, 164, 165, 174
Derbyshire, 21, 45, 112
Detcheverry, Gratien, 174, 176
devil, 2, 6, 9, 30, 31, 32, 37, 38, 46, 48–49, 61, 63, 77, 79, 110, 114, 166
Devon, 10, 25, 46, 72, 77, 82, 84, 85, 87, 100, 106, 110, 114, 149, 159, 192
Digby, Kenelm, 132
Domingo, James, 87
Dömötör, Tekla, 181
Dorset, 62, 70, 72, 86, 88, 107, 112, 129
Douglas, Mr Akers, 189
Drage, William, 77, 79
Drake, Edward, 106
Drayton, Robert, 73
Drinkwater, Peter, 127–28
Dublin, 41, 42
Dudley, 111
Dunton, John, 38
Durant, John, 150
Durbin, Henry, 46
Durham, 2, 15, 17, 78

Edward I, 1
Edward VI, 4
Eliade, Mircea, 178
Elizabeth I, 6
Elton, Hannah, 190
Essex, 9, 11, 12, 13, 16, 17, 18, 33, 57, 67, 68, 71, 73, 78, 87, 127, 133, 193
Evans, Benjamin, 22
Evans, Daniel, 159
Ewart, Dr, 105

Ewen, Cecil, xi–xii
exorcism and exorcists, 35, 36, 81, 103, 104, 111, 170, 172

fairies, 68, 70, 84, 95, 182–84
Fare, Ann, 87
Farmer, Dr, 117
Farmer, Mary, 109
Farnworth, Richard, 37
Faust, Dr, 176
Ferguson, Donald, 166
Filmer, Robert, 35
Finland, 168, 179
Fisher, Mary Ann, 102
Fletcher, J. S., 133, 143
folklorists, 53–54
Foot, Emma, 64, 105
Forfar, William, 57, 58–59
Forman, Simon, 95
fortune-telling, 10, 23, 46, 47, 71, 72, 73, 79, 87, 116, 142, 187
Fox, George, 36
France, 130–131, 163, 165, 167, 174, 175, 176, 177,
Freake, James, 121, 127, 139
Freare, Elizabeth, 14
Freman, Cristina, 3
Freman, Nicholas, 3
Fynes (cunning-man), 82

Gadbury, John, 127, 136
Gaule, John, 30, 60–61, 121
Garmann, Robert, 14
Geneva, 166
Germany, 130, 163, 167, 169, 177
Geyte, John, 3
Gibson, Elizabeth, 99
Gifford, George, 32–33, 61, 62
Giles, Clara, 26
Giles, Maria, 25–27, 56, 72, 85, 87, 88, 90, 98, 99, 102, 143
girdle-measuring, 84
Glanvill, Joseph, 80

Gloucestershire, 4, 18, 22, 24, 86, 97, 112, 127, 140, 153, 187, 189
Gore, Susanna, 86
Greaton, Nicholas, 37, 97
Green, Hannah, 86
Greene, Ann, 13
Gregory, Emma, 27, 99
Grey, Jane, 99
Griffiths, H., 117
Gunter, Anne, 106
Gunter, Joseph, 88, 90
gypsies, 40, 51, 57, 68, 96, 103

Hallett, James, 115
Hammer, Christopher, 177
Hampshire, 71, 95, 98, 102
Hancock, Agnes, 70
Harding, Thomas, 67
Hardy, Thomas, 57
Harries, Henry, 134, 144, 160
Harris, William, 155–56
Harrison, F. Bayford, 59
Hartlay, Edmund, 36
Hausselet, Jean, 174
Hawkins, Thomas, 48–50, 104, 105, 112, 149
Haynes, Joseph, 87
Hayward, Ellen, 188–92
Haywood, James, 106
heart, 109
Heathcote, Deborah, 72
Heather, Thomas, 10
hedge witch, 196
Henry III, 1
Henry VI, 1
Henry VIII, 4
herbs and herbalism, 74, 75, 77, 79, 81, 83, 106, 109–11, 116, 133, 189, 191–92, 193, 194
Herefordshire, 117
Hertfordshire, 10, 67, 77, 87
Heydon, Christopher, 135
Heydon, John, 124, 137, 142, 143

Heywood, Thomas, xv, 35, 70
Hillman, William Henry, 25
Hills, William, 73, 87
Hockley, Frederick, 138–39, 155
Hogsdon, wise woman of, xi, 35, 71, 114
Holland, Henry, 30, 31, 32
Holland, William, 63, 87
Holond, John, 3
Holy Roman Empire, 164
Homes, Nathaniel, 32
Honorius, 120–21, 131
Hopkin, Jacob, 16
Hopkins, Matthew, 14, 169
Horsley, Richard, 167
Hoser, Katherina, 169
Howell, Thomas Bayly, 23
Hume, David, 49
Hungary, 164, 165, 166, 168, 180, 181
Huntingdonshire, 30, 121
Hutchinson, Francis, 39–40

Inquisitions, 165, 172–73, 182
Isle of Man, 113
Italy, 165, 171, 172, 175, 176
Ivors, Lord, 99

James I, 8, 34, 123, 179
Jefferies, Ann, 70
Jewel, John, 6
Jones, Edwin, 155, 156
Jones, John, 22
Jones, Walter, 99
Jonson, Ben, 124
Jourdayne, Margerie, 1

Kemp, Ursula, 12, 110
Kent, 16, 18, 34, 36, 55, 87
Kingsbury, Anne, 20, 73, 95, 96
Kipling, Rudyard, 57
Kitch, Richard, 96
Kittredge, George, xi–xii
Klanickzay, Gábor, 181

Lackington, James, 142
Lambe, John, 27, 73
Lamkyn, John, 4, 120
Lancashire, 36, 43, 63, 90, 101, 136, 150, 154
Langton, Walter, 1
Lattimer, William, 107
Laukiston, Richard, 2
Leicestershire, 16, 70
Leigh (cunning-man), 96
Leo III, 131
Lilly, William, 73, 80, 95, 136, 137, 139, 151
Lincolnshire, 4, 16, 18, 51, 69, 72, 73, 82, 87, 93, 100, 113, 115
Locke, John, 49
London, 2, 3, 5, 12, 17, 23, 32, 47, 68, 71, 73, 87, 94, 95, 99, 100, 108, 114, 120, 121, 123, 127, 139, 141, 144, 147
Long, Hannah, 98
Long, Moses, 140–141, 143
love magic, 2, 101–2, 172–73
Lupton, John, 98
Lyne, Richard, 62

Macfarlane, Alan, xi–xiii, 76, 181
Machyn, Henry, 5
Magnus, Albertus, 121, 131, 132, 133
Malfrey, Thomas, 5
Manchester, 85, 137, 153
Manning (cunning-man), 106
Maple, Eric, 193
Markey, George, 189
Markey, John, 188–189
Marsh (cunning-man), 31
Martin, John, 55
Martin, William, 154
Mary I, 35
Mason, James, 31, 61
Mayes, Joan, 19
Mayhew, Henry, 47
McVeagh, Mr, 189

Melton, John, 36, 68
Merret, François, 176
Methodism and Methodists, 46, 49, 52, 58, 82, 90, 128
Middleton, John, 134
midwifery, 72
Miles, Martha, 87
Miller (cunning-man), 56
Monter, William, 167
Moon, Mr, 47
Moore, Mrs, 50, 51
More, Hannah, 57, 58
Morgan, Christopher, 5
Morris, James, 137
Morris, Richard, 22, 45, 72, 73, 84
Morrison, Arthur, 57
Morrison, Richard, 137
Moses, 130
Moulton, Thomas, 122
Moussall, Humphry, 148, 149
Murray, Mary Catherine, 64, 88, 106, 159
Murrell, James, 57, 133
Mysdene, Robert, 3

Napier, Richard, 79–80, 172
Napoleon, 103, 137
Nasche, Edmund, 4
Netherlands, 163, 166, 167
newspapers, 54–56
Niblett, Mrs, 24
nightmare, 184
Norfolk, 5, 18, 22, 88, 94, 102, 105, 106, 108, 109, 120, 121
Northumbria, 62, 98, 101
Norway, 168, 177
Nostradamus, 135
Nottinghamshire, 151
novelists, 56–60
Nowell, Alexander, 33

Olive (cunning-man), 68
Owen, Elias, 54

Owldring, Thomas, 121
Oxfordshire, 122

paganism, 177, 185–86, 193–94
palmistry, xi, 30, 71
Paracelsus, 122–123, 137, 138, 140, 150
Parker, Thomas, 159
Parkes, David, 137
Parkins, John, 51–52, 62, 72, 73, 101, 102, 103, 110, 115–18, 140, 141, 143, 148, 160
Parson Joe, 82
Patridge, John, 42
Patriche, John, 4
Pepper, Mrs, 36
Perigo, Mrs, 51
Perkins, William, 15, 18, 29–30, 31, 39, 48
Peronet, Aymon, 166
Peterson, Joan, 12, 104, 106
Philips, Judith, 35, 71, 95, 114
Philips, Samuel, 156
Pickingill, George, 193–94
Pócs, Éva, 181
Pole, 120
Poletto, Francesco, 171
Polwhele, Revd, 82
Pope, Richard, 10
Porta, Giambattista della, 122, 134
Porter, John, 2
Portugal, 163, 165
Pot, Henry, 3
Powell, Elizabeth, 10
Price, Mr, 117
Pyle, Robert, 36

Quakers, 36–37

Railey, Joseph, 137, 158
Ramsey, David, 95
Raphael, 137–38, 142, 144, 150
Ravenscroft, Edward, 20

Read, John, 129
Read, R., 124
Read, Sophia, 89, 105,
Remy, Nicholas, 77
Rendle, Thomas, 64, 88
Rhodes, John, 137, 138
Richards, Margaret, 159
Rigden, Paul, 16
Rollison (cunning-man), 136
Rooks, Thomas, 124, 147
Rosimond, Father, 108, 111
Rough Robin, 86
Roxborough, Sarah, 23, 56
Rump Parliament, 9
Ryves, William, 123

Saami, 178–79
Sadyngstone, William, 16
Salisbury, John of, 1
Salmon, William, 134, 141
Salter, William, 25, 85
Satan, *see* devil
Saucin, Joseph, 174
Sault, Richard, 38
Savage, Edward, 74
Scot, Reginald, 34–35, 39, 47, 67, 114, 125–27, 132–33, 134, 139, 145, 148, 150, 151, 155, 156, 157, 159
Scotland, 166
Scott, Walter, 137
seventh sons, seventh daughters, 50, 70, 74, 115
shamanism, 177–86
Shakilton, Thomas, 5
Shemaya, Ebn, 136
Shipton, Mother, 130
Shropshire, 14, 18, 45, 74
Siberia, 178, 184
Sibly, Ebenezer, 73, 135, 139
Sicily, 182, 183
sieve and shears, 5, 11
Simmonite, W. J., 137

Simpson, W. Sparrow, 143
Sjulsson, Olaf, 179
Skeat, Walter, 152
Sloane, Hans, 124
Smith, Robert Cross, *see* Raphael
Snelling, Margaret, 10
Solomon, 94, 120–21, 123, 126, 131, 138, 139, 141, 142, 145, 159, 175, 176
Somerset, 11, 15, 20, 25, 30, 54, 56, 64, 68, 70, 72, 73, 74, 80, 84, 87, 95, 96, 99, 111, 113, 129, 153, 192
Southey, Robert, 68
Southwell, Thomas, 1
Spain, 163, 165, 172
Spence, Hannah, 72
spiritualism, 53
Stacey, James, 25, 74, 75, 111
Staffordshire, 15, 23, 37, 38, 56, 88, 97, 108, 141
Stagg, James, 88–89, 90, 105
Stapleton, William, 94, 126
Starkey, Mrs, 112
Starkey, Thomas, 112
Stearne, John, 13, 30
Steward, John, 90, 94, 120
Stoekhlin, Chonrad, 177, 182, 183
Strasbourg, 166
Suffolk, 3, 78
Surrey, 62, 105, 109, 184
Sussex, 18, 57, 95, 115
Swain, Mrs, 27
Swan, Alice, 15
Swapper, Susan, 95
Sweden, 179
Swedenborg, Emmanuel, 132
Swift, Jonathan, 41, 42
Switzerland, 167

Tailer (cunning-man), 16
Tailor, Steeven, 114
Talbot, John, 14
Talonpoika, Juha, 179

Tatterson, John, 13
Taylior, William, 16
Taylor, Thomas, 97
Teare (cunning-man), 113
Tennant, Ann, 106
Thatcher, James, 99
thief detection, 2–3, 4, 9, 10, 11, 15, 16, 17, 22, 25, 26, 27, 38, 39, 43, 64, 68, 70, 87, 90, 96–101, 114, 143, 151, 167, 180, 188
Thomas, James, 56
Thomas, Keith, xi–xiii, 181
Thurlow, Grace, 12
Titi, Placido, 136
toad doctors, 84
Tomlinson, Sarah Ann, 101
Tongue, Ruth, 192
torture, 169
Tóth, Örzse, 180
Train, Joseph, 113
treasure-hunting, 10–11, 20, 59, 73, 93–96, 120, 126, 174–75, 176, 177, 180
Trent, Council of, 170
Tuckett, James, 25, 114
Tunnicliff, James, 88, 89, 112, 141
Turner, Robert, 122–23, 126, 127, 139, 140, 142, 147
Turner, William, 23
Twyford, Thomas, 10

Udal, John, 28, 54
urine scrying, 105–6, 107, 141

Vaux, John, 78
Veare, Thomas, 16
Villefranque, Jeanne-Marie, 174
Violett, Alexander, 16
Vowles, William, 11, 87, 99

Wagstaffe, John, 35
Wales, 22, 133, 137, 138, 144, 155, 158, 159–60, 184, 193

Wales, George, 137, 155
Wallys, Robert, 11
Walsh, John, 70, 73, 143, 182, 184
Walton, Richard, 72, 90, 148, 149
Ward, Thomas, 16
Warren, Susanna, 60
Warwickshire, 106
Watson, W. Willis, 54
Watts, Ann, 127
Webster, John, 35
Wecker, John, 124
Welford, John, 16
Wendore, John, 106
Wesley, John, 46, 111
Wesley, Samuel, 38
Weyer, Johann, 123, 125
Wheeler, James, 100
Wheeler, John, 100
Wherrall, Ann, 26
Whisker, Sarah, 102
Wicca, 193
Wilkinson (cunning-man), 63, 133, 143
Williamson, Margaret, 2
Williamson, William, 10
Willimott, Joan, 70
Wilson, Christopher, 12
Wiltshire, 10, 17, 36, 71
Windsor, witches of, 8
witch bottle, 108
witchcraft, accusations against cunning-folk, 12–13, 25, 63, 64, 71, 111–12, 190
witchcraft, curing of, 13, 16, 25, 62, 63, 78, 80, 87–89, 103–11, 117–18, 180, 190, 193
witch scratching, 108
Wolsy, Johanna, 3
Woodhouse, Dr, 77
Worcestershire, 11, 73, 190
Worsdale, John, 116
Wrightson, John, 53, 84, 85, 115
Wycherley, William, 5, 67, 94, 100, 121, 196

Yonge, Charlotte, 56, 58–59
Yorkshire, 10, 11, 13, 14, 16, 17, 22, 23, 36, 48, 50, 51, 53, 55, 62, 72, 82, 86, 90, 94, 105, 109, 113, 115, 137, 141, 145, 151, 155, 156

Zadkiel, *see* Morrison, Richard

www.ingramcontent.com/pod-product-compliance
Lightning Source LLC
Chambersburg PA
CBHW072138290426
44111CB00012B/1913